Gray Matters

D1592364

Global Perspectives on Aging
Series editor, Sarah Lamb

This series publishes books that will deepen and expand our understanding of age, aging, ageism, and late life in the United States and beyond. The series focuses on anthropology while being open to ethnographically vivid and theoretically rich scholarship in related fields, including sociology, religion, cultural studies, social medicine, medical humanities, gender and sexuality studies, human development, critical and cultural gerontology, and age studies. Books will be aimed at students, scholars, and occasionally the general public.

Gray Matters

~

Finding Meaning in the Stories of Later Life

ELLYN LEM

FOREWORD BY MARGARET CRUIKSHANK

Rutgers University Press
New Brunswick, Camden, and Newark, New Jersey, and London

Library of Congress Cataloging-in-Publication Data

Names: Lem, Ellyn A., author.
Title: Gray matters : finding meaning in the stories of later life / Ellyn Lem.
Description: New Brunswick : Rutgers University Press, 2020. | Series: Global
perspectives on aging | Includes bibliographical references and index.
Identifiers: LCCN 2019044056 | ISBN 9781978806313 (paperback) |
ISBN 9781978806320 (hardback) | ISBN 9781978806337 (epub) |
ISBN 9781978806344 (Mobi) | ISBN 9781978806351 (PDF)
Subjects: LCSH: Older people—Social conditions. | Old age—Social
aspects. | Gerontology. | Aging—Cross-cultural studies.
Classification: LCC HQ1061 .L457 2020 | DDC 305.26—dc23
LC record available at https://lccn.loc.gov/2019044056

A British Cataloging-in-Publication record for this book
is available from the British Library.

♾ The paper used in this publication meets the requirements of the
American National Standard for Information Sciences—Permanence
of Paper for Printed Library Materials, ANSI Z39.48-1992.

www.rutgersuniversitypress.org

Manufactured in the United States of America

For my parents, who inspire me every single day

Contents

Foreword

MARGARET CRUIKSHANK

Two propitious epigraphs begin *Gray Matters*, one from Miriam Toews and one from Doris Grumbach: "I think you have what it takes to endure" (Toews) and "I am ready to begin the end. . . . Until death, it is all life" (Grumbach). The book fully lives up to the expectations created by those observations. Creative, wide-ranging, and well-written, *Gray Matters* offers a many-sided, complex understanding of late life. It demonstrates that this period of our lives interweaves our past and present, takes grit, and offers opportunities for positive experiences. For some, learning becomes more enjoyable, as the phrase "senior college" indicates. *Gray Matters* also skillfully shows that aging occurs in a social context, a fact often overlooked when the process is understood as solely an individual matter.

Many older adults in North America age comfortably and lead meaningful lives despite media stereotypes of decrepit elders who either drain social resources or fill up gated communities. As the aging population increases, the need for more nuanced accounts of late life is urgent, as are challenges to ageist attitudes. People aged sixty-five to one hundred are extremely diverse and, as much scholarship indicates, perhaps more so than any other segment of the population. Thus the blanket identity "old" is ill fitting. The various identities elders have besides their age shape who they are. Even a narrower category such as "frail" tells us little by itself.

In recent years, the importance of narratives, such as creative work, interpretations of literary texts, and oral histories, as gerontological knowledge has been recognized. Members of the European Network of Age Studies and the North American Network of Age Studies further this work. Narratives convey the many-faceted aging process, as *Gray Matters* demonstrates.

The book's range of topics is impressive: parent-child relationships, housing, sexuality, living alone, gender differences, work/retirement/money issues, dementia and death. Books on aging cover some of these topics, but none I know of takes up all of them.

Another unique feature of *Gray Matters* is the inclusion of results from the author's own survey of 200 people. Real-life experience—good ballast for an academic book.

I particularly liked the chapter on sex and the one on dementia. "Sexual bereavement," considered by Lem, is a significant subject for both general readers and gerontologists, especially since many heterosexual women will be widows by their late sixties. The dementia chapter added to my knowledge of this important subject as it emphasized the value of a humanities perspective on late-life disease. The fear of dementia seems to intensify generalized fears of getting old, although increased risk of dementia mostly occurs only after age eighty-five, and some people diagnosed with mild cognitive loss either stay the same or develop increased function when tested a year later.

Gerontologists do not often discuss the role of luck in living a long, healthy, meaningful life. Our genetic inheritance may be lucky or unlucky or some of each. Our individual efforts, zealous as they may be, cannot *insure* a healthy old age. As we think of friends who have died prematurely and others who thrive despite multiple challenges, we can surely see that luck plays a role in determining who survives and who thrives. It may be hard in the United States, where we are hampered by the myth of rugged individualism, to concede that luck partly influences our late-life condition.

How do we find meaning in late life, when so many cultural messages tell us to deny it, try to fix it cosmetically, or pretend we are ageless? *Gray Matters* sheds light on this question as it explores the lives of elders through many examples from a range of sources, including from popular culture, literature, and everyday reflections. Individuals' paths to meaning differ greatly, of course, but the tribe of elders share commonalities, including the gradual, sometimes imperceptible, decline in our bodies and the inescapable social fact of marginalization. But these borders do not begin to tell the possibilities of late-life growth and change. For some, late life brings multiple problems and understandable despair. Often, though, these outcomes not only co-exist with growth and change but also interconnect.

I have heard of a bedridden woman who reads widely and leads a book discussion group in her bedroom. Evaluated by the white, middle-class, myopic standard of "successful aging," she has failed. By her own wiser self-evaluation and by the humane and capacious norms of *Gray Matters*, she is not only aging well but contributing to the lives of others.

Recently seeing a car with a license plate that read NOT OLD, I drove alongside the car to guess the age of the driver. She was probably in her fifties. Since the ageism that afflicts us in mid-life is thought to be especially virulent, I wanted to give her a copy of *Gray Matters*. "Until death, it is all life" won't fit on a license plate.

Gray Matters

1

Introduction

"Where Do I Begin?"

I think you have what it takes to endure.
—Miriam Toews, *All My Puny Sorrows*

I am ready to begin the end.... Until death, it is all life.
—Doris Grumbach, *Coming into the End Zone*

Our stories are ourselves, and our well-worn stories
are our well-worn selves.
—Michael Perry, *Montaigne in Barn Boots*

Gray Matters: Finding Meaning in the Stories of Later Life is the title of this book for a number of reasons. First and foremost, "gray matters" owes a debt of gratitude to the Black Lives Matter movement for recognizing that our society benefits from showing visible support for under-represented groups that have not often been given the respect and fair treatment that they deserve. Although "gray" is not universally embraced as a coveted symbol of age, it has been championed through the Gray Panthers, organized in 1970 by Maggie Kuhn to unify those who are actively resisting ageism's harmful effects. For me, "gray matters" is also a way of showing that older adulthood is a significant time of life that should be valued and not shunned.

The "stories of later life" that are mined for "meaning" are rich in detail and come from authors, artists, and performers of all ages, but mostly, those over sixty-five. Their creative offerings are examined and intertwined with first-hand experiences of over two hundred seniors who shared their personal reflections with me in a twenty-five question survey on various facets of their lives. The "matters" covered in these sources are sometimes practical (e.g., ways to combat loneliness) and at other times, philosophical (e.g., coming to terms with death), but they are always thought-provoking and shed light on the rewards and challenges of this time in a person's life. The literary critic Susan Gubar's 2019 book *Late-Life Love* addresses the power of stories not only to enable us to "sympathize" with others but also to "see ourselves anew" (261); she believes they also can be "clarifying [of] the issues we confront" (92). Finally, "gray" connotes a zone of complexity that arises in many of these age-inspired stories and avoids simple binaries. *Gray Matters* often delves deeply into topics affecting seniors' lives from multiple angles without endorsing or rejecting positions on these topics. We may not always be able to see what is absolutely "right," but there are many truths on display from which to learn.

Resisting Age Stereotypes

An example of a text that challenges our understanding of age is the popular young adult novel *Miss Peregrine's Home for Peculiar Children* by first-time author Ransom Riggs. Published in 2011 and adapted into film in 2016, the novel contains haunting vintage photographs of children in strange poses. One young girl, for example, appears to elevate several inches off the ground. Almost as strange as the freakish photographs is the central role Abraham Portman plays in the story of his grandson Jacob's discovery of the Welsh island of Cairnholm, a time-defying place, where "peculiar" children do not age. While not the first narrative to rely on a grandparent's stories to spur a plot into motion, *Miss Peregrine's* breaks new ground when young Jacob begins a romantic entanglement with one of the "peculiars," Emma, who had been his grandfather's sweetheart as well for many years before his death. This contemporary book shows respect for the elder Abraham by demonstrating that Emma's desire for him does not fade over time—even as she becomes involved with his teenage grandson. Such respect is not typically seen in popular culture, which tends to portray older individuals in demeaning ways. In contrast to the novel's portrayal of elders, on the long-running animated series *The Simpsons*, a better-known Abraham, patriarch of the Simpson family (who first appeared in a short on the *Tracey Ullman Show* in 1988), does not tell stories that reveal information of personal or historical significance to his grandchildren, as does Portman. Instead, the Simpsons' grandfather rambles incoherently, falls asleep in the middle of his own diatribes, and is mostly ignored by those around him. Author Bruce Evan Blaine writes that Grampa Simpson reflects many stereotypes of older people: "doddering," "senile," and "dependent" (160). A 2017 *New Yorker* piece on ageism adds that "Abraham (Grampa) Simpson . . . is a senile galoot . . . the butt of every joke" (Friend). While some viewers may not be worried about creator Matt Groening's unflattering portrayal of age on his almost thirty-year-old sitcom, a growing chorus of others argues that this type of representation both reinforces the negative perception of older individuals in society and prevents the average person from embracing this time as a rewarding period of life.. In fact, children start receiving negative messages about aging early on in popular Disney classics such as *Sleeping Beauty*, *The Little Mermaid*, and *The Emperor's New Groove*, all of which feature aged villainesses as angry, bitter individuals seeking to destroy the lives of innocent youth. It is not surprising, then, that Margaret Morganroth Gullette, one of the foremost age studies scholars, identified in her 2004 book *Aged by Culture* a profound "age anxiety" plaguing our society, much of which stems from negative cultural portrayals. Anne Karpf in *How to Age* goes as far as to term this widespread fear of growing old as "gerontophobia" (35).

What could remedy this almost pandemic dread of aging? Hearing diverse, complex stories of aging, such as the one illustrated in *Miss Peregrine's Home for Peculiar Children*, can counter stereotypes and misinformation that have long corrupted many individuals' thinking on the subject. As the literary gerontologist Barbara Waxman reminds us, stories "have the potential to change readers' minds by humanizing elders and offering new versions of old age" (22). In contrast to damaging stereotypes, Mary Pipher in *Women Rowing North: Navigating Life's Currents and Flourishing as We Age* (2019), believes that "stories of joy, kindness, and courage empower" audiences and allow them to see possibility rather than limitations (149). Introducing these types of stories is the worthwhile endeavor at the heart of *Gray Matters*, which offers a multitude of narratives centered on later life and allows readers to move beyond standard, yet superficial, conceptions of aging.

Preparing for the "Elder Boom"

Why the subject of aging has moved to the forefront of public discussion should surprise no one. Shifting demographics, not only in the United States but also worldwide, reflect a burgeoning population over sixty-five, with the most growth in the eighty-five and older bracket. The U.S. Census Bureau predicts that between 2010 and 2050 the number of people aged sixty-five to eighty-nine will double, and the number of those over ninety will quadruple (Larson and DeClaire xiii). Or, as Ai-Jen Poo explains in the *Age of Dignity: Preparing for the Elder Boom in a Changing America* (2015), there have never been as many people over sixty-five in the United States as there are presently; moreover, this trend will continue since "every eight seconds an American turns sixty-five"—that is, "more than ten thousand people per day, almost 4 million per year" (3). Even more startling, by 2035 one out of every three households will include someone over sixty-five. And by 2050, projections estimate that there will be "twice the number" of those sixty-five compared to the "very young" (Armstrong 11).

With this "elder boom" in motion, one might reasonably expect bookshelves at the local Barnes and Noble to be teeming with titles on the subject of aging, capitalizing on this large segment of the population, which includes many affluent "baby boomers" with considerable consumer capital. The reality, however, is that books on the subject of aging are still rather scarce, usually one shelf at best, while entire walls are devoted to childcare and the latest diets. Sometimes "aging" and "death" are combined for a slightly larger section, but this pairing is problematic itself, especially if too many people already fear aging as nothing more than the prelude to death. Gerontologist Louise Aronson in her 2019 book *Elderhood* comments that death still seems to receive more attention in books and other media due to its "abbreviated trajectory" and its "finiteness," while "aging, its longer and messier cousin," is a less popular topic (372). In a sequel to the internationally best-selling novel *The Secret Diary of Henrik Groen*, the curmudgeonly octogenarian narrator supports this viewpoint by commenting on a number of real-life books "published for or about the elderly," which he does not like reading due to his "loathing old age and everything to do with it" (Groen, *On the Bright Side* 391). Perhaps the pervasiveness of this attitude explains why most of the general books on aging these days seem to promise to turn back the clock and, strangely, become less old. Books such as *Aging Backwards: Reversing the Aging Process and Look Ten Years Younger in Thirty Minutes a Day* (2014) by Miranda Esmonde-White attempt to assuage the worries of those who are dreading their future aging selves, but, in fact, these books' emphasis on nonacceptance of one's later years sends a negative message about getting older. Similarly, the bevy of works promoting "successful aging" have been taken to task by age scholars who find the idea behind people being able to control how they age to be wrong on many levels. The phrase "successful aging" became popular after physician John Rowe and psychologist Robert Kahn used it for the title of their 1998 book, based on a ten-year MacArthur Foundation study, which found that older people could take steps to age better—"avoiding disease and disability, [maintaining] high cognitive and physical function, and engaging with life" (Stowe and Cooney 43).

Challenges to "Successful Aging"

One outspoken critic of "successful aging" is Andrew Scharlach, professor of social welfare at the University of California-Berkeley, who in a 2017 plenary talk at the Age and Society Conference in Berkeley, California, noted that Rowe and Kahn's idea of "successful aging" can be applied to at most 12–15 percent of older people and leaves out minorities and those with disabilities. The reason "successful aging" is so limited in its scope stems from the fact that research indicates tremendous inequality in terms of who has access to mechanisms that assist in an easier aging process (e.g., quality health care, gym memberships, financial wherewithal for travel and continuing education). Martha Holstein in her book *Women in Late Life* (2015), for example, points out that various minority groups, such as African Americans, "live fewer years than whites and more years with chronic health problems" that can be connected with "income, education, access to medical care and racism" (121). To give proper attention to the various barriers that limit older adults' ability to age "successfully," scholars have called for an "intersectional" approach to aging, which looks at how certain groups of people may experience multiple categories of identity that contribute to inequalities (e.g., ethnicity, poverty, gender). Rather than focus on individuals' "choices" to age well, this approach recognizes that not everyone has the same "access to social and material resources" and that this inequality can impact the experience of "old age" (Calasanti and Giles 71).

Another criticism of the "successful aging" movement that Scharlach put forth focused on concern that working hard to erase the signs of age sends the message that we are to wipe out signs that we are living our lives. Gerontologist Margaret Cruikshank also objects to the concept in *Learning to Be Old* (2013), where she points out that "successful aging" leaves out "luck and mystery" and sets up a dynamic that "failure [of aging] is possible" (3). She argues instead for the term "aging comfortably," which means working with one's own strengths and limitations toward an old age that meets one's own expectations, not others' (4). Additional sources show older individuals changing the definition of "successful aging" to meet their personal criteria. Thus, for example, one of the women interviewed in *Women Rowing North* describes "successful aging" as "having loving relationships and a life of engagement and meaning" (149). In addition, international critical perspectives on "successful aging" can be found in Sarah Lamb's edited collection, *Successful Aging as a Contemporary Obsession* (2017), in which anthropological studies with "real people" reveal that there is not one definitive definition of aging successfully that should be used as an evaluative measure (16).

Emerging Stories on Age

For those who are aging, students studying the field, and professionals working with older populations daily, the dearth of insightful literature on the topic creates a definite need for a more enlightened approach to aging and one that *Gray Matters* intends to fill. Several recent books on aging have called for "authentic writing on the subject of getting older," writing that is "original, truthful . . . and authentic" and includes "vibrant, complex stories about older people" (I. Brown x; Poo 121). The stories in this volume are primarily from recent literature (mostly novels and memoirs), as well as television, plays, films, and even art. In addition to the stories from the surveys of individuals over sixty-five, *Gray Matters* draws insight from interviews and field research observations to bring direct experiences to light. Despite age scholars like Cruikshank and others having argued that the humanities "so far have had little influence on gerontology as a whole," the body of creative work addressing aging is expanding significantly and is being recognized for encouraging "deeper considerations of challenging subjects" (Cruikshank, *Learning to Be Old* 182; Marshall, "Thinking Differently" 522).

An outstanding example of a work from the humanities that shows the value of literature for investigating aging is a powerful novel by Margaret Drabble, *The Dark Flood Rises* (2016). The central character, Francesca Stubbs, who is in her seventies, still works evaluating housing prospects for her senior contemporaries. Meanwhile, one of Francesca's dearest friends Josephine, who is also in her senior years, teaches a weekly course entitled "On Old Age and the Concept of Late Style" on poets such as Dylan Thomas and W. B. Yeats. During one of the classes, a sixty-year-old student named Sheila, who takes care of her mother experiencing dementia, when she herself is not working part time, writes a poem about dementia, inspired by Yeats's "Dialogue of Self and Soul." Drabble contrasts how poetry helps Sheila make sense of her burdensome life responsibilities while the "carer's guide to dementia," which uses the acronym "piglet"—"Person I Give Love and Endless Therapy To"—to refer to the cared-for person, only objectifies the person needing care. Sheila may pick up useful tips in the guide, but she finds the language demeaning: "Her mother is still a human being, an old woman, albeit demented, not a piglet, not a nursery rhyme toy" (126–127).

In addition to novels such as *The Dark Flood Rises*, *Gray Matters* looks to graphic memoirs. Art Spiegelman's *Maus* (1986), an illustrated rendition of his father's experience during the Holocaust using mice and cats, demonstrates that using a comics-style technique can help audiences be more receptive to issues that otherwise might be too disturbing or overwhelming. In fact, medical research now recognizes the potential of graphic literature to communicate with patients and families about end-of-life decisions. In an essay "Comics and the End of Life," M. K. Czerwiec notes that at the Narrative Medicine Program at Columbia University the "combinations of image and text" in comics can "serve as a window into the stressors, rewards, challenges, and experiences of hospice and palliative care" and "make this difficult reality more manageable." One of the suggested texts in the article is *Can't We Talk about Something More Pleasant?* (2014) by Roz Chast, which is discussed in several chapters of this book. Not only does the title demonstrate the challenge of having conversations about unpleasant end-of-life topics, but the graphic memoir also movingly details the experience of being an adult child of elderly parents. Chast must learn a whole new set of skills when confronted with her aging parents' needs (e.g., arranging an ambulette) and struggles with feelings of guilt about not doing enough to help, along with boredom and frustration when trying to assist. Another graphic memoir entitled *Special Exits* (2010) by Joyce Farmer, also treated in later chapters, frankly addresses family members' changes as they become older and the series of decisions that must be made as unforeseeable circumstances arise.

Gray Matters also considers representations of older people in films and television shows. Of late, Hollywood seems to be reflecting the changing senior demographics. Releases such as *Grandma* (2015), *The Best Exotic Marigold Hotel* movies (2011, 2015), *Lucky* (2017), *The Leisure Seeker* (2017), *Book Club* (2018), and *Poms* (2019) have major elder star power at the center of the narratives (Lily Tomlin, Judi Dench, Henry Dean Stanton, Donald Sutherland, Helen Mirren, Candice Bergen, and Diane Keaton). Even films such as Amy Schumer's *Trainwreck* (2015), a traditional blockbuster, incorporate a side plot of the main character's interactions with her father in assisted living. Another popular mainstream movie *Star Wars: The Last Jedi* (2017), though spoofed on *Saturday Night Live* for its elderly cast, has characters such as Luke Skywalker and Princess Leia played by the original actors, with the filmmakers making no attempt to camouflage their ages, and being respected by the other characters for their knowledge and experience. Some of the other films that will be discussed are also well-known Hollywood productions like *The Intern* (2015) with Robert De Niro, while others had more limited releases due to smaller budgets (*Columbus*, 2017) or foreign productions (Israel's *The Farewell Party*, 2014). Using a wide range of films is beneficial due to the ongoing limited representation of older people in this popular media form notwithstanding some recent improvements.

Despite this recent trend of better senior representation in movies, a University of Southern California study looked at the films nominated for Best Picture between 2014 and 2016 and observed that less than 12 percent included actors over sixty and that 78 percent of the films did not have a female actress older than sixty in a central or supporting role (Friend). Even more alarming, a 2017 AARP study of the top films that year revealed dramatic ageism and sexism in that films starring actors aged forty-five and over, only five were women, while thirty were men (Appelo). Other research has examined film dialogue in thousands of movies and noted that older women are given significantly less dialogue as they age (Anderson and Daniels).

Compared with film, television seems to have more prospects for aging actors and actresses as new networks and media companies continually develop programs beyond the limited traditional offerings of the past and, in the process, display improvements in representation as well. For example, the popular show *Grace and Frankie* (2015–) stars Jane Fonda and Lily Tomlin, both of whom were in their late seventies at the start of the series. In addition, 2018 saw the debut of *The Cool Kids*, with Vicki Lawrence, also in her seventies, set in a retirement community, as well as the award-winning *The Kominsky Method*, starring Michael Douglas as an acting coach and Alan Arkin as his agent. Yet, as social gerontology researcher Becca Levy has found, only 2 percent of the characters on television are over sixty-five, and they usually take on "extreme" roles—"absurdly fit, funny, and sexy or the severely disabled" (qtd. in Basting 31).

While other studies show that that number may now be closer to 9 percent, most scholars agree on the importance of effective representation of aging, especially on television, since "older adults who watched television had significantly worse attitudes about aging than those who did not" (Smith et al; Basting 29). An example of a recent television program that projects its older characters with less caricature and more realism and humanity is *Better Things*, created in 2015 by Pamela Adlon and Louis C.K. Unlike *Grace and Frankie*, which focuses almost exclusively on the central senior characters, *Better Things* concentrates on a single-mother, Sam Fox (played by Adlon), and her complicated life raising three daughters mostly on her own, while her mother, Phil (played by Celia Imril), lives nearby. The episodes featuring Phil, a former actress with a mercurial personality, and her family members, who are also in their later years, demonstrate fully fleshed out characters that defy most ageist stereotypes and show the often delicate family dynamics between parents and their adult offspring.

Television and films affect not only older individuals and their attitudes about aging, but they also influence others who are envisioning their future or interacting with their own aging family members. Thus, it is important to consider how popular media forms are contributing to a wider understanding of later life and which ones may be contributing to ageist ideas that perpetuate negative feelings about the inevitable aging process. Critics notice that with more baby-boomers in their "twilight years," there is hope for media that offer a "cultural reappraisal of old age" and provide "cultural relevance" (Meeuf 154).

Learning from the Surveys

In addition to representations of aging in literature and popular media, *Gray Matters* also includes the voices of lived experience drawn from survey results from over two hundred people over the age of sixty-five across the United States. With a written version distributed to recreational and residential facilities catering to seniors, and an electronic link to the survey that could be passed along to others (using a "snowball sampling" method to grow a larger sample size nationwide), the survey included twenty-five open-ended questions, which allowed respondents to reflect on different topics dealing with aging, ranging from their general mood each day to health challenges, ageism, finances, and advice to their younger selves. More women than men ended up taking the survey (the ratio was around three to one), and greater socioeconomic diversity was displayed in the responses than racial or ethnic diversity. The answers seniors provided, then, are somewhat limited to a homogenous mostly white U.S. population and thus do not illuminate various minorities' perspectives on the aging experience.

Still, allowing older individuals to speak for themselves in this book, alongside cultural representations of aging, creates a dialogue that presents a wider and deeper picture of aging.

Responding to a need for more involvement by the elderly in discussions of the later years, Meika Loe's 2011 book, *Aging Our Way: Lessons for Living from 85 and Beyond*, includes in-depth material from qualitative interviews. Making "elder voices" central in studies of this time enables Loe to treat them as "starting points for understanding age, aging, and the life course, at a time, when aging is changing" (xiii). Since this stage of life is often considered a great unknown for most people, learning what others have gone through is helpful preparation for the future. Psychologist Molly Andrews believes that "to learn about the selves we will become," it is imperative that individuals "listen to what the old have to say about themselves in old age, in all its complexity" (qtd. in Bouson 146). Also making this plea is Kathy Greenlee, former assistant secretary of aging for the U.S. Department of Health and Human Services, who argues, "We need more older people talking publicly about themselves and their lives" (qtd. in Graham 1). Seniors might not regard their recounting of day-to-day experiences as valuable, but studies demonstrate that this is a useful methodology with much to offer.

Take, for example, the story from one of the surveys for this book of a seventy-eight-year-old man who visits his wife of fifty-two years every day from eight A.M. to seven P.M. in the memory care clinic, where she now lives since he can no longer take care of her at home by himself. He writes that when he walks into her room every day, "her beautiful face" makes him smile. His mission is "trying to make her last days on earth as good as they possible can" and wanting to "stay happy for her." This man's explanation of caring for his wife disrupts the common view of the "burden" caused by Alzheimer's and allows alternative and poignant realities to emerge. These surveys, along with interviews with individuals over sixty-five and field research observing seniors in different facility settings, help us recognize that to examine culture and aging together, often called cultural gerontology, the "voices and visions of older people" must be pervasive (Twigg and Martin 355).

Scholars who have studied aging from a universal perspective and have what Cruikshank refers to as "gerontological knowledge" are also included in this study in order to provide context for and bring additional clarity to the topics being discussed. It also is helpful to include the views of experts in medical and sociological fields, particularly with regard to subjects such as retirement on which there is divided opinion. Many of my survey participants celebrate this time of life as freedom from the "ball and chain" of the workplace while others bemoaned the loss of identity and the invisibility that come from no longer having a vocation. Sociologists, for example, might focus on the economic disparities in groups of people, and how work is a financial necessity for many who have limited resources, which could illuminate why there are vastly different views on retirement. Medical research, on the other hand, could focus on how certain types of physical labor affect longevity and explain why life expectancy is so different for people who have spent decades doing certain types of work, which may influence conflicting attitudes about work. Having professional opinions from these various disciplines, then, on working vs. retirement helps make sense of the incongruities and gives a clearer understanding of the factors leading to the diverse opinions in the surveys.

Ultimately, then, *Gray Matters* takes an interdisciplinary approach to the topic of aging. The benefits from this approach are manifold and, as I discuss below, help in

- avoiding the false duality of aging as mostly negative or positive
- emphasizing the variability and individuality of older people who tend to be regarded homogeneously and stereotypically
- countering myths about age that often lead people to fear aging or disengage from the subject of aging altogether
- creating more balance in age studies, which tends to be dominated by medical science.

Picking up almost any book on aging, one can tell right away if it is in the upbeat, positive camp of "aging is not the end" or the negative, often jokey, narrative of decline. Karpf's often-quoted *How to Age* (2014), which encourages readers to age "zestfully" by "embracing age," is an example of the former. On the other side of the spectrum are books such as William Miller's *Losing It* (2011) and Nora Ephron's popular *I Feel Bad about My Neck* (2008), both of which lament about the cruel ravages of time. Miller finds almost nothing good to say about growing old, despite being healthy and teaching law into his sixties at the University of Michigan: "Old age represented everything that is vile about embodied existence. The precursor of death, it looks like death except it reproduces all the disadvantages of childhood with none of its excuses or hopes or loveable bodies" (40). While slightly more balanced than *Losing It*, the best-selling *The Secret Diary of Hendrik Groen 83 1/4* and its sequel *On The Bright Side* also overemphasize the negative with multiple references to "diapers" for incontinence and passages that have eighty-three-year-old Henrik grumbling about old people's "walker shuffle, . . . their endless complaints, . . . their bellyaching" (1). The Groen books and others like Fredrik Backman's popular *A Man Called Ove* (2012) now even have their own literary category unfortunately deemed "geezer . . . grump lit" (Swinnen). Prominent age scholars have noted the problem of this dualism in that it sends over-simplified messages that leave out shades of gray in between the two camps. Gullette, in *Ending Ageism, or How Not to Shoot Old People* (2017), describes the two sides as the "happy gerontologists" who write books like *Why Almost Everything Gets Better after Fifty* and the "opposing faction" who believes "'old age can be nasty, brutish and long'" (xvi).

Both sides draw on convincing research to support their arguments. Proponents of the positive aspects of aging frequently tout the advantages of growing old: freedom from social expectations, better decision-making, increased gratitude and forgiveness, less anxiety, greater emotional stability and satisfaction, and time for contemplation. While "wisdom" is often included in this list, aging scholar Kathleen Woodward has written convincingly that the term has problematic implications in that it is a stereotypical term feeding into an ageist conception of old people as passive and not assertive or angry enough to express dissatisfaction ("Against Wisdom" 187, 202). Additionally, Woodward argues that wisdom does not carry much value in "contemporary Western societies" (205). On the other hand, the list of common complaints about growing old is nearly as long: decline of physical abilities, social isolation, powerlessness/dependency, dwindling energy, economic instability, potential dementia, invisibility and shame.

In representing both positive and negative aspects of aging, *Lucky* (2017), Henry Dean Stanton's final movie before his death, avoids a false dichotomy of "good" and "bad" and instead reveals important facets of the later years, which are not easily categorized. Lucky, the title character, is a ninety-year-old creature of habit stuck in his contradictory daily routine of smoking a pack of cigarettes and doing yoga exercises. While he relishes his freedom and independence, living alone without family, he seeks connection at a local diner and a bar where he is a regular—another apparent contradiction. The beauty of the film comes from its refusal to make extreme claims about the quality of Lucky's life; he is "lucky" that he is still alive and can secure small pleasures, but the slow pace of his life, medical uncertainties, and the few activities he engages in reveal that he is also subject to limitations due to age. In this way, *Lucky* avoids oversimplification and creates a more comprehensive representation of aging.

Scholars have noted that films such as *Lucky* and other cultural texts are noteworthy for neither glorifying nor vilifying the aging process. As the introduction to *A Guide to Humanistic Studies in Aging* (2010), edited by Thomas Cole, Ruth Ray and Robert Kastenbaum, convincingly argues, integrating humanities with age studies helps move past positive and negative thinking about age and promotes "examining the *complexities* of aging, teaching us to 'appreciate the multidimensional richness of older lives'— both individual and collective" (19). By avoiding an impossibly optimistic view of aging that could bring disappointment or a paralyzing negative portrayal based on fear, these balanced portrayals of good and bad reveal greater realism, which can only be healthy and should be desirable.

Variability and Individuality

Work in the humanities and research from other disciplines—including the aging surveys—can further bring out the differences among older individuals, who are too often are lumped together in one amorphous category. A headline to a 2017 *New York Times* Sunday Review article, "Old People Are Not All the Same," employs a truism that should be common knowledge, but, according to the author, geriatrics professor Louise Aronson, is often ignored. She criticizes the Centers for Disease Control's vaccination guidelines that list seventeen different categories for children from infancy to eighteen, but only one group for those sixty-five and older, who apparently "don't change over the last half-century of life" (6). The idea, then, of a "one-size-fits all" grouping for seniors is problematic both in the medical realm, which is not acknowledging different bodily changes that happen over decades of time, and in general since looking at older people as one homogenous entity perpetuates stereotypes of them as "miserly, cranky, obsessed by sex but sexless, incompetent, drunken, bitter, childish, demented, and worthless because they may die soon" (Cruikshank, *Fierce* 3). The irony of such blanket statements is that research has found that when people reach their later years, they become more unalike one another than similar. In *The Fountain of Age*, Betty Friedan cites an influential Duke gerontologist whose research showed that "chronological age" could not be associated with certain characteristics. His research revealed "the incredible variability of older people in the community. When you've seen one older person, you haven't seen them all. Older people do not become more alike by becoming old. In many areas, they become more varied" (117). Age scholars Margaret Cruikshank, Margaret Morganroth Gullette, Martha Holstein, and Leni Marshall also have stressed this important observation in their work. Susan Jacoby points out that the "five septuagenarians" running for president in 2020 highlights how diverse that decade in life can be and cites AARP administrator Jean Accius, who argues we must replace "outdated assumptions that people over a certain age are monolithic" ("We're Aging Fast" A25).

The interdisciplinary research in *Gray Matters* helps rectify the tendency to see seniors as a uniform group; the surveys additionally bring out striking contradictions that demonstrate how differences in health, wealth, temperament, and other factors can determine attitudes in age that defy easy generalities. The rich and diverse examples from literature, film, and more also show divergent perspectives on the aging experience and offer testimony to counter fallacious generalities about older people. Elizabeth McKim and William Randall comment on how a humanities approach can "prevent . . . age-ist [sic] attitudes that swirl around in society . . . that all older people are more or less alike" (qtd. in Bouson 188).

The graphic memoirs *Can't We Talk about Something More Pleasant?* by Roz Chast and *Special Exits* by Joyce Farmer, which are discussed in later chapters, illustrate this diversity of experience. In those works, which represent the parents of the author-illustrators, readers see very different outcomes in terms of physical and mental health for family members even though they are roughly the same age. In *Can't We Talk about Something More Pleasant*, Chast's father, George, becomes increasingly worried about the safety of the family "bankbooks" and develops greater food idiosyncrasies, but continues to be a loving presence for his daughter. Her mother, in contrast, who was an assistant principal, retained an off-putting, domineering authority even as she weakened physically but developed a warm and positive bonding relationship with Goodie, one of her caregivers. *Special Exits* also shows age diversity through the portrayal of her stepmother, Rachel, becoming mentally and physically incapacitated before her husband, Lars, the author's father. Farmer depicts these differences when showing Rachel's near complete dependency on others, especially when she loses her eyesight, but Lars can at least attempt to maintain their household despite the daughter's concern that his wife's "needs are killing him" (135). Both of these memoirs remind readers that "getting old" does not involve achieving a stage in life with set circumstances; people age individually and often interdependently, as seen in *Special Exits*, which should serve as a good reminder to banish simple generalities about seniors' lives.

Countering Myths of Aging

Despite the increase in older populations worldwide, scholars recognize that there are currently not enough people going into the gerontology fields, even as that need becomes greater each day with people living longer than ever. Atul Gawande makes this observation in *Being Mortal* about doctors. Marshall offers the same assessment about health workers in *Age Becomes Us*, and Poo recognizes this reality for caretakers in *Age of Dignity*. At least part of the reason that occupations involved with the elderly are not being filled is a general lack of understanding of this demographic. Myths about being old abound, and negative associations with this time in life not only affect people's attitudes about their future identities but can also prevent prospective job seekers from considering meaningful work with older populations, despite the growth of opportunities. Replacing overly simplistic myths with interdisciplinary stories allows for engagement with more complex realities and offers "counterstories," or "alternative" narratives, with wider possibilities (Bouson 25; Segal 18). Cruikshank's *Learning to Be Old*, like other gerontology sources, begins with an entire chapter devoted to "cultural myths and aging." Some of the most prominent ones involve self-reliance and the perception that any diminishment of this capability over time is a diminishment of self, which creates a burdensome situation for another. Another myth concerns the loss of some physical or mental abilities leading to an inevitable and irreversible decline. The idea that older people are a drain on society and do not contribute in any worthwhile way is also a false idea widely held. In

Gray Matters, multiple cultural works challenge these myths and reinforce interdisciplinary research that reveals weaknesses in these common but faulty ideas.

For example, both the novel and HBO mini-series *Olive Kitteridge* (2008, 2014) demonstrate that even if a person loses the ability to speak, as Olive's husband Henry does after he has a stroke and is in a nursing home, it does not mean the person is no longer "there." Olive continues to talk to Henry and share her daily frustrations with him. Despite an imperfect marriage, Olive's faithful attention to Henry every day for years when he is unresponsive and her belated appreciation after the stroke of the "loyal" and "kind" husband that he was throughout their relationship show that instead of seeing Henry as a "burden" when he becomes impaired, Olive wants to be taking care of him; his condition brings out the generosity of her spirit and the depth of her love for Henry that she could not reveal enough prior to his illness. A large number of studies on caretaking and its impact points to the psychological and physical strain that comes from this role, especially in families. However, research also supports the positive aspects of caregiving that correlates with Olive's devotion to Henry. Gail Sheehy's *Passages in Caregiving* (2010) discusses how looking after a loved one in need of care "opens up the greatest possibilities for true intimacy and reconnection at the deepest level" (qtd. in Loh, "Daddy Issues"). A recent poll by the Associated Press–NORC Center for Public Affairs also supported the less publicized aspects of caring for others, such as the feelings of value for the caregiver, which again contradicts the myth that caretaking is mostly a "burden" to be endured. According to this poll, 90 percent of respondents indicated that the caregiving experience was "worthwhile" for them (Swanson and Alonso-Zaldivar). The reality, of course, is that whether the caregiver is a family member or a paid worker, taking care of someone who is incapacitated can be difficult work and emotionally taxing, but usually only the challenging parts make it into the wider mythology of aging; as a result, fear of not being fully independent takes center stage and marks this time of life as one to be dreaded and avoided as long as possible.

Other aging myths that can be countered by integrating interdisciplinary material include the deeply ingrained "decline narrative" and, perhaps as a result, the idea that older people are a "drain" on society. Very likely, the "decline narrative"—that as we age, there is an inevitable downward direction of health and well-being from which there is no recovery—comes from the medical field's long-held domination of age studies (Marshall, *Age* 9). Since bodily capacities and functions do inevitably change with age—for example, the brain shrinks in volume—science has tended to posit these changes over time as losses, leading many people to refer to "senior moments" as the start of the end to mental functioning. Reinforcing the idea of the old body as flawed and always getting worse occurs in popular media, in addition to medical journals. A September 2017 edition of *The New York Times Magazine* posed this question for readers: "If you could live for 200 years in a healthy young body, but with an old person's brain, would you do it?" ("Dear Reader" 6). This question sets up a false dichotomy between young = healthy and old = unhealthy/undesirable. Literature reviews in medical journals reveal a similar bias in projecting aging as a negative trajectory. Gerontologist Anne Basting in *Forget Memory*, for example, cites research that shows for a decade leading up to 2001, articles on Alzheimer's were told "almost exclusively from the medical perspective," showing that it was "fearsome, relentless and aggressive" (39). Problems with the "medicalization" of aging also are addressed directly in Aronson's book *Elderhood*, based on her experiences as geriatrician. She writes that too often the "disease" model of aging creates work "opportunities" for some at the expense of providing "helpful" assistance to older patients (248). Her book closes with a plea for not thinking about aging through the "single approach" of "science" and embracing disciplines as diverse as "history, literature, philosophy, anthropology, [and] sociology" (403).

Once interdisciplinary investigation of aging challenges the "downward spiral" view of aging, it can also mitigate the equally spurious claim that the old are not contributing anything valuable to society and simply leeching off the young. Other scholars have written about the problematic terms used to describe the growth of a graying population. Cruikshank, for example, in *Learning to Be Old*, explains how terms such as "senior tsunami," "epidemic," and "time bomb" incite fear that of disaster for the population as a whole (26–27). Those who hold this perspective and worry about dwindling economic resources such as Social Security will benefit from seeing the many ways older individuals are contributing even into their later years and not being parasitic at all. The film *The Intern* (2015), which will be explored in greater detail in the chapter on "Money, Work, and Retirement," provides a striking example of the potential older people have to be productive and guiding presences to younger generations. Robert De Niro plays seventy-year-old Ben Whittaker, who decides to participate in a senior-citizen internship program for an e-commerce business after he retires from his company. The plot revolves around on how much Ben has to contribute to his younger co-workers, despite his not being up to speed on recent technology, including the harried CEO, Jules Ostin (Anne Hathaway), who at first resists any of his assistance.

Lest anyone think *The Intern* is merely a Hollywood Cinderella story for seniors—the prospect of a second chance to offer valuable service to others—studies show older individuals are both working in record numbers and volunteering countless hours of their time. In other words, the film is merely showing what is happening daily as those sixty-five and above defy the misleading representations of themselves as "worthless." The Bureau of Labor Statistics predicts that increases in labor-force participation for those seventy-five and older will rise from 8.4 percent in 2016 to 10.8 percent in 2026 (Dreifus). Meanwhile, 30 percent of those aged sixty-five to seventy-four are regular volunteers; in 2015 alone, there were with 21 million volunteers over the age of fifty-five, whose labor has been estimated to have been worth $77 billion if it had been paid work (Karpf 174; Stoecker). These figures do not even take into consideration the amount of uncompensated childcare that grandparents supply, which some studies estimate to be as much as 14.3 hours a week (Huddleston). Again, it becomes apparent that a fuller picture of aging needs to be present in order to alter the faulty mindset that old people do not contribute and merely take from others.

When medical sources on aging emphasize bodily and mental decline, the astronomical costs of medicine readily come to mind, fueling the idea about how costly old people are to keep alive and healthy, not what they provide. In place of this model, *Gray Matters* uses an age studies approach, which Gullette defines as a "multi-disciplinary field" bringing together "humanistic, anthropological, and other social science approaches" and "highlighting (depending on the needs of one's topic) narrative, popular culture, especially the media" and "literary fiction" ("Ageism and Social Change" 319). When scholars examine aging through multiple disciplines, they are able to move beyond the single-minded focus on the "body," as Marshall points out, and concentrate on other "micro" and "macro" facets of old age and its "effects" (*Age*, 92, 149). Age studies, by being more narrative-based, allow subjective experience to be relevant in ways that strictly scientific fields do not permit (Cruikshank, *Learning* 198). The hope, then, from this interdisciplinary study of aging is a broadening of perspective on later life whereby prejudices, deeply ingrained misconceptions, and generalizations about old people are dismantled and gerontology and the aged themselves are no longer loathsome or scary.

With all of these new possibilities for investigation, one likely can see why it is so exciting to study aging at present. Besides the demographics pointing to an "elder boom," writers, artists, and researchers are wrestling with the meaning of growing old more now than at any other point in time. Silvia Stoller, who compiled a collection of essays on Simone de Beauvoir's own multidisciplinary study of aging, *La Vieillesse (Coming of Age)* from 1970, suggests that "age might . . . be one of the key issues of the twenty-first century"(8). In addition to having so many different thinkers and creators reflecting on old age in scholarly and creative works, there also is a willingness for the populace at large to reimagine the later years. The *New York Times* runs a column in its *Science Times* section entitled "The New Old Age," which captures the latest developments pertaining to aging such as the rise of cohabitation among seniors and new developments to aid seniors' dental health. Begun in 2008 by Jane Gross, it continues as a twice-monthly feature by Paula Span, who reports that the column receives a tremendous amount of feedback from readers and that it even helped challenge the discriminatory practice of barring assisted living residents from eating in the waterfront dining area of one fancy nursing home in Virginia by publicizing the issue in a column. "The New Old Age," going strong almost ten years since its inception, shows that people remain interested in learning more about this time of life and are receptive to developments and changes in perspective on aging.

Another popular media outlet on issues pertaining to age comes from Ashton Applewhite, who maintains a blog entitled *This Chair Rocks*, which launched her notable 2016 book by the same name. When Cruikshank wrote in the 2013 edition of *Learning to Be Old* that "aging is emphatically not a trendy subject," she may not have been able to imagine the current environment where there is more openness to frank discussion on old age realities. One indication of this changed climate is the fact that Gawande's *Being Mortal* was on "best book of the year" lists in nearly every major newspaper in the country in 2014 and on the *New York Times* best-seller for over ninety-nine weeks. Gawande, a surgeon, staff writer for *The New Yorker*, and professor at Harvard Medical School, approaches end-of-life issues from his experiences as a doctor and as a son of aging parents. One of his many achievements in the book is to highlight misconceptions on the part of the medical community when dealing with older individuals. He wants readers to recognize that the aged "have priorities beyond being safe and living longer" (243). Perhaps the highest priority that *Being Mortal* emphasizes is the desire people have for a "meaningful . . . old age" that "requires more imagination and invention than making them merely safe" (137). Gawande also champions the power of stories and believes that "life is meaningful because it is a story"

(238). This perspective is shared by *Gray Matters*, which explores aging in all its contradictions and complexities, most often through "stories," to help figure out what matters most in the later years of life. Gawande believes that "there is arguably no better time in history to be old" (22). Even Miller, the pessimistic author of *Losing It*, agrees: "It is better to be old now than it ever was" (6). While some might disagree with this appraisal, one can say with great certainty that it is an exceptional historical moment to learn about age.

"What do you know about aging?" is the inevitable question asked of a researcher studying late life, and one that was directed at me several months ago after describing this book project to some of the seniors at the YMCA where I exercise. The question is legitimate, though, especially since, as indicated earlier, too often older people's voices are not included enough in age studies. The thought of one more academic in her fifties setting the record straight on being old could be cause for alarm, especially when that academic is an English professor, who has no "certificate" in gerontology studies or medical training. In place of those conventional qualifications, I am someone who deals with age issues on a daily basis. As a daughter and daughter-in-law to four family members in their eighties, I know that this subject is far from mere scholarship to me. Have a parent turn sixty-five and a whole new world of Medicare versus Medicaid, long-term care policies, fall prevention, cataract surgery, hearing aids, and more presents itself with no simple instruction book.

When I first became interested in the topic of aging due to my mom and dad encountering age-related issues, I presented a paper entitled "What to Expect When You're Parenting Your Parent" at the national Popular Culture Association Conference in 2016. I decried the absence of good guides on how to navigate the complexities that emerge when age causes parents and children to take on different roles over time, but I have since learned those books do exist. Workman Publishing, the same publisher that puts out the famous, trusty *What to Expect When You're Expecting* guide to pregnancy, also has a book *How to Care for Aging Parents* (2004) by Virginia Morris; other titles on the same theme include *Should*

Mom Be Left Alone? Your Q & A Companion for Caregiving (2005) by Linda Rhodes and *My Mother, Your Mother: Embracing 'Slow Medicine,' The Compassionate Approach to Caring for Your Aged Loved Ones* (2008) by Dennis McCullough. While these books are practical and can be useful for addressing specific questions or problems, they do not deal with the wider experiences of aging. Like the character in *Dark Flood* who appreciates poetic insight over a reductionist "how to" book to care for her mother, I continue to value how creative works bring out the humanity of what older individuals grapple with, including the ordinary satisfactions and frustrations of a many-decade life. Hence, this English professor went to work analyzing these sources, along with background reading from different disciplines on aging, to see what could be learned in order to better understand what older people go through today—both my own family members and those I have not met—living independently at home or with assistance at some type of senior residence.

Now, I also teach a gender, sexuality, and women's studies humanities course that looks at aging from an interdisciplinary perspective with both traditional-age students and, when I am lucky, older returning adult students. The class helped shape the aging survey that I reference throughout the book, which was first designed by my mother, Joanne, a former family and martial therapist now in her eighties.

My father, Darryl, who recently retired from law at eighty-four, and his wife, Iris, have done field research checking out Aging Expos, so that I could have the brochures that were disseminated there to get a sense of what businesses are trying to market to seniors. Older people in my life, including my hairdresser, who is in her sixties, have distributed the surveys, cut out relevant articles for me to look at, and shared their first-hand experiences to make sure I had an exhaustive look at the topic. In addition, my teenage son and I have spent time with residents at an assisted-living facility where I have given talks on literary topics; every person whom I have met there has something to teach me that can illuminate a facet of aging. One time, for example, I was leading a discussion on Gawande, and a man kept asking the woman next to him if she was ready to leave, every five minutes! Apparently, not everyone, even those dealing with age-related issues, finds talking about them with a stranger to be a good use of their time. This reminder proved helpful as well for me and reinforced the idea that studying aging is a communal process; no one person holds all the knowledge. Many people have worthwhile contributions to offer: older people themselves, adult children of aging parents, caregivers, and researchers such as Basting, a MacArthur Genius Award winner, who works here in Wisconsin with those having memory loss to find the creative potential that remains. The more stories one accumulates, the more panoramic the view, and the greater chance that "meaning" can be found in the later years, which reinforces this book's central idea that "gray matters."

2

Senior Parents and Their Adult Children

"Can't We All Just Get Along?"

What on earth are we going to do with our
old, old, old very old parents?
—Erica Jong, *Fear of Dying*

We become instead the sons of our sons.
—Colum McCann, *Thirteen Ways of Looking*

She always possessed an air of invincibility, but my mother,
like everyone else, is a mere mortal.
—Marita Golden, *The Wide Circumference of Love*

More than one critic has noted that William Shakespeare's *King Lear* is currently experiencing a "renaissance" as the topic of aging family members and their relationship with offspring resonates for growing numbers of people. *King Lear* even appears on television with a BBC/Amazon Studios collaboration featuring Anthony Hopkins in the title role. But before the dramatic worldwide population increase in older adults seen today, *Lear* captivated audiences both in its original form and in various artistic adaptations, most notably Akira Kurosawa's film *Ran* in 1985 and Jane Smiley's Pulitzer Prize–winning novel *Thousand Acres* in 1991, later made into a film as well. The pull of the story comes from Lear's inability to see his three daughters for who they are. Two of them, Goneril and Regan, use false flattery in order to inherit large portions of the kingdom, while Cordelia, who earnestly cares for her father, refuses his request that the sisters compete to show who loves him the most. Audience members are riveted by Lear's blindness to the true nature of his filial relations and cannot help but wonder if a similar type of blindness happens in real life—one that prevents people from accurately assessing the true nature of ties among friends and family. Despite *King Lear* bringing to light questions of loyalty and perception, it remains unmistakably a play about growing old, and, hence, has contemporary topicality.

In the first scene of Act I, Lear discusses his desire to "shake all cares and business," so that he can be "unburdened" in his "crawl toward death" (41–43). Comments on "age" versus "youth" permeate *King Lear*, which focuses on generational interplay and, particularly, how parents and their adult children get along with one another. According to Martha Nussbaum in *Aging Thoughtfully: Conversations about Retirement, Romance, Wrinkles and Regret* (2017), the "age theme" is what has contributed to the "play's recent surge in popularity" (Nussbaum and Levmore 8). While Nussbaum sees this interest as "narcissistic" in that audiences connect the play to their "own future, near or far," it is also possible that large numbers of individuals are interacting with parents who are seniors and coming to terms with the shifting dynamics of those relationships. This is a present reality, not a future one.

Statistics tell one side of the story: at least ten million adult children in the United States are looking after their senior parents, three times more than fifteen years ago (Geewax). Put another way, by 2020, one in three adults will have some kind of "elder-care responsibility," a practice that begins earlier on in various ethnic and racial minority communities, especially in intergenerational households (Slaughter 240). One other noteworthy statistic is that due to increases in longevity, parents generally have "twice as much time" with their grown-up offspring than they did when their children were young. (Applewhite, *This Chair Rocks* 194). Numbers like these also show that parents increasingly need care from their children, as does a wave of literary works that deal this new reality. Such books include Roz Chast's 2014 graphic memoir, *Can't We Talk about Something More Pleasant?*, about her relationship with her parents in their later years, as well as Richard Ford's latest Frank Bascombe story collection, *Let Me Be Frank with You* (2014), in which Frank observes that "complications and unfathomables in dealing with one or another's aging parents seems to be the new norm for modern offspring" (126).

Role Reversal

An important facet of these relationships, which often appears in fiction and nonfiction works, is the shifting power dynamic between older adults and their adult children, particularly in the United States and other predominately white Western countries. For instance, Lauren Fox's 2015 novel *Days of Awe* captures the difficult and poignant moment when the grown-up child is looked to for comfort and reassurance by the parent who no longer fills that role. The protagonist, Isabel Moore, shares that she "sometimes wants to crawl into the lap of the person who has loved me the longest and the best," but now sees that her mother, Helene, looks to her daughter as if she is the "only one" who can "save her" (135). This wistfulness also comes through in Jonathan Kozol's memoir, *The Theft of Memory: Losing My Father, One Day at a Time* (2015), in which Kozol is struck by how his father, a brilliant neurologist, had become "an almost . . . totally dependent child" (212). The typical "balance of power" shift for Kozol is accentuated by the mental degeneration that his father experiences and that eventually necessitates Kozol's looking after the best interests of his parent. He describes the process as a full circle, starting from "his father's exercise of competence and judgement and authority in helping" Kozol "get through the some of the most uncertain and unstable times" to his "own responsibility" to use "competence and judgment to protect" his father in his final stage of life (269). These role reversals can understandably be difficult for parents as well, as psychologist Mary Pipher points out in *Women Rowing North: Navigating Life's Currents and Flourishing as We Age*. After years of being consulted for guidance on everything from riding a bike to making a pot roast, parents must face not having their "advice and opinions" sought as adult children want to demonstrate their independence. This change in "power relationships," Pipher explains can be "confusing and painful," but is part of normal individuating (29).

Estrangement

The willingness to take responsibility for an aging parent in need is complicated for those who have not had a strong relationship with that parent. Lynne Segal in her 2014 book *Out of Time: The Pleasures and Perils of Ageing* explains that the "role reversal" from being the one "cared for" to the "carer of," especially in midlife, can be jarring enough, but it is "all the more challenging if the earlier relationship with the parent was tense or ambivalent, as is quite often the case" (261). People's responses in the surveys for this book gave a sampling of those types of parent-child interactions that were difficult to rectify later on and rendered future caregiving by those offspring unimaginable. One eighty-four-year-old woman described giving her son "unappreciated and hurtful advice which separated him from" the family "forever." A sixty-eight-year-old man shared regrets that in his first marriage he spent very little time with his children, which he felt contributed to his son being in and out of jails later on as the son struggled with drug addiction, possibly the result of growing up without a "father figure." Some respondents noted that they let their jobs overshadow their personal lives. A former electrical engineer, now seventy, explained on behalf of himself and his wife, a retired lawyer, "There were lots of times where we could have been home, but we decided to stay at work." Others were less specific about their insecure relationship with their adult children but noted that they had not parented very well and, as a result, there is not much closeness in their families now.

This type of "estrangement" was the subject of a *New York Times* article entitled "When Families Fall Out," based on the research of Lucy Blake in *The Journal of Family Theory & Review* and Kristina Scharp's findings from a study on the topic as well. Scharp believes that separating from one's family is actually difficult to do since "our culture" makes people feel badly if they do not repair broken familial bonds: "Achieving distance is hard, but maintaining distance is harder" (qtd. in Louis D1). Research has also revealed that when these relationships remain "broken," the parents experience significant declines in happiness. Gerontologist Karl Pillemer, who heads the Cornell Legacy Project, which gathered practical advice from over 1,500 older Americans beginning in 2004, reported that those who were no longer in contact with their adult children were the "unhappiest" among all the people studied (Applewhite, *This Chair Rocks* 189). New medical reports also link dementia risk to older people with negative relationships with their adult children, citing reasons such as more "stress" arising from that missing familial contact and less communication on health-related issues such as medication complications and the importance of exercise ("Study: Seniors' Relationship with Adult Children" 2).

Several recent films depict how a ruptured relationship between parent and offspring is challenging to repair, despite time and the erosion of parental power. The debut film of video essayist Kogonada, *Columbus* (2017), for instance, features a Korean American son, Jin, whose famous architect father has fallen into a coma during a speaking tour in Columbus, Indiana. While Jin is expected to stay in town to look after his father rather than return to Seoul, where he currently lives, Jin seems unwilling to do so. As he explains to Casey, the young woman he befriends, who looks after her mother struggling with drug addiction, "He never paused his life for me." The contrast between the two young people's sense of responsibility toward their aging parents demonstrates that often adult children make the decision of how much care they are willing to provide their family member based on their perceptions of how well the parent had looked after their well-being. The fact that Casey still wants to help her mother despite the drug problems shows that personal flaws and struggles are not necessarily deal breakers for some children; in other situations, physical or emotional distance often proves to be a greater future barrier.

Another 2017 film, *The Hero*, directed by Brett Haley and starring the indomitable Sam Elliott, depicts the struggle to make amends for negligent parenting with one's adult child, as the main character, Lee Hayden, a famous former western film star desperately tries to reach out to his daughter, Lucy, who has had many years to "get over" her absentee father. Viewers see how Lucy has hardened her heart toward her father who has consistently disappointed her by prioritizing his film career over the needs of his family; she struggles with the conundrum of whether she owes him anything or even wants to forgive him for years of being devalued by him. A twist on this theme of the struggle to forgive a flawed parent in adulthood can be seen in the 2015 film *Trainwreck*, written by and starring Amy Schumer and directed by Judd Apatow. The movie begins with the father of two young girls, Amy and Kim, explaining why he can no longer be married to their mother by using an analogy of how children need more than one doll for companionship; the speech ends with his instructing them to repeat after him, "Monogamy is unrealistic." Twenty-three years later, the sisters are shown having to make decisions for the father's medical care. The younger daughter Kim argues, "We should put him in a shithole" as her feelings toward her dad, whom she calls a "dick," have left her bitter and less sympathetic now that he needs their assistance. This example differs from the others in that the audience sees contrasting responses from offspring to the same parent. While one sees the dad as the "worst father ever" and wants to reciprocate the years of "bad parenting" now that the power dynamics have shifted, the other sister recognizes that he was "not that great of a guy" but was the "greatest dad" by making her "feel loved." Adult children's contrasting attitudes toward aging parents are a reminder that there is not one objective standard of "good parenting" and that people growing up in the same household might come to different conclusions about a parent's treatment of them, which, in turn, can affect their willingness to be involved in the parent's life later on. Households, too, shift as years pass; factors such as work, divorce, and extended family may create entirely different environments in the home, some more positive or more negative, that can color siblings' memories of their parents and their attitudes about them over time.

Reconciliation

For those wondering how individuals are able to reconcile the past and the present with their aging parents, Chast's graphic memoir shows her stepping into a caregiving relationship with her mother and father while unresolved conflicts from her youth linger. In *Can't We Talk about Something More Pleasant?* Chast chronicles the slow decline in health of her parents, George and Elizabeth, while providing background information on their family history as well. Despite George's dementia, which makes him highly forgetful (e.g., not remembering his wife Elizabeth is in the hospital and asking for her repeatedly) and somewhat paranoid (e.g., obsessing that someone will want to steal their outdated "bankbooks"), Chast recognizes that he and she were "kindred spirits" and that she would remember him after his death "with great affection" (227). Her mother, on the other hand, proves more challenging. Chast recounts how she struggles to come to terms with the end of her mother's life because of Elizabeth's abrasive personality and her inability to ever express approval. A moving scene that demonstrates the chasm between them occurs in a full page with nine panels labeled June 24, 2009. Chast begins by revealing her intentions: "I wanted to have a final conversation with my mother, about the past, and finally worked up the courage to say something." She tells Elizabeth that she wishes they could have "been better friends" and hopes her mother would agree. Instead, the response is a question, "Does it worry you?" Both, then, somewhat disingenuously say "no," and that leads to a quick departure by Chast, whose last panel reads, "It was time to go" (208). She expresses sadness and anger that her mother never "tried harder to know" who she was as a person (202).

A week before Elizabeth's death, the two share a less muted conversation and are able to exchange words of love (209). However, a lifetime of strife between a parent and a child does not often end with an easy salve. Toward the end of the memoir, after her mother's death, Chast writes, "I'm still working things out with my mother. Sometimes I want to go back in time and warn her: 'Don't do that! If you're mean to her (me) again, you'll lose her trust forever! It's not worth it!!!'" (227). Although Chast's parents provoked contrasting emotions in her, the depictions of the care that she provided for them do not display any sort of imbalance. She sorted through all their belongings when they no longer could reside in their Brooklyn apartment, made the necessary arrangements for their medical and residential care, and spent time with them consistently, even when it involved travel after she no longer lived in New York. Her commitment and dedication to both her parents, as depicted in the visuals and the writing of the memoir, nearly masks the unresolved conflicts with her mother.

Offering Support

Chast is typical of many adult children who look after the welfare of their parents in old age, often while raising families of their own. The surveys reveal that for a majority of those over sixty-five, their children are one of their main sources of emotional support. Many wrote of the financial and emotional assistance they receive not only from their sons and daughters, but also from the spouses of their children. Those living closest appeared to provide the most support, but even those living some distance away make an effort to visit and keep in contact. Although spouses and friends were frequently cited in response to "who helps you out," "children" seemed to evoke more impassioned responses, suggesting it was not just the tasks that were being done that were helpful, but the ongoing heart-stirring feelings connected with that primal relationship that were sustaining. Several were similar to what an eighty-seven-year-old expressed: "Our children are our biggest supporters. They help clean the yard, cook, clean, and help with anything that we cannot physically do any more. We are grateful for our children." Some people just concentrated on the emotional connection, as did an eighty-year-old woman without a marital partner who said that her children "are my reason for living." Other responses demonstrated appreciation not only for adult children's acts of kindness, but for their offspring's symbolic significance as testimony of having lived a purposeful life. Given these strong bonds in some families, one can imagine that a major motivating factor for adult children to give back to their senior parents in their later years is to return the investment of time, energy, and love. Diana Athill in her moving memoir *Somewhere towards the End* (2008) explains this logic aptly in relation to caring for her mother: "If you are the child of a loving, reliable and generously undemanding woman[,] you owe her this consolation in her last years. I think that for people to look after their children when they are young, and to be looked after by them when they are old, is the natural order of events" (54).

Athill is not alone in recognizing that "positive parenting" is more apt to yield involved children when older parents are in need of aid. University of Chicago law professor Saul Levmore, who with his colleague Martha Nussbaum wrote different sections of *Aging Thoughtfully*, comments on reciprocal care (173). He writes that some older people can rely on this investment to be "forthcoming" from their families: "Each generation provides unwavering support for its children, and so when these beneficiaries age, it seems right that they should care for those who brought them into the world and supported them" (Nussbaum and Levmore 32). When an aging parent is satisfied that his or her child is fulfilling expectations looking after that parent, a common reaction might be "I did something right," a response one interviewee gives in John Leland's *Happiness Is a Choice You Make* (2018) when asked about her attentive daughters (181).

Reciprocity

A term for this transaction that is practiced around the globe is "intergenerational reciprocity," in which, as described by anthropologist Sarah Lamb, "adult children are morally obligated to care for their elder parents in exchange for the consistent support and sacrifice the parents extended to their children in producing and raising them" ("Beyond the View of the West" 38). The story "No More Maybe," published in *The New Yorker* in 2018 by the Chinese American author Gish Jen, shows how the message of care expectations can be transmitted in families. The narrator remembers that before she and her husband, Wuji, were even married, they decided that their parents could live with them in old age. The couple mutually agree that "our parents are our responsibility" (79). When her in-laws come for a prolonged visit while she is pregnant, the narrator expresses some concern about the couple's prior largesse, but the father-in-law at the end of the story reinforces the dictates of reciprocal care. He tells her, "You will be a good mother. . . . You will manage things very well for your child. . . . And then one day your child will have to manage you" (83). Despite the exasperating experiences of the in-laws' visit, the narrator knows "he is right" and affirms his status by referring to him in the final lines as "the professor," when most of the story shows him slowly losing that professional identity in age-related fogginess. Jen indicates in this story that within Chinese culture, even in the United States, the idea of paying back parents for their efforts is reinforced within families. Some commentators, however, believe that this age-old principle of "intergenerational reciprocity" is losing its hold on younger generations today. As a result, countries that have for years enshrined the idea of "filial piety," the Confucian idea of taking care of one's elderly relatives, now have enacted laws to guarantee the tenets are carried out by all members of society. In China, for example, the Elder Rights Law stipulates that, under threat of punishment, adult children look after their parents to make certain that "their parents' financial and spiritual needs are met" (Lamb, "Beyond the View of the West" 39).

In Western countries such as the United States, there is not the same sense of duty to compensate one's progenitors for their support earlier in life. Besides a lack of societal expectation to look after the elderly, care for older family members also can be challenging due to lack of governmental support for this important endeavor. Some private companies may offer paid leave to their employees to assist their parents who are gravely ill, but more often than not, that time off is uncompensated; in addition, expenses for chronic illnesses at the end of life are costly and not always covered by insurance. A 2019 study reported that adults over sixty-five needed to take $22 billion from their "long-term savings accounts the previous year" in order to cover medical costs outside of Medicare (Jacoby, "We're Aging Fast"). The U.S. idea of individualism espouses that families should be able to manage the conundrum of elder care on their own without government assistance, but too often that can lead to economic devastation and emotional stress for all parties involved.

Ideological complications for parental care occur when adult children contemplate the negative aspects of their childhood and want to hold the older generation be accountable for their wrongdoings, consciously or unconsciously. Levmore addresses this reality when he mentions that not all families will enact a positive cycle of care from one generation to the next, especially in "dysfunctional" and "quarrelsome" families and those who remember growing up as painful (Nussbaum and Levmore 32). The situation can be further complicated by the fact that parents' treatment of their children also does not always remain the same over time and may not be consistent due to fluctuating circumstances. The writer Anna March in her essay "Gone Girl" points to this dilemma when she wonders "what to do with and for our aging parents . . . if they weren't [good to us], but are now?" Also, she raises the problem of the "solid F" parent who is "obnoxious without merit" due to a "mental health issue" (31). Chast was able to support both parents equally despite the negative emotions she still held toward her mother, but other adult children are left with the question of how to rise to the occasion of providing assistance and care to their aging family members if the relationships still bear unhealed wounds from the past? Is there hope for those seniors and their children to establish a positive relationship despite a bumpy shared history and unresolved conflicts?

The Desire to Be "Good"

Several creative works take up this question and show that there are different motivating factors behind helping one's senior family members whatever the quality of that relationship may be. One such factor is the desire to be "good." An interesting perspective on "goodness," as a reason to devote energy to assisting aging family, can be found in the graphic memoir *Displacement: A Travelogue* (2015) by Lucy Knisley. When Knisley's father and his siblings do not offer to accompany her ninety-year-old grandparents on a cruise, despite everyone's worries that the couple is not physically or mentally up to the challenge, Knisley volunteers to take them herself, but she is not quite prepared for the level of care that is needed. Her grandfather experiences incontinence that requires she wash his pants each night, and she discovers that her grandmother is losing her mental faculties and has to be prevented from wandering around the ship. In the middle of the book, Knisley takes a full page of panels to reflect on "goodness," since she wants to figure out whose interests must be privileged when they seem to be in opposition. In one frame she is bowing down to her grandfather and thinking, "Life is spent balancing acts of making yourself happy and making others happy . . . in the hope that making others happy will lead to more personal fulfillment and general social beneficence" (84). This idealism, however, is challenged shortly thereafter as she recognizes that her own unhappiness in caretaking is also very real, and she is left wondering if "enduring close proximity to the mortality and decline of people" she cares about would still make her "good" or if that is just a ploy to gain adulation from others. The last scene on that page shows Knisley offering to take her grandparents on an excursion to the deck, which will involve challenges due to their limitations, but the act nonetheless shows that "goodness" has prevailed and that she has put their interests above her own.

Others adopting this mindset of "being good" to take on difficult eldercare responsibilities appear in various nonfictional and fictional works. Atul Gawande's *Being Mortal*, for instance, includes the story of a woman named Shelley whose father, Lou, comes to live with her and her husband and two teenage children after a series of falls that stem from Parkinson's disease and render him unable to live alone. As Gawande notes, "Taking care of a debilitated, elderly person in our medicalized era is an overwhelming combination of the technological and the custodial"—everything from managing medications, specialists, tests, and appointments (85–86). Despite feeling "her sanity slipping," Shelley's reason for prevailing under these difficult circumstances is that "she wanted to be a good daughter" (86). This frame of mind, thus, focuses less on the past and what a parent might deserve or not based on one's upbringing, but instead locks onto the idea of individuals wanting to achieve admirable behavior to satisfy their own expectations.

Evidence that literature often faithfully represents real life, a character in Erica Jong's 2015 novel *Fear of Dying* uses the almost same language as Shelley to explain what motivates her to be the adult daughter who remains on the home front to look after family while her other sisters are "gallivanting around the world"—"I felt I had to be the good daughter" (13). Similarly, Noah Baumbach's 2017 film *The Meyerowitz Stories (New and Selected)* also showcases a dutiful daughter whose kindness to her arrogant and dismissive father baffles the other siblings. When one brother asks Jean, "Why do you always show up for dad?" she responds, "Because I am a decent person."

This independence of action has its own logic, which may not be understood by others because it satisfies a personal code or commitment. In an essay on coming to terms with her abusive estranged mother late in life, Claire Johnson describes her own sense of "loyalty," both a "blessing" and a "curse," that helps her reconnect with the woman who treated her horribly growing up; recognizing that "everyone is damaged," she is able to "forgive" someone who is part of her "tribe" and even finds "compassion" for her (127). However, as the graphic memoir *Displacement* reveals, the desire to be "good," which can lead individuals to behave altruistically in relation to older relatives, is not without its complications and hardships. Being unable to determine when doing too much for others creates harm for oneself, Shelley, for one, seemed to push herself beyond what she was capable of, to her own detriment. The Jong example demonstrates other concerns with acting out of "goodness" since it leads to dissension among the siblings when they do not all share the same ethic of self-sacrifice. Studies show that "sibling disagreements" over caregiving can be a greater "source of stress" than caring for the family member (Poo 62).

Still, at times, the need to act righteously with regard to a loved one who requires assistance can be a motivating factor to take on responsibilities that might not always be pleasant. Joan Wickersham's short story "The Tunnel, or The News from Spain," included in *The Best American Short Stories 2013*, demonstrates that one's actions toward aging parents do not always stem out of unconditional love, but often from a sense of "doing the right thing." The story centers on a time when the mother, Harriet, is in a nursing home and is visited regularly by her daughter, Rebecca. The visits involve four hours of travel to Connecticut from Boston, where the daughter lives, but they are often manageable because the two discover that late in life "they liked each other" (290). However, as Rebecca goes through some personal crises in her own life, she recognizes that sometimes the visits are "more like Honor Thy Mother than . . . like running into a burning building to save someone you love who is trapped inside" (302). This passage reveals that on occasion following "commandments" in order to be "good" will suffice in order to be there for a relative even if one's heart is not fully engaged.

Creating a Sequel

Literature illuminates other strategies for adult children who may not feel a natural closeness to their aging parents to connect with them. Margaret Cruikshank in *Learning to Be Old* recognizes that parents' identities often change as they get older, and, as a result, they may be more approachable and open as they become increasingly "vulnerable" (175). Jong's fictional character Vanessa Wonderman experiences this transformation in her mother "deep into her nineties" since she is "much nicer than she was" during childhood; hers is a "sweetness" that comes with the "sagging arms" and "bunioned feet" (9). Kozol, in his memoir, also notices that he can have a better relationship with his father, even after dementia sets in, since the "diminished" parts of the elder Kozol still left the "essence of the person he had been," and the two develop a closeness that had not been possible previously. This opportunity to repair a damaged relationship with parents during their senior years is referred to as a "chance in Second Adulthood" by Gail Sheehy in *Passages in Caregiving* (2010). She encourages people to create a "sequel" to "troubled family drama" by adopting a new and honest relationship with parents who likely do not bring out the same kinds of conflicts as they did in the past (qtd. in Loh, "Daddy Issues").

Quite a few survey responses addressed the issue of elders wanting their children to let go of the past and envision a new relationship. One senior wrote that she wishes she could convince her son to "let go of anger and realize that some happiness is in his own hands." Another similarly urged her children to "let go of pettiness and old angers," which "poison life." The comments show that these older individuals believe in the possibility of rectifying former patterns by recognizing the changes that develop over time and by willingly giving up "old problems and disagreements" that create unnecessary "stresses."

One has to wonder, too, if the finding from happiness research that shows life satisfaction becoming greater as people become older might be connected to applying the advice of "letting go" of anger that seniors advocate for their offspring. These studies, such as one from the Brookings Institute by Carol Craham and Milena Nikolva, have been replicated worldwide and consistently show individuals' happiness high between eighteen and twenty, dropping to a low point at forty before steadily increasing to its apex at ninety-eight (Larson and DeClaire 92). Another scholar, remarking on the consensus in the research, states, "With age comes happiness" (qtd. in Rauch 122). Although various theories exist to explain why individuals who are likely dealing with some physical and or emotional difficulties, such as loneliness, would be among the most contented, it is not hard to see that adjusting one's expectations of others and not holding on to negative feelings from imperfect relationships can contribute to a sense of well-being and peace.

Dealing with Disappointment and Loneliness

While anger might diminish at some point for older adults, an emotion that is prevalent in gerontology stories from both real life and art is disappointment, particularly with the amount of time seniors are able to spend with their grown-up children and grandchildren. Respondents in the surveys repeatedly voiced their desire for more time with and attention from their loved ones, even while recognizing their offspring had full lives of their own. One question on the survey asks, "What do you look forward to?" and typical responses were "time with children and grandchildren." However, some people brought out their dissatisfaction with the frequency of interaction with comments such as "Seeing grandchildren when daughter can fit me in her schedule (works full-time—3 toddlers) and seeing son—not as often as daughter-in-law obstructs more visits." The need for more time with adult children also emerged from a question about what older adults would like to tell their families. Some variation of this response was prevalent: "I wish they would come to visit." People mentioned feeling "sad" that family members do not "call" or "stop over" nearly enough, and some went as far as saying that they wish they could let their children know how lonely and isolated they felt. As one woman explained, "I cover it [the loneliness] well and don't want to whine or complain."

Loneliness is often not communicated due to a lingering stigma attached to it. Susan Jacoby writes about the embarrassment surrounding loneliness in her 2011 book, *Never Say Die: The Myth and Marketing of the New Old Age*. She explains, "Loneliness is considered somewhat shameful—one of the last social taboos in a country where people are willing to appear on television and talk about nearly every other form of intimate unhappiness" (138–139). Since loneliness and isolation can also have serious health consequences—most notably, a dramatic increase in mortality rates and significant cognitive decline—it is imperative that the issue be given more attention and focus (Aronson, *Elderhood* 295). Nussbaum and Levmore offer one compelling innovation from Great Britain to combat senior loneliness—the "Silver Line—whereby older individuals can call a number and an empathetic person will talk with them (204). However, given that research shows that family members are more coveted companions than strangers, it is questionable how effective this "Silver Line" may be in ameliorating the harms of feeling too isolated from loved ones (Brody, "How Loneliness" D7; Carstensen 113; Friedan 384). Research is also looking into whether technology may be able to lessen some of the harmful effects of loneliness. The AARP Foundation, for example, has developed a project of giving seniors the Amazon smart speaker, "Echo," to do everything from telling jokes, to playing music, or seeing what is going on in the community. The hope is that residents in the housing complexes involved in this project will connect with one another, compare notes on what they are using Echo for, and feel less disconnected from everyday life (Ianzito 30). If the idea of using technology to combat loneliness seems too impersonal, Japan has taken steps to personalize technology by developing robots that are viewed as "iyashi," meaning "healing," since they are able not only to do physical tasks such as lifting older adults, but to express emotions and act as a "social companion" (Aronson, *Elderhood* 302). Commentary on the idea of robots as caregivers appears in the sequel to the pseudonymous Dutch novel *The Secret Diary of Hendrik Groen*, entitled *On the Bright Side*, which was published in the United States in 2019. The central character, Hendrik, who lives in an assisted living facility in Amsterdam, quotes a fellow resident who states, "'If a robot ever comes to help me get dressed, I'll yank the batteries out'" (253). Despite this resistance to being "cared for by a machine," Hendrik also recognizes that if a robot can perform some "tasks," the "human staff" may be more available for quality in-person "attention." Likely due to his ambivalent feelings about technology being used to minimize loneliness, he states his preference for an alternative developed in Flanders of letter carriers who are paid to check in on and visit with older people who are living alone to see if they are in need of services— an interesting initiative that quite possibly could be developed elsewhere (268).

Creative works such as the *On the Bright Side*, which highlight the problem of loneliness and the need of older people to be surrounded more often by family, can perform a public service by bringing the issue out in the open and taking away some of the shame associated with it. Margaret Drabble's novel *The Dark Flood Rises* is just one of countless examples featuring seniors who express a need for more time with their offspring. The central character, Francesca Stubbs, an active seventy-year old who travels around England as a housing expert for the elderly, spends part of her time looking after her first husband, Claude, once a doctor, now in poor health and permanently confined to bed. "Physically . . . imprisoned" in his household, Claude longs for his grown son Christopher: "Though he doesn't admit it even to himself, he wishes he'd come to see his old father more often" (107). The novel accentuates Claude's longing for this important family connection by highlighting his inability to move beyond the walls of his home, except for hospital visits. He is described as "bored, with the unalleviated boredom of inert old age," and readers recognize in Claude an example of an older adult with a disabling condition that challenges that person's ability to actively seek out desired companionship and necessitates others coming to him.

A different example that also shows how the onus is on the younger and more able family member to make an effort to see the relative who is incapacitated in some way comes from Elizabeth Strout's *Olive Kitteridge*. Although the title character, Olive, always desires more time with her son, Christopher, after he marries and moves from the family's home in Maine, in the chapter "Tulips" she is most emphatic about his visiting once Henry, her husband and Christopher's father, is immobilized by a stroke. Even though Henry has limited sensory responses, Olive announces the visit to him, "Christopher is coming," and, then, directs her son to communicate with his father: "Talk to him. . . . Tell him you're here" (147). Despite Christopher ending his trip early, Olive continues to bring up the visit to Henry and promises him future ones based more on her wishes than reality. Like Claude in the Drabble novel, Henry is another character without physical mobility who must rely upon others' good will to make the effort for connection.

These literary examples are a powerful reminder once again that adult children often have greater opportunities to facilitate quality time with an aging parent whose travel may be restricted by physical limitations (e.g., even the constraints of not driving at night). Olive's insistence that Henry is worth visiting despite his questionable mental responsiveness also sends the message that effort should be made regardless of whether acknowledgement of the interaction can be registered. In our technologically savvy era, one might think that Skype, Facebook, email, or even the phone may be suitable replacements for in-person interactions, but both the surveys and the creative sources emphasize the greater fulfillment offered by personal visiting, perhaps for the physical connection that human touch can provide. Visiting also reveals effort and time that can make older people feel they are being prioritized and not just "fit in" to a busy schedule.

Olive Kitteridge reinforces this idea of the potentially solitary nature of aging and its harmful effects. One character, Bessie Davis, described as the "town's old maid," is said to wear "loneliness" like a "lesion on her face" (102); others, whose husbands die, are "drowning in the emptiness" (257). Perhaps the clearest declaration of the dangers comes from Olive herself, who notes that "loneliness can kill people—in different ways can actually make you die" (68). Naming the culprit directly takes away any possible ambiguity that this is a real condition that can affect everyone, but is more likely to affect older individuals who often have unstructured time on their hands and perhaps less opportunity to take active steps to remedy the situation. Strout continues examining the theme in another linked short story collection, *Anything Is Possible* (2017). In "The Gift," for example, two older gentlemen have a chance meeting after a production of *A Christmas Carol* and confide their loneliness to each other. Another piece in the collection "Windmills" features a middle-aged woman named Patty bringing food to her mother, who practically begs her to stay: "I won't eat anything sitting alone. Can you stay and eat with me? . . . Pretty please?" This story has particular pathos in that Patty's mother has a spotty memory, which means she cannot remember that her daughter does visit often. The mother remarks, "I never see you anymore," to which Patty responds, "I was here three days ago." In an interview I conducted with Dan Anhalt, a college financial specialist whose parents both experienced significant memory loss, he mentioned that this inability to recall family members' visits is very common with older adults whose short-term memory is impaired. As a result, he and his siblings set up a white board to leave a lasting record of those who stopped by to help his parents remember the individuals spending time with them. The story "Windmills" is particularly effective for capturing both the point of view of the mother, who hungers for company but may not remember the attentiveness she does receive, and the adult daughter who tries to be present for her mother while balancing other life responsibilities, but often feels unacknowledged.

Both Perspectives

Strout is adept at representing adult children and their older parents' perspectives in *Olive Kitteridge* as well. Scholars have noted that fiction treating old age helps present situations from more than one viewpoint. Mike Hepworth in *Stories of Ageing*, for example, points out that novels "require author and reader to extend her or himself imaginatively into the minds of other characters," thereby, allowing multiple ways of viewing the older individual's experience (5). Thus, in *Olive Kitteridge*, the reader anguishes when the son, Christopher abruptly shortens his visit home, leaving his father in the nursing home tended to by Olive alone, as well as when he scolds Olive, who flies for the first time to visit him in New York, because she does not have a cell phone that would help him find her at the airport. And yet, Christopher's rationale for his actions is also aired. In one tirade, he explains, "You have treated me poorly for years. . . . You make people feel terrible. You made Daddy feel terrible. . . . I'm not going to be ruled by my fear of you, Mom" (230). Having the benefit of both perspectives prevents anyone from simply siding with the older generation or the young. Even though aging parents need the companionship of sons or daughters close to their hearts, the grown-up child has a side to the story as well that merits knowing, though, it is not always easy to share due to the possibility of unearthing vulnerabilities that are easier left buried. The difficulty of an adult child sharing her perspective on family relations is on display in Rachel Khong's 2017 novel, *Goodbye, Vitamin*, about a father's struggle with memory loss. The mother asks the main character, Ruth, why she did not visit them more. Ruth responds that it is a hard question to answer, but explains, "I didn't want to see you suffering. I didn't want my fears confirmed. It was less terrifying this way: not helping you, not saving you, just leaving you all alone" (128–129).

The raw honesty of the passage helps people understand that the distance that older people face from loved ones is not always the result of the younger generation's focus on the busyness of their lives. Clearly, there is an emotional and psychological aspect as well that makes it difficult to see one's parents in a weakened or compromised state. Rick Moody's 1997 story, "Whosoever: The Language of Mothers and Sons," which became part of his novel *Purple America* (1997), offers a similar explanation. The narrator has finally come home to take care of his severely disabled mother, whom he has not visited for months. Although the son recognizes he has been "neglectful," he tries to justify his absence by noting how painful it is for him to address the reality that "her condition is worse, always worse" (21). These examples serve as a reminder that the reason for adult children not being present may not be lack of care, but just the opposite—caring too much and not being able to watch a loved one's well-being compromised.

Intrusive Adult Children

A different type of problem confronting seniors and their families that appears in literature but not as much in the stories from the surveys is intrusive adult children, who are more involved than their parents would like. Susan Gubar in her memoir *Late-Life Love* suggests that it is rather commonplace for older partners, especially in second or third marriages, to face resistance from their grown children, who may see the "match as an outrage, a joke . . . or an act of disloyalty to a biological parent" (23). An example of this type of disapproval is shown in the novel *Our Souls at Night* (2015), by Kent Haruf, which was made into a 2017 film starring Robert Redford and Jane Fonda. It looks at neighbors Addie Moore and Louis Waters, who come together at night for companionship years after their spouses die. Much of the plot derives from the objections raised by their children who live out of town and do not approve of their respective parents' unconventional nocturnal activity. Louis's daughter, Holly, finds the arrangement between the couple "embarrassing," and Addie's son, Gene, questions Louis's motives, thinking he may be trying to bilk her for money. In contrast to the lack of attention on the part of some adult children, Gene and Holly's concern might seem welcome, but their cluelessness as to the needs of their parents—a desire for intimate closeness and a second chance at partnership—makes the two adult children appear inexplicably negative. Unless the grown children are worried about their financial inheritance, it is puzzling why there could be any objection to their senior parents seeking companionship, physical or otherwise. A *New York Times* article on the financial conflicts over later-life relationships, "When Your Parents Remarry, Everyone Is Happy, Right?," revealed that older couples often worry how future romantic relationships will affect money intended to be left to their children. Online comments on that article showed mixed perspectives, with one vocal group thinking parents should be able to spend their money in a new relationship however they desire while others shared horror stories of second marriages leading to bankruptcy and the inability to pay for nursing care when needed later on (La Gorce).

Another work featuring "helicopter" children, but with less selfish motives, is Michael Zadoorian's novel *The Leisure Seeker* (2009), which also became a film, featuring Helen Mirren and Donald Sutherland in 2017. "The Leisure Seeker" is the pet name of the Winnebago that Ella and John Spencer decide to dust off for a road trip from their home in Detroit to Disneyland in California, in order to revisit important places from the couple's time line. The problem with the plan that concerns their son, Kevin, and daughter, Cynthia, is that John is experiencing the effects of Alzheimer's and Ella has late-stage cancer. In a series of phone calls with Kevin and Cynthia, Ella must defend the trip, which is against her doctor's orders, and no one feels altogether comfortable with John at the wheel. Since the couple does experience a number of misadventures that lead them to the brink of danger, their children's objections have merit, in contrast to the offspring of Addie and Louis in *Our Souls at Night*, who come off as puritanical or selfish. Gerontologists have noted that adult children tend to prioritize safety for their parents while the older adults put more emphasis on maintaining their independence, these "mismatched goals" can lead to conflicts (Aronson, *Elderhood* 308; Span, "Aging Parents' Willfulness" D5). However, it is hard not to side with Ella, who admonishes her daughter, "Dear, what's going to happen is going to happen" (163). The ending also challenges the reader not to doubt the couple's decisions. We are asked to believe that the Spencers made a "happy ending" for themselves, and if doubts remain, the final words of the book are, "It is not your place to say" (272). Thus, whereas *Our Souls at Night* ends with the older adult characters, especially Addie, heeding the unfounded concerns of her adult child, *The Leisure Seeker* fully endorses the parents' ability to decide for themselves, over their children's objections, how to spend their final days.

When Death Descends

The death of one's parents that the children in *The Leisure Seeker* seek to delay is for many people a loss from which they never quite recover. Multiple survey responses discussed that event as life-changing and one that still affects them years later. A fairly representative response to the question of "significant losses" illustrates this reality: "The loss of parents has been my hardest. They have been gone for twelve and fourteen years and I still miss them." This same sentiment was shared by a ninety-year-old woman named Helen in Leland's book *Happiness Is a Choice You Make*, based on extensive interviews. Helen still cries when talking about her mother who died in 1969 and feels "lost" without her (58).

Besides reflections on the death of parents, several survey respondents shared stories of their children's deaths. Some were miscarriages or involved infants who died when under a year, but others chronicled the pain of an adult child's death, which is rarely represented in mainstream literature or film. Larry McMurtry's 1975 novel and later film *Terms of Endearment* is one memorable exception, and Joan Didion's 2011 memoir, *Blue Nights*, on the unexpected death of her daughter, is another. A previously unpublished manuscript by Harlem Renaissance virtuoso Zora Neale Hurston, *Barracoon: The Story of the Last "Black Cargo"* (2018), a nonfictional account based on interviews with Cudjo Lewis, one of the last slaves transported to the United States from Africa, has a memorable passage on the subject as well. When Lewis finds out another one of his adult children has died, he explains his sorrow: "We old folks now and we know we ain' going have no mo' children. We so lonesome" (88). Those who wrote in the surveys about their children's death also were remarkably candid. A sixty-six-year-old woman alluded to the suicide of her son at twenty-six. She asked, "How do you cope with suicide?" Fourteen years later, the mother is still in counseling and has taken to releasing a "birthday balloon to the heavens" to "keep his memory alive." Some individuals had experienced the deaths of multiple offspring and struggled with the unexpected tragedy since almost no parent expects children to die first. According to Marsha Malick, a professor at the University of Wisconsin–Madison who researches bereavement, a child's death for an older person is a "trauma that doesn't go away" (qtd. in Span, "A Child's Death"). Unlike parents of child-bearing age, elderly parents may no longer have a spouse to share the grief, much less the possibility of having more children. This was the situation for an eighty-six-year-old widow taking the survey. She described barely recovering from the death of her husband, who went from a "man who loved to walk at a brisk four miles an hour" to "slowly deteriorating health" from renal failure, when shortly thereafter her son was killed by a "driver who ran a stop sign and struck him as he was riding home from work on his bicycle." She wrote that the shock was "even more difficult" than the loss of her husband, and one that she still cries over: "The loss of a child is just not right." Perhaps the dearth of creative works taking up this topic validates the point that older individuals mourning for children who precede them in death is not an emotional landscape many people want to encounter.

Accepting Imperfect Relationships

Amid all the stories on the painfulness of loss that comes from death, there are some notable artistic renderings that inspire hope and promise. A story previously mentioned, "The Tunnel, or The News from Spain," is one such example; in it the mother and daughter share an imperfect relationship, but one of mutual understanding and growing appreciation. Rebecca becomes closer to her mother, Harriet, when she thinks that her mother is not going to live after she has been diagnosed with stage-four colon cancer. At that time, Rebecca takes on a helping role—using connections to get Harriet the best surgeon, indulging Harriet by reading reports of international intrigue and gossip, such as news about Princess Diana, which captivate her mother, and being present for multiple rounds of chemotherapy. Rebecca's sister, Cath, who lives in Colorado away from all of this medical activity in Boston, still carries grudges from the past, including some very petty grievances (after taking her to a Broadway musical as a child, Harriet did not buy the original cast album for her). Cath considers Harriet a "monster." Over time, Cath suggests that their mother "live closer," but takes no initiative to make that happen, while Rebecca repeatedly asks her to move nearer to her home in Connecticut. As the more involved daughter, Rebecca makes sure the nursing home staff treats her mother compassionately, brings beef tenderloin to the facility since Harriet is not mobile enough to go out to eat, and, generally, hopes for her mom not to die.

While the story never quite pinpoints what Rebecca receives from her efforts, the gaping hole that is left when her mother dies answers the question: "She wants to call Harriet, more passionately than she would have believed, an hour ago, that is was possible to want that, or to want anything" (306). The story of Harriet is interwoven with Rebecca's pursuits of romantic love, always with complications, and at the end, she needs her mom "to guess, to analyze, to explain, to make predictions" that will help her understand how to find and keep love, which so naturally developed between herself and Harriet. All the "work" of finding a partner ends up more taxing than traveling to the nursing home filling her mom's "many requests" because at least with her mom and the years of fostered understanding, she knew what to expect.

A final example of a complicated relationship with an aging parent, one in which both parties find a way to get along, can be seen in the contemporary television show *Better Things*. The comedy-drama series, which premiered in 2016, was co-developed by Pamela Adlon, who stars in it as an actress raising three daughters by herself after a divorce. *Better Things*, hailed by *Time* magazine and the *New York Times* as one of the best contemporary shows on television, stands out for its inclusion of an older parent who is interwoven into the family narrative and not played for laughs the way that elders typically are in this medium (D'Addario 118; Poniewozik). Jerry Seinfeld's parents (and George Costanza's) on *Seinfeld*, along with most of Betty White's roles, show this tendency of the small screen to caricature older individuals as comedic types without complexity and depth. In contrast, on *Better*

Things, Celia Imrie plays Phyllis (usually called "Phil") as the eccentric mother to Adlon's character, Sam Fox, and her actions are unpredictable in each episode because she defies simple characterization. Phil is usually a minor character, but an exceptional episode, entitled "Phil," in season two is devoted fully to her character. The episode begins with Phil playing cards with friends, complaining about Sam. She mocks her in a somewhat cruel fashion, but it is nonetheless refreshing to see an elderly character portrayed as independent and not always in need of assistance from their children. When Sam comes to the door to chastise her for seeking refinancing on a mortgage without Sam's permission, Phil returns to her card game unrepentant. The scene shows the tension between them (Sam also warns her mom about making unannounced "pop ins" to her house) as natural, given their living in close proximity to one another and both having strong personalities. Phil's bravado at the start of the scene makes her vulnerability shortly thereafter all the more dramatic. After volunteering as a docent in a local museum, she becomes disoriented and cannot find her car; she ends up falling and breaking bones in her leg.

As in the Wickersham story, in which one sibling is removed from direct care of an older parent by living far away, Sam's sibling, Marion, lives out of state, holds grudges from the past, and does not know the best way to proceed with care for Phil, due to physical distance and perhaps emotional distance as well. Sam complains to him that she needs an "accomplice" and does not want to "carry all the weight" herself in deciding if their mother needs to move to assisted living. Ultimately, though, Sam finds that she does not need her brother's input and figures out that the best decision is to "keep her home" until it is no longer possible. The final scene directly contrasts with the first one as Phil tells her daughter, "You know I am so proud of you, so grateful you take care of me, that you keep me." Some might interpret this interaction as Phil giving up the fiery independence that is on display with her friends at the beginning, but another way to look at the scene is that parent and "child" are figuring out together the next best steps and that this forges a closeness and appreciation that can be overlooked in day-to-day interactions and conflicts. The impact is made stronger by an earlier scene in which Sam's manager, Tressa, shares her own "war story" of dealing with her father, whom she took care of when he had dementia. Tressa warns, "You get used to things being hard where you can work to make them better. But this isn't that. There's no good end to this. It doesn't get better. Your mother is gonna get worse and worse and then she'll be gone." Rather than following this negative trajectory, however, Sam and Phil do arrive at a "better" place in their relationship with one another in a way that leaves hope that stories do not always have predictable endings, even for those deep in their later years.

Location, Location, Location

Better Things demonstrates that living near one's older parents often results in front-line caring responsibility that can be onerous but also worthwhile. There are now increasing numbers of families who are going one step further and revisiting the tradition of multigenerational living, which was the norm for nearly 25 percent of the population in 1940 but dipped to 12 percent in 1980 ("The Return of the Multi-Generational Household"). Demographers consider "multi-generational households" to be those with two adult generations or more or one with grandparents and grandchildren under the age of twenty-five. In the United States, various minority groups have commonly used this type of living arrangement for economic and social purposes, with as many as 40 percent of African American, Latino, and Asian American families including three generations in the home (Poo 127). The practice is especially prevalent among those who are foreign-born, but the trend is gaining for "nearly all U.S. racial groups," according to a 2018 Pew Research report, with a record 64 million people in the United States, or one in five families, living in multigenerational households, many of which include a family member over sixty-five (Cohn and Passel). This type of arrangement introduces a whole host of other issues that naturally develop out of sharing one's most intimate space. Gish Jen's 2012 story "The Third Dumpster" shows the Lee family encountering this dilemma as the aging parents believe "Chinese people . . . did not live by themselves," while the sons fix up a home for the parents so that they can be autonomous. Another variation on the dilemma can be seen in *One House Over*, a 2018 play by Catherine Trieschmann, in which the daughter, Joanne, takes her father, Milos, into her Chicago home, along with live-in caregivers, and chaos and conflict ensue as their overlapping lives do not fit together neatly. Still, research has indicated that older adults who live with children are "healthier" and possess "sharper mental and social skills" (Loe, *Aging Our Way* 182). Increased opportunities for engagement and less time alone, which can be up to seven hours for the average seventy-year-old, help to explain the physical and mental advantages for seniors who live with family members (Pipher, *Women Rowing* 84).

Geographical distance between family members, in contrast, definitely poses challenges of its own in the later years. Hearing my in-laws' struggles with problems regarding technology, house maintenance, and caregivers, but being in a different part of the country, made it difficult to assist them in any concrete ways other than regular phone communication. Very often, an out-of-town relation may offer financial support for a parent, but some assistance for older people can only come in person. A dramatic moment in *One House Over* occurs when the father, upset with his daughter's choice of hired help for him, announces that he is going to live with her brother out of state instead. The daughter replies with frustration, "He sends a check, so he doesn't have to see you."

Being close by to one another on a daily basis is sometimes the only way for adult children and parents to make important decisions together. Joyce Farmer's graphic memoir, *Special Exits*, about caring for her father and stepmother, shows how adult children must be the "eyes and ears" for their parents at times, especially within the medical maze many older people must navigate. For example, the daughter, Laura, angrily yells at hospital staff when she notices her stepmother's fingers have cuts all of over them from diabetes tests that she does not need (143). By being present at the hospital, Laura both sees the problem, which easily could be missed, and can vocally advocate for her stepmother in an intimidating manner that would be hard to muster on the phone. Recognizing that there is a growing need for adult children and their parents to live near each other, real estate developers are no longer concentrating exclusively on building senior housing in warm weather locations that older adults flock to upon retirement; they see an increased demand for communities closer to where seniors' grown-up children live. A 2018 *New York Times* article on "The Parents around the Corner" highlighted the new construction of different types of senior housing in locations not previously sought out by older adults for their proximity to family members (Miller 10). Being nearby clearly can be an advantage to parents and their adult children, as one daughter in the article expressed when considering the possibility of her mother falling, "How am I going to help her when she's in Walnut Creek, Calif., and I'm in Brooklyn?"

Aside from both the size of the United States, which allows for greater geographical distances among family members, and the fact that the country's population is more mobile than most others, another reason family members might not make arrangements to live near aging parents is that the rewarding aspects of looking after one's elders are not very publicized; instead, the potential problems receive much more attention. An adult child is more likely to share the gritty details involving cleaning up after a parent loses control over bowel functions or the hand-wringing over whether dad should give up driving after a few "fender benders" rather than express satisfaction in maintaining a connection of fifty, sixty, or more years with someone who was there from the beginning of one's life.

Final Reflections

Writing about older individuals and their relationship with their grown children is bound to leave out some people's experiences. For example, the subject of financial ties between the generations leads down a path with different kinds of outcomes. Wills, trusts, and inheritances have instigated many family conflicts in both literature and real life as money can cause various emotions to surface, some of them potentially good but many not. Several people in the surveys mentioned that they wished they could ask their children for financial help but expressed how hard it was to make such a request. Another story emerging from the surveys brought out how difficult it was to continue taking care of a daughter with physical and mental disabilities, both financially and otherwise, since the older adult does not know if her daughter will ever be independent or will need assistance for life. According to a Pew Research report, 40 percent of parents who are eighty-five or older have recently provided financial support to their adult children (Aronson, *Elderhood* 186). These topics all merit further exploration, but they were not the ones that came up repeatedly in the surveys or recent literature on aging. More often than not, the stories—both in the creative works and in the surveys—touched on the way that the central relationship of parent-child changes over time and must be navigated with care.

Just as sharing horror stories of seniors and grown-up children does a disservice, idealizing parent-child relationships in the later years is also not helpful. In reality, the children may hear more than they ever wanted to know about bodily breakdowns and who has recently died while parents may be dismayed that their loved ones cannot carve out more time for face-to-face visits and even lengthier phone conversations. But amid these conflicts of interests often lies an appreciation on both sides for the moments, days, and even years of this primal and nourishing relationship, which outlasts most others and always feels like "home."

3

Surveying the Housing Options

"No Place like Home"?

Am I the only one ashamed that we care so little for our parents that
we shove them in these most expensive of scrap heaps?
—Patch Adams, foreword, *The Senior Co-Housing Handbook*

I beg you to find a way to take care of me in my own home.
—Joyce Farmer, *Special Exits*

As we age, we are less able to care for each other,
but we still care about each other.
—Susan Cerletty, personal interview

Upon hearing the title *The 100-Year-Old Man Who Climbed Out the
Window and Disappeared* (2009) of the book by Jonas Jonasson,
one can easily imagine from where centenarian Allan Karlsson is
trying to escape: the "Old Folks' Home," of course. Institutions
that house seniors generally do not fare well in literature or in general public opinion. In the case of Karlsson, readers learn that the
Home is dominated by rules that "sucked the joy out of Allan's life"
(e.g., banning alcohol and smoking) and a rigid schedule for meals
that limited residents' opportunities to eat when they were hun-
gry. Upon hearing the prescribed protocol for everything, Karlsson

asks Director Alice, "Can you take a shit when you want to?" He soon realizes that his autonomy is truly gone as "he had lost control of his own spirit" (377).

Condemning senior care facilities is not a new phenomenon. The 1887 short story "A Mistaken Charity" by Mary Wilkins Freeman features the sisters Harriet and Charlotte, who escape the "Old Ladies Home" that do-gooder Mrs. Simonds thinks will be better for them than their own ramshackle domicile. While the "Home" in the Freeman story is "comfortable" and even serves wholesome food, the sisters feel like "prisoners" because they have had to give up their comfortable ways of dressing and eating back at their household. Both works, then, written over 115 years apart, lodge a similar complaint against old-age homes—they impinge on the freedom of individuals to do as they please due to the confines of large group setting with set agendas.

Nursing Home Critique

Although it may sound extreme to think of nursing homes—the term most people think of first when referring to these facilities—in terms of incarceration, even well-known gerontologists have made similar claims. William ("Bill") Thomas, an age activist and physician who wrote *What Are Old People For?* (2004), characterizes the traditional nursing home as a mixture of a "hospital and a prison" (qtd. in Durrett 119). His dissatisfaction with the "prison" aspects led him to develop innovations in these types of facilities, most notably, the Eden Alternative and the Green House models, which emphasize making senior living facilities more personal with greater individual care. Outspoken institutionalized care critic Betty Friedan devotes an entire chapter to "The Nursing Home Specter" in *The Fountain of Age* (1993). In that chapter she makes the bold claim that in the ten years of research that she examined, nothing changed her perception that nursing homes were "death sentences, the final interment from which there is no exit but death" (510). Friedan justifies her use of language associated with the penal system by making a "death row" analogy, noting that people died frequently once moved to a nursing home, often within a month (510). Evidence, in fact, does show that a "majority of people institutionalized in nursing homes die within two years of their arrival" (Poo 31). Another parallel Friedan draws is that just as prisoners often are known solely by their crimes, nursing home patients are viewed mainly "in terms of their infirmities," according to Barry Barkan, a gerontologist she cites (522). Her main complaint, though, stems from the discrepancy between what older people want in their living situation—"independence, flexibility, and freedom"—and the lack of those elements in nursing home facilities. Finally, the use of drugs to subdue residents in these types of "board-and-care" institutions in order to make them more manageable is also common in penitentiaries, a problem that Friedan mentions and that gerontologist Margaret Cruikshank notes in *Learning to Be Old* as well (Friedan 514; Cruikshank 57–58).

Adding to the negative perception of senior care residences, evoked in articles such as Tara Pour's 2016 *Washington Post* "Promise You'll Never Put Me in a Nursing Home," are their portrayals in visual media. Elizabeth Strout's novel *Olive Kitteridge* has a few gentle stabs at nursing homes once Olive's husband Henry is put in one after a stroke (e.g., her son asks, "My God, how can you stand this place?"), but the HBO mini-series in 2014 expanded the critique and extended its reach with added scenes. Before Olive leaves on a short trip to visit her son in New York, she gives the nursing staff explicit instructions about how she would like Henry to be taken care of in her absence, down to the detail of changing the water in his flowers. Upon returning from New York, she shows up at the facility and learns that he has died, apparently not having received phone messages to that effect. While the nursing home appears to be a pleasant place in this scene, with a piano player entertaining people and residents doing stretching exercises in the background, Olive's conversation with one of the workers becomes increasingly fraught with criticism and rebuke. When she realizes that during her conversation with Henry the night before, half an hour before he passed away, someone just propped the phone by his ear and walked away without noticing or informing anyone that he showed signs of last breaths, Olive is irate and levels this stinging diatribe: "So you just left the phone off the hook; you couldn't be bothered. You let the old woman babble on to her old husband as he drifts. You didn't give a damn about my husband. He was just one more stupid old man to wash and fill a bed. You can go to hell. I will slit my throat before I end up in a place like this." Since the worker does not respond to any of Olive's accusations after admitting that she did not change the water of his flowers and did not check on Henry's responsiveness when putting the phone by his ear when Olive called, these biting words are left undisputed and contribute to the general image of nursing homes as unresponsive to the individual needs of residents. As a miniseries primarily designed for entertainment, this adaptation leaves out possible reasons for such neglect. Among them are the fact that workers in most nursing care facilities, especially for-profit ones, are tasked with too many responsibilities and patients to watch over on their long shifts, are often poorly compensated for their time, and change jobs frequently.

Another visual media source that expands criticism of senior care residences from its literary predecessor is the 2006 film *Away from Her*, Sarah Polley's adaptation of the short story "The Bear Came over the Mountain" (1999) by Alice Munro. Much of the criticism in this film is subtle and may be easy to miss if not focused on nonverbal clues. When Madeline Montpellier, the supervisor at Meadowlake, a nursing home with different levels of care, offers to take Grant Anderson on a tour of the "brand spanking new" building before his wife Fiona, who has been experiencing memory lapses, becomes a resident, she comes across as insincere in rattling off all the positives of the place, such as its "natural light," "state of the art entertainment center," and "lovely new dining room." Grant's impassive face reveals that he is not impressed with her showmanship and that proves true as well when she talks about the policy of no visitors in the first thirty days, after which the residents are "happy as clams." Additional scenes added to the movie from the story that offer criticism include a young woman visiting relatives who claims the place is "fucking depressing" and the fact that Fiona is put into clothing that does not belong to her, an unflattering, orange sweater that Madeline calls "pretty" and Grant says is "tacky." It also shows that no one appears to know or care what belongs to his wife; she has become one of the masses. Grant is aware of how the facility uses words to mask problems; for example, moving to the second floor, for patients whose conditions worsens, is referred to as "progressing"—an "interesting choice of words," he remarks. When Fiona is thought to be declining and the staff warns that she will likely have to move to the second floor, Grant's frustration at this compartmentalizing of levels of care into bureaucratic policy is apparent when he tells Madeline, "I am aware of your bloody policies."

The power of both these works comes from the absence of sensationalism in their critique of these facilities. Patients are not shown being abused by hostile and impatient workers, but questions are indirectly asked as to whether institutions that are home to large groups of elderly are doing a good enough job. Given the negative portraits of institutions housing seniors from these different types of sources, no one should be surprised that research shows that most Americans want to age at home and not in a care facility. A study by AARP found that 90 percent of respondents said that "institutions are not the appropriate place for elders to spend their final moments, months or years" (Poo 2).

Stories from the Surveys

The survey responses for this book mirrored these findings, with dozens of seniors answering that one of their worst fears was ending their lives in a nursing home. Several people gave short explanations to support their desire to avoid institutionalized care if at all possible. A seventy-seven-year-old woman mentioned that she hopes not to end up in a nursing home because she saw her mom "decline and deteriorate there," a process she described as "awful." For eight years, every day, she would go to the nursing home and was struck by the "dreary, depressing atmosphere surrounding everything and everyone." One might ask why this woman did not seek a different place for her mother, but often relatives want to minimize relocations since the process is stressful and even has a psychological term: "relocation stress syndrome" or "transfer trauma" (Derrick). Moving for everyone is difficult and often dreaded, but for those late in life it can be particularly "destabilizing" as routine and familiarity are normally important constants when so much else about getting older can be unpredictable (Durrett 104). The woman's decision not to move her mother to a better facility also could have been dictated by cost. High-quality care facilities can be very expensive, especially when not covered by Medicare, and families are not always able to help defray these monthly expenditures and any needed add-on necessities, such as individualized nursing care.

Others' stories offered more details and made a convincing case for why many people continue to be wary of this living arrangement. One such story came from a sixty-six-year-old woman who described how her mother died from injuries sustained when nursing home staff dropped her during a shower and proceeded to "cover up" what happened. Eventually, a doctor discovered that both of her femurs had been broken in the fall, leading to other complications that contributed to her death; the incident required litigation, and eventually, the nursing home provided a financial settlement. The money clearly did not assuage this woman's lingering anger at the facility that treated her mother poorly. She explained, "Being an RN for 33 years, I have always treated my patients like I would have wanted my own family to be treated. Someone in that nursing home just didn't care enough to treat my mother with the same care I would have afforded to their mother."

Not all the responses from the surveys included terrible experiences with senior care facilities. A ninety-two-year-old woman in assisted living who receives care with bathing, meals, medication distribution, and housework addressed the positive aspects of her living situation. She included a number of social activities that she participates in, including "cards, lectures, word and group games, art classes, library, visiting group presentations, church and religious presentations." This diverse collection of social opportunities stands in contrast to the situation of some of individuals in the surveys who live alone in condominiums or houses. A seventy-seven-year-old, for example, said that she enjoys her "independence" and wants to have her "own place as long as possible," but stays in touch with friends more by phone than in person and feels "lonely." Several respondents observed that senior care facilities can be less isolating and called for a change in how people view nursing homes. In the words of a sixty-six-year-old, "I would like to address the overwhelming fear some have regarding moving into senior facilities. My personal observation/experience is that many people are significantly happier/more active/more social in senior facilities. Rather than a person that lives alone in a home, curtains drawn, refusing to go outside . . . without contact beyond the child that may come or call once a week. To me, that is not independent; it is more like prison." Recognizing that we should not have a stagnant one-size-fits-all view of senior care facilities, a woman in her eighties declared that nursing homes don't have to be "warehouses for the elder [sic]" and asked, "What can you and I do to make them better?" These opinions from those over sixty-five are particularly important to highlight, not only because of their first-hand experiences with housing issues but often because of their parents' experiences as well. With increases in life expectancy, seniors often are likely to have surviving parents in their eighties and nineties who also are trying to figure out where they should reside. Their opinions matter and need to be heard since scholars have noted how too often in the past "older people's voices" have been "muted in academic analyses of housing issues" (qtd. in Jamieson 13).

Literary Approaches to Senior Housing

The significance of having older adults evaluate housing options themselves is also shown in Margaret Drabble's novel, *The Dark Flood Rises*. Francesca Stubbs, the seventy-year-old central character, is an expert in the field and is paid by a charitable trust for

"examining and improving the living arrangement of the ageing."
Early on in the novel, readers meet Fran's much younger colleague
Paul Scobey. While she credits him for his knowledge of "adaptation" (making a "dwelling space . . . adapted to the ageing and the
disabled"), Fran also comments that his youth makes him unable
to understand how older adults might think about their housing.
She explains that "he is far too young to share her first-hand empathetic familiarity with some of the needs of the elderly" and
"doesn't expect people to want what they ought to want" (6). To
show just how crucial a direct understanding of senior housing
needs are, the novel includes an account of a woman who died
because she could not open the door to her bathroom due to the
type of doorknob, which prevented her from reaching the phone
to call for help after a mild stroke. Fran recognizes that being "well
ahead . . . on the road of ageing" herself, her younger colleagues
need her to "advise" them and "offer insight" (8).

Since the novel centers on an expert on housing for older adults,
it includes reflection throughout on different types of living
arrangements and how and why they appeal to various characters'
preferences and needs. Paul asks Fran to accompany him on a visit
to his Aunt Dorothy, who resides in a home specializing in schizo-
phrenia and those like Dorothy who are also experiencing dementia. The description of the "home-cooked food with the menu
changing weekly, access to local church and local shops, medical
attendance" does not reveal "any hint of hidden or underlying
neglect"; it is a "very small outfit, a domestic operation, a 'home
from home'" (39–40). The details contrast sharply with May Sarton's 1973 often-cited novel *As We Are Now*, which depicts a home-
care facility providing insufficient meals, medical care and social
engagement. *The Dark Flood Rises* also displays a retirement complex named Athene Grange, which is designed to "give its residents
the illusion that they are living in a Cambridge college" and which
appeals to Fran's friend Josephine, who is happy to have "down-
sized" into an apartment there and found great opportunities to
socialize. Those who live in their own private houses or condominiums seem to fare less well, especially those without a partner,

since they often seem isolated with scarce companionship. Fran's ex-husband, Claude, for example, whose health is declining, lives in an expensive "second-floor mansion block apartment with polished floors and brass fittings," but he spends most of his time alone "bored," seeing only his visiting care worker, whom he tries to lure to his bed for sexual relations, and his tabby, Cyrus, which provides some distraction and company for Claude. This detail mirrors several survey responses indicating that pets can become older adults' new "best friends," appreciated for the unconditional love they provide.

If the novel slants toward presenting those living in private dwellings as more vulnerable to loneliness, it does acknowledge some of the potential nightmares of institutionalized facilities that continue to evoke public distrust of them. There is mention of residents becoming ill at one care home after a worker deliberately contaminates food; once prosecuted, the worker is sentenced to a mental health facility. But this is an isolated incident, and by including so many different types of housing situations—many of which are continuing to be developed—the novel has the effect not of adding to the negative stockpiling on senior housing, but of opening for examination the varied options out there for older people to consider.

The Price

Something that Drabble's novel and other literary works that comment on senior housing share is recognition that many facilities catering to older adults are expensive. Fran notes this after visiting one new development, hearing about the various costs, and reflecting on the steep prices attached to quite a few of the "care homes and accommodations for the elderly": "It's expensive, getting old." Roz Chast's *Can't We Talk about Something More Pleasant?* goes into even greater detail about the price of assisted living. In the section on "The Place," she lays out the costs of the facility that she finds for her parents in Connecticut, including, per month, $7,400 for rent, $200 for furniture, and $600 for a "personal support plan," assistance beyond the six hours a week that an aide would provide for showering and dressing help—none of which would be covered by insurance. Drabble's novel includes some prices as well for the different types of housing (in British pounds), but Chast goes beyond the numbers to share the fear and shock of how the costs will be managed given that her parents have a fixed income based on pensions and social security. On a page with a drawing that simply says "Extra help?" Chast describes her worries about "the astronomical amount of money" that was needed for her parents in "The Place" and "whether their money would hold out till the end" (144). The next page continues a detailed look at the expenditures that mount on the minus side, while only the pensions and social security appear on the plus side, followed by a question in all capitalization and underlined: "HOW MANY MORE YEARS???" (145). Adding to the scary financial reality for her family, Chast includes on this page the fact that her parents' health insurance, "catastrophic" life insurance, and Medicare cannot not be drawn upon to pay for any of these costs. This information may be helpful and eye-opening for seniors and their adult children, who might think that insurance and/or Medicare would help pay for a living arrangement that requires care for health-related issues.

Despite some variations in different U.S. states and in the amenities at individual facilities, Chast's financial picture seems realistic. According to a 2017 Genworth Cost of Care Survey, assisted-living facilities on average charge $3,750 a month, while semiprivate rooms in nursing homes costing $7,148 a month (Holmes 3B). A 2017 *Consumer Reports* article entitled "Who Will Care for You?" corroborates these numbers and gives a state-by-state breakdown, which notes that in some states (such as Chast's Connecticut) assisted living costs over $60,000 a year (Wang 32). The article also points out that Medicare does not pay for long-term care facilities, but that Medicaid can in some states; however, Medicaid usually requires seniors to exhaust all of their financial resources before qualifying. As a result, some older adults end up in nursing homes when they are "mostly healthy" since Medicaid will pay for those who are eligible. According to the Kaiser Family Foundation's research, 62 percent of nursing home residents are on Medicaid (Terrell 15). Clearly, more alternatives for affordable senior care facilities are needed, given that costs are exorbitant, especially for people on fixed incomes, and that depleting one's savings to qualify for a Medicaid-funded facility, when that might not even be the right level of care, makes little sense.

Marketing to Whom?

Besides pointing out the problem of high costs for many care residences catering to older adults, Chast's memoir and other sources also comment on how too often these places try excessively hard to appeal to the adult children by highlighting the facilities' amenities rather than the care that elders themselves will receive. In fact, according to these works, the initial problem can be deceptive advertising in the residences' publicity materials. On the first page of "The Place" section in *Can't We Talk about Something More Pleasant?* Chast cleverly shows the disparity between how the assisted living residence appeals to the adult children more than their parents with a series of posters, which she looks excited about, but her parents think otherwise. In one frame, Chast exclaims, "And look-there's a GYM, and little bar if you want to get a drink before dinner. And BINGO ALL DAY LONG!" (126). Meanwhile, the mother's thought bubble reveals, "My daughter = nitwit," and next to a picture of her parents are the words: "Have never been to a gym, don't drink and don't play bingo." The page ends with Chast's mother saying she is "fatigued" and wants to get back to their room. The message is clear that the two generations do not agree on what is important in such a residence and that the facility seems more focused on what a younger generation might find appealing.

Atul Gawande in *Being Mortal* emphasizes that care facilities catering to adult children's interests and not their parents' is a significant problem. He brings in the opinions of Keren Wilson, the developer of Assisted Living Concepts, which operates 184 residences nationwide. Wilson points out that "the children usually make the decision about where the elderly live, and you can see it in the way that places sell themselves. They try to create what the marketers call 'the visuals'—the beautiful, hotel-like entryway. . . . They tout their computer lab, their exercise center, and their trips to concerts and museums—features that speak much more to what a middle-aged person desires for a parent than to what the parent does" (106). Wilson believes that the offspring already wield too much power in the decision of where their parents will live and often cannot help but to evaluate places through "their own lens" and not their family members'.

Brochures and material distributed at the now popular "aging expos" throughout the country provide real-life examples of how senior residences are reaching out to adult children in the hope that they will, in turn, influence their parents. My dad and his wife attended an expo in Northwest Indiana on my behalf and brought back brochures and giveaways that places were handing out to promote their offerings. One Indiana facility named StoryPoint has a separate handout directed at adult children with the header, "8 Signs that Your Aging Parents Aren't Ok to Live Alone Anymore." The flyer asks relatives to basically spy on their older family members during the holidays to determine if they can see "signs of trouble." One piece of advice is to "rifle through the mail" to see if there are "unopened bills," a possible indication that the "loved one" is "having difficulty managing finances," which is said to be "one of the most common first signs of dementia." Another spying technique is to give the relative a hug to see if there is a "strange body odor" or "obvious weight gain" that could mean "money trouble" is resulting in eating too much "dried pasta and bread." After this two-page list of possible signs that aging parents need to leave their current residences, StoryPoint encourages people to reach out to one of their "community specialists" who can "provide peace of mind," supposedly for adult children and their parents, even though the material was addressed only to the children. The material from StoryPoint that is intended for the "future resident" still seems focused on the younger generation with its lavish descriptions of gourmet food prepared by executive chefs ("pan-seared crab cakes with lemon aioli" and "fresh strawberries with mascarpone and limoncello crème"), a business center and "friendly games of poker." Some of the individuals who move to this type of facility likely would appreciate these amenities as well, but lack of attention to the cost, size of rooms, available medical services, and other practical matters that would concern seniors themselves is a serious omission.

How the rhetoric of senior facilities can mask the realities within is apparent in Marita Golden's *The Wide Circumference of Love* (2017). In the novel, when Gregory Tate, a sixty-year-old successful architect in Washington, DC, experiences significant memory loss, his wife, Diane, needs to find a care residence for him after the changes in her husband become too severe and potentially dangerous. As she and her closest friend, Paula, start the process of trying to identify the right facility for Gregory, they examine a "stack of booklets and brochures" given to them by a social worker, most of which sound ideal. The women note that even the names "Lighthouse," "Morningside House," and "Heartlands" all have a rosy association with them, conveying positive imagery as Paula remarks, "They sound like synonyms for heaven" (183). When the two go to visit one of the places, the reality is in stark contrast to the halcyon name. The inside was "beautifully decorated, colorful, serene," but upon closer examination, they observed the reality behind the scenery and flowery language: a "tall pecan-colored woman pacing the halls and hovering around the exit, her eyes as large as saucers, distant and suspicious . . . and the woman sitting in a rocking chair, holding a doll in her arms in an ironclad embrace" (184). Former poet laureate of the United States Donald Hall in an essay on aging called "Death" also notes the "encouraging names" given to facilities for the aged, which he calls "old folks' storage bins"; among the names he singles out are "Happy Valley," "Paradise Pastures," "Pleasures of Plenty," and "Golden Heirloom" (97). The cynical narrator of *The Secret Diary of Hendrik Groen* also chimes in on the subject, saying that any place that has "happy" in its name makes him wary; he is "leery" of facilities like the "Happy Days Nursing Home" and wonders what the upbeat name is concealing (257).

The Reality of Senior Care Facilities in Literature

Other literary works also present stark contrasts between what one senior housing activist Arthur Okner calls the "Del Webb model of elder life"—an "illusion-based advertising campaign that puts a picture of a white-haired couple playing golf and tennis and sitting around the pool"—and the sadder side of senior residential care (Durrett 220). Joan Wickersham's short story "The Tunnel, or The News from Spain" (2013) depicts the experience of a woman named Harriet who lives in a care residence; in one scene, in which she "slid down out of her wheelchair," she attributes the mishap to the facility being "short-staffed" (302). A 2017 *AARP Bulletin* cover story on "How Safe Are Our Nursing Homes?" reveals that "inadequate staffing" continues to be a significant problem for nursing homes, which are required to have a nurse on site only eight hours a day (Terrell 15). Additionally, recent investigations examining payroll records (as opposed to nursing homes' reports on staffing) on over 14,000 senior care facilities revealed "large [staffing] shortfalls on weekends," with one-fourth of the places having no registered nurses at least one day for three months. These shortages are a serious problem in that they usually go hand-in-hand with "health code violations" (Rau 1+). Joyce Farmer's graphic memoir, *Special Exits*, also showcases problems with the care that seniors receive in assisted living facilities—often not disclosed in promotional material and even ratings of places—in a scene where her stepmother, who is losing her eyesight and mental faculties, falls out of bed because the rails have been left down by staff (135, 138). It may be too easy to criticize this action as carelessness on the part of the worker, but blame should be leveled at the institutions that are maintaining these staffing shortages, which result in too few workers being able to look after the needs of too many patients.

Literature does not focus only on the shortcomings of these types of care facilities; other works highlight the progress that has been put into effect to make assisted living and nursing homes better than they were in the past. One such example can be seen in Richard Ford's connected short story collection, *Let Me Be Frank with You*. The central character, Frank Bascombe, who appears in Ford's other critically acclaimed novels, is now sixty-eight and learns that his former wife, Ann Dykstra, will be entering an "extended-care community," Carnage Hill, which his daughter Clarissa informs him is not a stereotypical "old folks' home" (135). Unlike other literary works that show the discrepancy between the promotional rhetoric of facilities and their stark realities, *Let Me Be Frank with You* demonstrates that this senior residence embodies the ideals set out in its advertising and publicity. A brochure for Carnage Hill touts it as a "living laboratory for Gray Americans" since "aging is a multidisciplinary *experience*." Other material on display in the lobby touts its "Platinum Certification" from the "Federation of Co-axial Senior Life-Is-a-Luxury-Few-Want-to-Leave Society"; the idea that permeates all of this marketing is to "re-brand aging as a to-be-looked-forward-to phenomenon" (138). Rather than contradicting the positive promotion, Carnage Hill lives up to its billing, sending the message that there are institutionalized care facilities that indeed are as good as they seem, even though many may be too expensive for the majority of seniors.

Among the laudable features of Carnage Hill are its sustainability practices, the hand-painted murals and photography on the walls, which counter an atmosphere of "infirmity or decline," personable workers who do not wear "uniforms" so as to make the place less like a hospital, cutting-edge technology to help residents remember to take medication and stimulate their mental faculties, and activities, such as a book group, that attract a host of "wheeled walkers" and "oxy-caddies [portable oxygen]" (138–139; 149). The contrast between this facility and others that most people associate with residential care is brought out when Frank recalls the typical "one-dimensionality of most of these places," which he describes as "soul-less vestibules" with "unbreathable antiseptic fragrances" and "dead-eyed attendants" (138).

Ford's description of Carnage Hill's superior amenities is not just one fiction writer's fantasy. Significant improvements have been made in residential care institutions, rectifying many problems from the past. For example, the previously mentioned Eden Alternative and Green House movements, brainchildren of William Thomas, have paved the way to rethinking how these types of facilities should be run. The aim of the Eden Alternative nursing home is to focus on lessening the "boredom and loneliness" of the living environment by bringing animals and pets to diversify the residents' day (Cruikshank, *Learning* 12). Thomas is also credited for developing the Green House Project, smaller units that have consistent staff members working directly with residents for individualized care. In addition, attention is given to increasing sunlight and access to outdoor space and providing residents more autonomy over their days (e.g., wake-up and meal times). Thomas's goal was to create places that would "look to the government like a nursing home, in order to qualify for public nursing home payments, and also to cost no more than other nursing homes," but that would feel like a "home, not an institution" (Gawande 142). Some of the home-like touches are "family-style meals around one big table" and "ordinary furniture" in comfortable living spaces, along with private spaces, like bedrooms and bathrooms, all of which include "universal design" to make everything accessible (Gawande 143; Loe, *Aging Our Way* 285). Two of the seniors featured in Meika Loe's qualitative research for her book *Aging Our Way* move to a Green House from independent living once they require help with "activities of daily living (ADL), such as dressing, walking, and bathing"; they credited this alternative care facility for altering their "outlook" and said it "saved their lives" (Loe 61). The limited number of residents in each home, generally twelve, helps the multidisciplinary team of workers know each resident personally and reflect their interests, meal choices, and habits.

Another novel innovation was to establish Green Houses for specific populations such as veterans, people who identify as

LGBTQ, and those with dementia. Since evidence shows that many LGBTQ elders worry that they may be discriminated against in traditional nursing homes and some have expressed a need to "closet" themselves again to prevent ill-treatment in institutionalized care, these facilities offer the promise of security, acceptance, and community (*Gen Silent*). As of 2017, there were 242 Green Homes in 32 states with at least 150 more being planned. A research study by the Robert Wood Johnson Foundation found that Green Homes are not able to fulfill all of their ambitions just yet, but experts in the field note that the attempt to "deinstitutionalize nursing homes" is a "cultural change" that is long overdue (Span, "A Better Kind of Nursing Home"). Research also suggests that, compared with traditional nursing facilities, these types of homes can bring costs savings to Medicare and Medicaid because with better overall conditions for the people living in them and clearer communication among staff members, hospitalizations are less frequent (Zimmerman et al. 483).

Whatever future innovations will be made to transform care facilities, listening to the objections of those who have lived in the less-than-stellar ones will be crucial. One of the six seniors profiled by John Leland in *Happiness Is a Choice You Make: Lessons from a Year among the Oldest Old*, Ruth Willig shared that when she had to move to a nursing home, the greatest difficulty for her was the loss of her privacy and being able to "set her own schedule" (182). Ruth also mentioned the "ever-diminishing autonomy and control" over her surroundings, which is confirmed by studies in which seniors show reluctance in giving up living in their homes because "home" for many is associated with "independence and dignity" (Gonyea and Melekis 46). Thomas has recognized these important values in the establishment of his senior care facilities, which are viewed as models in the industry. Besides the amenities offered at these institutions, developers should remember that maintaining people's dignity and privacy helps individuals deal with losses of self-reliance and the status that come when they no longer maintain their own independent living situation. Too often, institutions focus on "cost and efficiency," which can negatively impact residents' daily experiences by not prioritizing their needs sufficiently (Aronson, *Elderhood* 297).

Despite all the focus and near-hysteria surrounding nursing homes and other types of care residences, the number of Americans who actually reside in them is small, and possibly even decreasing. Statistics indicate that between 3 and 5 percent of those over sixty-five and 10 and 13 percent of those over eighty-five are residents in nursing homes, giving a total of around 1.4 million people (Kinsley 71; Friedan 22; Leland 170; Glass 260; Aronson, *Elderhood* 71). These numbers support the consistent research findings that the majority of people in the United States do not feel that institutions are the proper environment for older adults to spend their final years, a sentiment that was voiced in the survey responses as well. Just as an often-cited AARP study found that 90 percent of seniors wanted to "age at home," respondents in the surveys for this book expressed repeatedly that living independently in their homes was their preference (Poo 31). They also wanted to make sure that their adult children understood that desire; in response to the survey question "What do you really wish you could tell your family?," an eighty-two-year-old woman said, "We are doing ok and want to stay in our home."

Staying at Home or Investigating Alternatives?

An effective illustration of how adult children and older individuals might be at odds as to whether the parents should remain in their own homes or seek residence in a care facility can be seen in the Netflix television program, *Grace and Frankie*, in particular the last episode of season four, "The Home." Grace (Jane Fonda) and Frankie (Lily Tomlin) have become friends after their husbands of over thirty years become romantically involved with each other. In season four, when the two women are living together, a number of problems occur (e.g., a corrupt contractor has stolen the copper wiring from their place, and there is an infestation of rats in their home), leading their families to convince the two women that they should both go to an assisted living residence with the idyllic name "Walden Village." Their adult children read from a check-list put out by the residence of "signs your parents are ready for assisted living," which includes items like "recent physical setbacks" and "neglect around the house"; Frankie argues effectively that on a different checklist with other criteria, the two women "would be just fine." While Frankie's first reaction to the idea is a feisty "Fuck no," they are manipulated into agreeing even after asking their children, "Are you forgetting what this house means to us?" Two months later, Frankie and Grace are shown living at Walden Village, but not quite assimilating. Frankie is not allowed to paint outside of the art room, and Grace is not able to continue her vibrator business from where she lives due to zoning rules about conducting business from one's residence. Some of their beloved belongings, such as Frankie's fondue pot, also are confiscated as being too "dangerous" and put in the "no-no room." Grace tries to repeat her children's logic when questioned about the move by her boyfriend ("the house was too much for me"), but the friends soon realize that they need to make the decision for themselves. They know that the only place for them to escape the "dumb rules" of Walden Village is, in their words, "our house . . . home," which is exactly where they return.

The lessons to be drawn from the episode are crystal clear. Older adults should trust their own instincts regarding what type of environment best fits their whole person and should not give up their rights to decide what type of housing is suitable for them before they are ready. A facility's checklist that is focused on disability and impairment cannot be an effective tool to gauge when it is time to leave one's household. The episode also provides some of the "why" behind the large majority of people who want to stay in their homes—at least 79 percent of those over sixty-five reside in private residences (Gonyea and Melekis 47). Part of the reason is that Grace and Frankie do not want to have to explain their personal choices to anyone, especially building administrators—such as Grace's refusal to show up at the designated lunch time and Frankie's possessing a blowtorch (for her art!). They also do not want to follow rules that they feel impinge upon their individuality.

Perhaps an even more central reason can be the emotional attachment that develops for a place where one has lived for many years. Paula Span's *New York Times* article "How to Age in Place?" quotes seventy-one-year-old home-owner Elliott Goldberg saying, "I have a lot of good memories here" (D5).

Modifications in Order to "Age in Place"

A logical question that arises, however, is what about those seniors who are experiencing physical or mental challenges that make living independently not feasible? A 2014 report on "Housing America's Older Adults" put out by the Joint Center for Housing Studies at Harvard University reveals that 37 percent of those over sixty-five will need care in a facility at some point in their lives (even if for a short time), especially if they live alone, which is true for 40 percent of households. Part of the problem is that few private residences have features needed by those who are aging, including no-step entrances, accessible light switches/outlets (especially for people in wheelchairs), extra-wide doorways and halls, one-floor living, and levers for doors and faucets that do not involve as much twisting and turning knobs. According to the study, only 1 percent of residences in the United States have all of these features and only two of five have even one (Joint Center 2, 5).

Just as Francesca Stubbs in *The Dark Flood Rises* notes some of these types of adaptations in buildings and reviews them positively for helping seniors in their day-to-day lives, respondents in the surveys also see them in a favorable light, with some mentioning the need to adapt their living spaces after a disability arose. An eighty-six year-old woman discussed having to find a "no-step" solution when her husband "became an invalid." The need for these changes to homes has given rise to a new category of expert for the National Association of Home Builders—namely, a Certified Aging in Place Specialist (CAPS), who can help older adults make the proper modifications to their homes as various disabilities arise. Besides some of the modifications already mentioned, bathrooms also can benefit from many changes, such as higher toilets, curbless showers, and grab bars. Although these renovations can be costly, Medicaid and the Veterans Affairs offices provide grants, and some states offer reimbursement through tax credits. They likely recognize that modifications to a home for senior needs may help to prevent falls, which occur half the time at home and are the primary "cause of injury and injury-related deaths" for individuals sixty-five and over (Gonyea and Melekis 49). For the many people who say they will leave their homes only "feet first," these accommodations may extend the length of time older adults can stay "in place" for longer than they may have in the past. Another organization that provides assistance is the National Aging in Place Council (NAICP), a "one-stop shop" of in-home aging services providers, who have been carefully screened to make sure they will not take advantage of elderly consumers (Sichelman).

Those who are hoping to "age in place" also have been pursuing long-term insurance policies that pay for caretakers to assist them with nursing and/or daily tasks to make living at home an option for an extended period of time. Critics have complained that these policies are too expensive for many seniors who do not have large amounts of savings and may be subsisting on Social Security. Issues also can arise with qualifying for these policies. The novelist Gail Godwin writes about her experience trying to obtain a long-term care policy in an essay entitled "Losing Ground," included in the anthology *Aging: An Apprenticeship* (2017). She is shocked to learn that her application is denied because by seeing doctors regularly for preventative medicine, she left a "paper trail" that an insurance company believed made her "not a good risk" (205). Godwin also writes about how these policies may cause one to be self-deluding in that it is too hard to predict one's future self, both body and mind, to know what one will really need and when:

> You want to die at home with your familiar views and no
> horrible institutional lighting and no one taking away your
> individuality . . . but when you're imagining this future, you
> can't quite get your mind around the fact that you may be much
> altered from the you who is now projecting this future. You may

be blind and unable to see any views or be disturbed by the institutional lighting. You may be gaga enough not to care where you are—or even to know you are an individual. But now you feel that if you can just qualify for the policy and get to stay at home, you'll go on being yourself and everything will be all right. (203)

This passage is a reminder that some of the proactive steps that people take to try to guarantee a certain outcome for their future self may not be effective when that future turns out to be not as planned, especially in the case of those who do not want to imagine changes in residence or changes to themselves. Despite not being able to determine one's future health path, Godwin comes to regard long-term care policies as being able to provide some peace of mind and a sense of security that one's future health and well-being are not completely up for grabs, even if that notion is somewhat of a self-delusion.

Not everyone in the surveys expressed a desire to remain in their homes forever. Some older adults recognized the burden of maintaining a home was too much of a physical struggle even if the desire was to remain there. One study showed that apartment residents over seventy were "more satisfied" than those residing at home due to less "upkeep" of the property (Golant 47). Besides the demands of keeping up with the outside of physical property (e.g., lawn maintenance), the struggles of keeping up with housework can be a monumental task as well. Both *Can't We Talk about Something More Pleasant?* and *Special Exits* illustrate how the demands of household chores can be too taxing once people reach a certain age and/or physical state. In her graphic memoir Chast devotes a full page to the "GRIME" that she notices upon entering her parents' place after not being there for over ten years. She is able to tell right away that they "haven't cleaned in a really long time" (15). When Laura visits her dad and stepmother in *Special Exits*, she cannot stop sneezing from the dust and thinks to herself, "It's at least eleven years since this room has been cleaned" (20). Both works also call attention to the clutter of objects that their respective parents have amassed over the years and have been unable to give up. But for one senior answering the survey, being liberated from countless possessions when giving up her home was something she anticipated. Her comment was that it would be "freeing to get rid of ¾ of our things and seeing some of our treasures in our kids' and grandchildren's homes." Whether family members, who likely have homes of their own, will be open to receiving these offerings raises other possible problems that adult children of older adults often discuss. Other survey responses mentioned the possibility of "downsizing" as well, not with dread, but just some uncertainty about finding the next right place that would be affordable and practical for their evolving needs.

Alternative Types of Senior Housing

Whereas in the past the only options for older adult housing were living independently in a home, condominium, or apartment, living with one's children, or living in a care residence (nursing home or assisted living), there are new options being developed, many of which have been successful in other countries for decades and are now being implemented in the United States. Their impact may not yet be felt since housing experts still decry that "thoughtfully designed housing for older adults is not being created on a scale commensurate with the growing need," as articulated in a 2017 *New York Times* op-ed piece by Allison Arieff. Regardless, one such alternative, senior co-housing, is capturing people's interest and expanding significantly. The idea of co-housing originated from Danish architect Jan Gudmand-Hoyer in 1964, though it took over ten years for his model to be actualized in Denmark. The idea has popularized in the United States due to the joint efforts of architects Charles Durrett and Kathryn McCamant. Their first intergenerational co-housing project was established in 1991, and since then, there are now over one hundred, with an additional 120–150 being planned. The first exclusively senior co-housing development, Glacier Circle in Davis, California, was built in 2005; the average age of residents there is eighty (Durrett 19, 203). Those who are organizing co-housing developments replace the idea of "aging in place" with "aging in community," one in which residents look out for each other and share responsibilities and some living spaces, while having their own private spaces as well. They also make many household decisions together, without a hierarchal leadership, and have opportunities to spend time in the company of others, if desired. Although co-housing has been confused with communes, due to the shared decision-making, people in co-housing usually own their own units (such as condominiums) whereas those living in communes generally own property together. Preventing loneliness and isolation is a main goal of senior co-housing, but it also can boast of environmental advantages with research indicating that "cohousers drive 60% less and use 50–75% less energy for heating and cooling than they did in their previous homes" (Durrett 21).

In order to introduce more Americans to the idea of co-housing, those interested in finding others who share an interest in co-housing are developing workshops across the country to study the principles behind it and figure out in advance if this type of living situation would meet people's present or future needs. I joined a ten-week session in Wisconsin with my mother, who is in her eighties, to learn more about senior co-housing and to see how older adults reacted to it as an alternative living option. The workshop uses a guide designed by Durrett and Jean Nilsson, which does not hide its bias as seen in the first chapter when co-housing is touted as "far and away the best option for many seniors." Still, the guide does ask workshop members to respond to questions in "homework," as well as in group discussions that allow for an exchange of ideas and conclusions in which co-housing is not always the "best option." According to the guide, 40 percent of participants in the first study group in Denmark went on to join a co-housing group. By contrast, in the study group I attended, nobody definitively committed to the idea, and many decided it was not for them. While most of the group did see how senior co-housing could be a more stimulating environment with more emotional support than living alone or in a care facility, questions remained about whether it was economically feasible for many seniors on fixed incomes, even if the monthly estimate of $2,000 for mortgage, food, and utilities is less than the estimated $4,000 for assisted living (Durrett and Nilsson 74). Other issues that contributed to reluctance in the workshop group concerned questions about incompatible personalities and doubt about finding strangers who could become family-like friends. Likely fueling this resistance is American individualism, a doctrine that most people in the United States are subtly brought up learning, which stresses a wariness of communal activity and the importance of maintaining one's own "borders."

While participants in the workshop had serious concerns about the viability of senior co-housing, they were drawn to an intergenerational model, which is an offshoot of the co-housing movement. In a 2018 report from Generations United and the Eisner Foundation entitled "All in Together: Creating Places Where Young and Old Thrive" researchers found that 74 percent of Americans believe that age segregation is destructive and prevents the young and old from benefiting from each other's "skills and talents." Innovative housing projects are finding ways to bridge this gap by bringing college students and seniors together in shared living spaces. In Cleveland, Ohio, a retirement community is offering room and board for students at nearby Case Western Reserve University, and other senior residences are supplying free room and board to students who are artists-in-residence there. Similarly, New York University has launched a program to provide housing for students in spare rooms that older people have in their apartments or homes. In Los Angeles the Anita May Rosenstein campus of the LGBT Center provides low-cost apartments to older adults and temporary shelter for homeless LGBT youth with a large commercial kitchen to feed homeless individuals in both demographics. This Los Angeles initiative is particularly timely as research indicates that seniors who identify as LGBT often experience "rental housing discrimination" and projections indicate that by 2050, there will be significant increases in the homeless population of adults sixty-two and older (Gonyea and Melekis 50).

At the senior co-housing workshop I attended, I was introduced to Susan Cerletty who is bringing intergenerational co-housing into her own home in Wauwatosa, Wisconsin. Drawing upon her years as a physical therapist, Cerlatty has reconfigured the 1878 house to accommodate possible physical challenges seniors may face, while still maintaining many of the original components of the house. Besides a state-of-the-art stair climber, the floors are covered in a vinyl that reduces slipping, grab bars are in a variety of locations from the front door to inside and outside of the shower, and all the passageways are wide enough to traverse with a wheelchair. Right now, Cerletty lives in the home with her mother, Joanne Hulce, who is in her nineties, and a graduate student from a local university. When I visited the house, I had a chance to talk to Cerletty and Hulce about the rewards and challenges of this kind of arrangement. Hulce, who moved from a life-plan community—a residential facility for seniors with different levels of healthcare—said she appreciates the "feeling of safety, comfort and companionship" in the new living environment because she did not enjoy the "large institution" feel of the other facility, where everyone being "old" tended to lead to the "sameness of daily conversations." Cerletty added that she appreciates that unlike in age-segregated facilities, with people staying in their rooms a lot, trying not "embarrass" themselves, in their current household, there is always someone to ask, "How did you sleep?" They are also very involved with their age-integrated neighborhood (one of the criteria when Cerletty was researching locations), such as hosting bike decorating for Fourth of July parties, so there is intergenerational activity inside and outside of the house. Hulce still misses her native Michigan roots, where some of her deepest personal connections are, and Cerletty mentioned that being in a household with people of different generations sometimes means that not everyone has the same expectations of shared living; still, they seemed overall very satisfied with the arrangement, especially in their ability to "shape the care environment" that they call home (Cerletty and Hulce).

Angela Peterson, photograph of the home of Susan Cerletty and Joanne Hulce, Wauwatosa, Wisconsin, 2018. (Courtesy of *Milwaukee Journal Sentinel*, ©2019 Journal Sentinel Inc., reproduced with permission.)

The developments to bring young and old together not just in a community center or school setting but in a residence are supported by various writers who have recognized the value of forging greater connections between different-aged groups of people. One of the first prominent writers on old age, the Roman orator Marcus Tullius Cicero, wrote in his 44 B.C. work, originally titled *How to Grow Old*, "What indeed could be more pleasant than an old age surrounded by the enthusiasm of youth?" (61). Celebrated anthropologist Margaret Mead also heralded the "mutually beneficial relationships" of multigenerational communities in the various cultures that she studied (Larson and DeClaire 151). Literary sources, too, advocate the potential good of bringing younger people in greater proximity to those late in years. *The Dark Flood Rises* has several older characters express that "young people" can "infuse . . . energy into the elderly" (Drabble 150). The memoirist

Diana Athill additionally shares how the interconnectedness of the generations can be good for all: "People who are *beginning* . . . is a reminder. . . . It enables us to actually feel again—that we are not just dots at the end of thin black lines projecting into nothingness, but are parts of the broad, many-colored river teeming with beginnings, ripenings, decayings, new beginnings . . . are still parts of it" (84). Athill's perspective, albeit somewhat philosophical, recognizes the common humanity between people separated by many decades in that we all experience a series of beginnings and endings at all stages in lives. Having meaningful contact with people from different ages through innovative intergenerational housing allows for this infusion of shared experience to happen with more frequency and regularity. Whether for financial reasons and/or because of cultural expectations, when people of different age groups live under one roof and defy the age segregation so common in education, work, and socializing, many positive outcomes are seen.

Two other housing movements that have developed some traction in the United States include the Village movement and naturally occurring retirement communities (NORCS). Most people credit Beacon Hill Village in Boston as the innovator of the Village movement, in which residents of a community contribute money to a collective fund in order to finance resources needed for individuals to remain in their homes. In some "Villages," the money goes to a repair person who can address everything from changing light bulbs to other broken appliances. Others hire a director to coordinate volunteers and nursing assistance. Often called a "neighbors-helping-neighbors membership organization," the Village model relies heavily on volunteers, and members are "encouraged" to volunteer as well; this may involve dog-walking, sharing computer knowledge, or helping someone with shopping (Baker 29).

Besides assisting with such practical living tasks, Villages also have a social component so that members can enjoy each other's company at group events, as well as initiatives to combat loneliness. Thus, for example, in Washington, DC, the Capitol Hill

Village has a "rise and shine" partners program in which people who live alone check in with each other daily. There are currently over 200 Villages across the country with 150 more in the planning stages. Researchers who have studied their influence, such as Andrew Scharlach at the University of California-Berkeley, see Villages as important for making assistance easy to come by, providing "social connection" for seniors who might otherwise feel isolated, and giving people a renewed sense of purpose in that they are being asked to contribute and help others (Baker 33–34). I had a chance to interview Ann Albert, the executive director of Sharing Active Independent Lives (SAIL), located in Madison, Wisconsin, which is part of the Village to Village network. Albert expressed the individuality of each Village (repeating a common saying that "to know one Village is to know one Village"), but commented that all seem to be guided by "incredibly talented pioneers" who are "banding together" and "helping each other" through the aging process. She also emphasized the importance of people being able to remain their "own decision makers," which may aid them in "maintaining self-worth" as well (Baker 32).

Credit for devising the term "NORC" (a naturally occurring retirement community) goes to University of Wisconsin–Madison human ecology professor Michael Hunt who first used it in a 1986 article that he co-wrote with his wife, Gail Gunter-Hunt, a social worker specializing in gerontology, to describe a number of apartment complexes in Madison that housed predominantly senior residents never choosing to move elsewhere. The general definition of a NORC is an area that has a high concentration of older residents; they can be found in places with apartments, condominiums, trailer parks, or individual homes in urban and rural areas. One estimate is that there are over 5,000 urban NORCs nationwide, consisting of upward of ten million people (Masotti et al.). Unlike senior facilities that use marketing strategies to encourage older adults to become residents, these places do not advertise or boast of amenities; instead, they cater to elderly who just happened to remain in a location over a long period of time. A main difference between Villages and NORCs is the absence of a membership fee from the latter. Instead of using that fee to finance assistance that may be needed by participants, NORCs work with social agencies already a part of the community and receive government funding to help those who want to remain at home rather than pursue expensive institutionalized care. Residents who are affiliated with NORCs also note that while Villages might help only those who are dues-paying members, NORC are willing to reach out to anyone who is in need. In an email conversation that I had with Hunt, he said that he noticed that in Madison, seniors seemed more inclined to move to a NORC than a "place that was designed and planned for older people." He pondered what "architects and developers" were "missing" and came to the conclusion it was "COMMUNITY." His co-written ground-breaking article on the subject also makes clear how important a safe "neighborhood" can be to older residents, especially for easy socialization, and close proximity to shops, services, and public transportation (Hunt and Gunter-Hunt 12, 15). One of the interviewees in Loe's *Aging Our Way* discussed how her neighborhood of "mostly retirees" has been declared a NORC, resulting in state grants to support community activities and a social worker for the area to address any issues that the residents might face (171, 284). No one who took the surveys identified as living in a NORC (or a Village, for that matter), but people did express a desire for more "funded home health services," which indicates that not living in one of these types of communities may make it more difficult to find resources on one's own. In contrast, a sixty-seven-year-old-woman who lives in a senior housing residence wrote about how her building connects residents with "agencies that can help people," including those with serious handicaps. Places that have been designated NORCS, including several in New York City, make health care a priority by providing nurses available free of charge to older residents in the community as part of the city's budget (Abraham).

Those who have studied housing for many years recognize that the place where a person lives affects many aspects of well-being and peace of mind. As Durrett writes about co-housing, "A home is more than a roof over one's head or a financial investment. It can provide a sense of security and comfort, or elicit feelings of frustration, loneliness, and fear" (15). As the literature, surveys, and housing resources reveal, many different options are available for those entering the later decades of their lives. While tradition has seen older adults stay fixed in their single-family homes for year after year, others are investigating alternative possibilities and weighing factors such as social engagement, physical/mental abilities, and financial realities in the decision-making process to figure out where they best belong.

4

Understanding Memory Loss
"Am I Losing My Mind?"

Please understand, I am still here.
—Richard Taylor, *Alzheimer's from the Inside Out*

Every story of Alzheimer's Disease—and this is true of any
terminal illness—must be different.
—Margaret Morganroth Gullette, *Ending Ageism,
or How Not to Shoot Old People*

It's a terminal disease, all the literature keeps saying. "But isn't
everything terminal?" is what I say to nobody, out loud.
—Rachel Khong, *Goodbye, Vitamin*

There is so much...hope—not for a medical cure at the
moment, but hope for a cultural cure—for meaning and
connection between families and staff and elders.
—Anne Basting, unpublished letter to *The New Yorker*

Susan Jacoby's discussion of Alzheimer's disease in her 2011 book
Never Say Die: The Myth and Marketing of the New Old Age is one
of the harshest treatments of how the degenerative disease may
affect the 5.1 million Americans who have received this diagnosis.

Jacoby makes readers painfully aware of the trauma that she experienced watching the person whom she loved devolve from a "bright mind" to "darkness," which can explain why she believes those afflicted with Alzheimer's might feel "like Job" and "curse the day" they "were born" (113). Several prominent scholars, Anne Basting among them, argue that such extreme negative viewpoints only fan the already disproportional fear that mental decline is inevitable with age and further alienate those with this severe form of dementia. Another debatable argument in Jacoby is that "people with dementia are largely invisible" in literature on the subject since much more focus tends to be on the caregiver, whose point of view tends to overshadow the individual with memory loss (121).

Representing Alzheimer's

Certainly there is evidence in both creative and scholarly works that focus on this age-related degenerating condition to support Jacob's claim. John Bayley's 1998 memoir *Elegy for Iris*, later made into the 2001 film *Iris*, based on the prolific novelist Iris Murdoch's experience with Alzheimer's, often showcases Bayley's frustration with taking care of his wife as her disease progresses, in addition to his grief over losing his intellectual equal. A similar, more recent book, which also has an eponymous title tied to the author's wife, *My Two Elaines: Learning, Coping, and Surviving as an Alzheimer's Caregiver* (2017), by former governor of Wisconsin Martin Schreiber, even includes "caregiving" as part of the subtitle to highlight the fact that writing about his wife's Alzheimer's disease necessitates discussing how the partner must take on new responsibilities due to the disease. The fact that many caregiving-focused books are written by men, when two-thirds of caregiving is done by women, is addressed in Susan Gubar's *Late-Life Love*, which notes that male spouses who writing of their experiences gain appreciation of the tasks that many women do every day, such as "shopping, cooking, and cleaning" (Poo 46; Gubar 203–204). Although these examples and countless others show a tendency to focus less on the individual with dementia and more on the person who is helping that individual adapt to the changes, writers and researchers are finding original ways to alter this trend.

One surprising medium for presenting Alzheimer's disease from the perspective of the person who is experiencing it is a dark, animated Netflix comedy series for adults entitled *BoJack Horseman*, which premiered in 2014. A season-four episode called "Time's Arrow," written by creators Raphael Bob-Waksberg and Kate Purdy, based on research and their own families' experience, imaginatively and effectively captures the mindset of someone with severe dementia. The episode begins with the title character, BoJack, a former sitcom star past his glory days (who happens to be a horse), taking his mother, Beatrice, to live in a nursing home. Right away, the viewer understands that something is not right with Beatrice as she refers to BoJack as "Henrietta." What follows next is a mental tour of Beatrice's meandering thoughts, which are deeply rooted in the past. Like many individuals who have Alzheimer's disease, Beatrice is able to access long-term memories of her childhood and young adulthood better than short-term memories (MacFarquhar 47). Researchers believe that memories retrieved most often in the course of one's lifetime stay with people the longest, even when dementia has set in; in addition, since long-term memories tend to be stored in the brain's cortex, they are preserved longer than the short-term ones tied to the hippocampus region, which is where late-life dementia first strikes.

Besides depicting what seems like a nonlinear slide show of Beatrice's painful memories from when she was younger, the episode goes one step further in its attempt to connect viewers with Beatrice's condition by giving them an almost virtual experience of what it is like to live with Alzheimer's. The words on signs are rearranged; faces appear devoid of any distinctive features, and particular characters that instill strong negative emotions, such as Henrietta, a former servant who became sexually involved with Beatrice's husband, have scratch marks over their faces. Even the flashbacks to her past are fragmented and incomplete, following the vagaries of her mind. But the episode is notable not just for its attempt to illustrate the perspective of someone suffering from severe dementia, but also for casting some light on the power of storytelling for individuals who are not mentally fully cognizant. In contrast to the lobotomy referenced in the episode, which Beatrice's mother was forced to have years ago when she was not acting normally, BoJack offers his mother a reassuring imaginative reflection in the final scene. He tells her about a "warm summer night" when "fireflies are dancing in the sky" and her whole family is surrounding her, saying that "everything is going to be all right." Since Beatrice's reminiscences into the past include memories of her father denying her ice cream when she was younger in order to "protect" her figure, this ending scene is particularly poignant in that BoJack incorporates Beatrice eating vanilla ice cream into the story. He asks her, "Can you taste the ice cream, mom?" Her response takes a moment, but she finds the words to say, "It is so . . . delicious." In the last scene of the episode, Beatrice's disorientation, seen at the beginning when she mistakes her son for Henrietta, is transformed into an awareness of the possibility of continuing to use her imagination and even language when inspired. The effect is to make viewers want to pay better attention to those with dementia and not write them off as "gone." Even in the first scene, when Beatrice is confused over BoJack's identity, she makes puns by saying "my son is a ball of gas . . . a star," while pointing at the sun, playing on the double meaning of sun/son and also "star," since BoJack was a former popular sit-com actor. This viewpoint showing creative possibility even amid extreme memory impairment stands in extreme contrast to Jacoby's projection of Alzheimer's as all loss.

Facts and Fears

Alzheimer's is the most common cause of dementia, with 5.7 million people diagnosed in the United States and 47 million globally (Kluger 4). Dementia is defined by Dr. Eric Larson, a leading expert in delaying and preventing Alzheimer's, as "cognitive impairment sufficient enough to affect everyday functions" (Larson and DeClaire 77). Although many people overestimate how many older individuals will experience dementia, Larson puts the likely figure at one-third of those between eighty-five and ninety and one half of those between ninety and ninety-five. At the same time, even as the number of people who will be diagnosed is expected to grow significantly, the rates of people developing various types of dementia are decreasing. Part of the explanation for this perplexing situation is that in the past, it was not uncommon for seniors to experience dementia for ten years or more; now, seniors usually are affected only in their last year of life, perhaps due to the incorporation of healthier lifestyles, which explains the 25 percent decrease researchers have noted (Larson and DeClaire 4; "Alzheimer's Disease: Working to Solve the Mystery" 4). Meanwhile the dramatic anticipated increase in those affected—160 million worldwide by 2050—reflects the sheer number of people who will be over sixty-five (Bredesen 15).

Despite decreases in the numbers of those affected by dementia and in the length of time that they experience it, the widespread fear of losing one's cognitive abilities when aging has not abated at all. In fact, studies have shown that after cancer, people fear having Alzheimer's more than anything else (Applewhite, *This Chair Rocks* 67). In a 2017 bestseller entitled *The End of Alzheimer's*, Dr. Dale Bredesen explains that this fear is the "number one concern of individuals" as they get older because when we think about ourselves as unable to "perform the basic functions of daily life," we tend to think that there is little distinguishing us from "mere sacks of protoplasm dependent on others to feed, dress, move and bathe" (12). The survey responses supported the existence of extreme fear of dementia, but there was a wider range of reasons provided beyond the notion of dependency cited by Bredesen. Some respondents listed their concern about dementia or Alzheimer's specifically as just one of their "fears," but others gave detailed explanations. A sixty-six-year-old woman mentioned that she feared dementia based on what she has seen as its effects on people whom she knows. Others listed family members or friends who struggled with memory loss and the difficulties it caused for loved ones. A few seniors who answered the survey worried that dementia would reduce them to a "state of nothingness," which created for them an existential crisis of psychological nonexistence. On the opposite side of the spectrum were answers with very practical concerns—especially the potential "financial hardship" of requiring paid care at home or in a facility. Other practical matters that came up in a survey in Anne Basting's *Forget Memory* (2009) on why people fear memory impairment included losing insurance, losing their driver's license, and being institutionalized (159).

Not Just Fear

Even though the surveys reveal great anxiety about losing one's mental faculties in old age, they also included countless stories of families accepting living with Alzheimer's disease and other forms of dementia, rather than describing the situation in catastrophic terms. One woman described her husband's Alzheimer's disease as a "challenge," but she went on to say "we are lucky." The fact that his "mild temperament" has stayed constant and that he is able to express gratitude for her help creates a dynamic that is tolerable for both rather than the nightmare that is often imagined. Another woman explained that she is able "to handle" her husband's dementia presently, but she is not sure if this is something she can expect to continue do. Even with families in which both parents have been diagnosed with Alzheimer's or another type of dementia, the narrative is not one of utter despair. An interview with the middle-aged son in one such family revealed coping strategies learned through trial and error and support groups; these strategies include the importance of not arguing with those who have dementia, accepting that one's efforts might not be reciprocated, and seeking respite from care (Anhalt).

Recent fictional works featuring characters with Alzheimer's also present a portrait of the disease that minimizes the fearful aspects. The novel *Goodbye, Vitamin* by Rachel Khong, for instance, features thirty-year-old protagonist Ruth Young whose mother asks her to come back home to help look after her father, a retired history professor who has been diagnosed with Alzheimer's. The novel brings some levity to situations caused by the father Howard's altered behavior as dementia sets in (e.g., it opens with his pants being returned by a neighbor since Howard has thrown them up in trees to protest his name being written into his clothes to identify him better); however, it also includes the significant challenges the family faces when Howard's behavior becomes too unpredictable and even scary, as revealed when Ruth says to him: "An hour today, you spent shouting. You said we'd stolen money from you. You threw your pillows over the fence and into the Grovers' pool. You broke the legs off of your dining table chair. You smashed almost all of our drinking glasses" (170).

Although this passage may describe the type of horrific actions that can create anxiety about dementia, it is followed by the dad "quietly" eating a banana and weeping. The disease is normalized as well by including many scenes in which Howard is still very much himself. When Ruth and Howard watch the Oscars, he "pokes fun at the actors and actresses—remembers all their names, like any regular, not sick person" (85). Moreover, when his memory and personality are still sharp, father and daughter also together take on projects for the house, especially building a patio cover, which had been started but unfinished for years. Seeing the different ways that Howard is still participating in the world, albeit not teaching his courses at the university, replaces the worst-case-scenario images that feed fear and worry about the disease as revealed in countless studies and surveys. The "nothingness" that one respondent identified as eliciting her fear of dementia is challenged in the novel through diverse examples of the father's actions, which are not all negative.

Another contemporary novel that depicts Alzheimer's disease with more complexity is Allison Pearson's 2018 *How Hard Can It Be?* Unlike *Goodbye, Vitamin*, which has the father's experience with dementia at its center, this novel incorporates the storyline into one facet of the central character's teeming life. At fifty, Kate Reddy is struggling with her adolescent children, her husband Richard's midlife crisis, and her own serious hormonal fluctuations. Since Richard is preoccupied with "finding himself," Kate feels responsibility to look after her in-laws, Barbara and Donald, who live independently in their own home, but not easily due to Barbara's accelerating mental decline. In this novel, as in *Goodbye, Vitamin*, there are also dementia-related incidents that create consternation for family members (e.g., Barbara buys a chainsaw with no clear purpose in mind), but, rather than use scare tactics to portray dementia as a descent into hell, as is typically done in literature and film, Pearson represents Barbara, for the most part, as faring well emotionally. After the chainsaw incident, Kate asks Donald if Barbara is "distressed," and he answers, "No, love, she's happy" (246). In another scene toward the end of the book, when Barbara is given soaps as a Christmas present from her granddaughter, they bring out reminiscences of her first holiday abroad. She recalls incidents from that trip in great detail, only not realizing how far in the past they happened. If the reader thinks this inability to put one's memories in the proper time frame is a terrible handicap, Donald offers a different, thought-provoking perspective. He tells his grandchild, "Sometimes, you know, it's funny. Sometimes I envy her, your gran, thinking it all happened last week like that. . . . If only, eh?" (284). Instead of viewing Barbara's problems with time as a weakness, Donald recognizes that having those memories nearer to one's consciousness could even be seen as desirable.

Mixed Portrayals

Other fictional works go into more detail about terrible outcomes that might do more to scare than inform readers who already dread the disease. *The Wide Circumference of Love* by Marita Golden is by no means all bleakness on the subject of Alzheimer's disease, but neither does it hide some brutal realities. Sixty-eight-year-old Gregory Tate's struggles with the effects of Alzheimer's, including wandering and eventually some physical violence, fill the entire novel, but passages written from his perspective in a journal he keeps provide balance. In one entry, he writes about his ambivalence upon learning more about the disease's outcomes:

I keep getting lost when I'm driving. Forgetting where I'm going. Arriving somewhere and not knowing where I am. So far, I've managed to keep it from Diane [his wife], from Mercer [his business partner]. But these days I'm always running late. Running behind. Running to catch up to where I'm supposed to be. I don't know what is happening to me. I should want to know. I do want to know. But if I find out[,] I am afraid of the cost I will pay for that knowledge. Losing my company. Everything I've worked to build. Shattered. (98)

Here, one sees why people are often afraid to receive a definitive diagnosis. Awareness that there are such outcomes, all connected to identity loss, results in individuals wanting to be shielded from medical forecasting. And yet, the novel simultaneously helps readers to understand the mindset of a person who knows that some mental abilities are waning and that this necessitates a "masked" double identity.

With this valuable insight into a person's struggle to know how best to deal with cognition changes, one would hope that the rest of the novel also would demonstrate the complexity of dementia, but it does not always do so, and instead further generates fears of this type of diagnosis. In one long passage toward the end of the book, Gregory's wife, Diane, describes his future suffering as an inevitable reality, seeing it not unlike Jacoby's depiction of Alzheimer's as a "curse." She bases her prognosis on the staging of his diagnosis from doctors and her own knowledge and predicts "more suffering to come" due to the "horror of the disease": "His immune system would gasp for breath, impossible to retrieve. That mind, devious and cruel, would disrupt his body's desire to move, his yearning to eat. Lethal blood clots and infections sown by the steady shutdown would ultimately stop the intricate and elegant system from working" (240). Although researchers such as Dr. David Holtzman, a professor of neurology and associate director of Alzheimer's Disease Research Center at Washington University School of Medicine in St. Louis, concur that during the "final" stages of the disease those affected will need "full-time care" as "brain regions atrophy and related functions break down," there is so much individuality in how the disease manifests itself, whereas the passage focuses on the worst outcome as an inevitable reality (qtd. in Heid 13). That Gregory is shown having an ongoing physically intimate relationship with another resident at his memory care facility at the time that Diane has said he is only "suffering" and is even able to identify one of his architectural projects on a car ride with his son serves as a reminder that one cannot always measure the degree of "suffering" of another when Alzheimer's is present. Thus, Gregory's mother, Margaret, offers this cautionary advice when Diane explains what will happen with perhaps misguided authority: "I don't care what those doctors say. All the studies and research . . ." (240). She argues for acknowledgment that science cannot always predict the outcomes for human beings, even those with a disease such as Alzheimer's.

That Alzheimer's does not routinely follow a predictable course and often affects people differently is an important point, especially in view of the great public trepidation of the disease's progression. Beyond literature, other specialists in the field emphasize this point as well. A 2017 article entitled "Dementia Stages and Strategies," published in a newsletter from the Icahn School of Medicine at Mount Sinai, notes that "Alzheimer's Disease affects people in different ways, and disease progression is very individual" (7). Geriatrician Louise Aronson in *Elderhood* also observes that "there is no single truth with dementia," so attempts to pin it down to a specific and guaranteed trajectory can be misleading (53).

Environmental Factors

Research has also found that the environment and the type of care received can influence levels of "capacities and impairment" (Friedan 75). In recognition of this reality, a "dementia village" movement has been spawned, first in the Netherlands, and now in the United States and throughout Europe as well. The idea behind a "dementia village" is to re-create an environment based on the past in which those who have dementia can stroll freely through restaurants, stores, theaters, and gardens, while health professionals (called "carers") interact with residents there as one community. People live in small bungalows with others with whom they have some connection based on personal history or interests. Drawing upon Robert Butler's "reminiscence therapy," which addresses ways that those with severe memory loss often feel less anxiety and more comfort in the past than in an uncertain present, these type of "villages" offer a chance to experience the past, which has been recreated in architecture and design. Typically stressful situations such as handling money are avoided by businesses not requiring money for purchases and being staffed by care workers, while problems such as wandering are circumvented by having large areas for walking (e.g., the Netherland's Hogewey is on four acres) with only one entrance and exit, which is locked. A few critics have expressed concern over the deception inherent in this type of arrangement. British dementia expert Graham Stokes, for example, objects to the creation of "artificial worlds," which he believes generates more confusion than assistance for people with dementia whose reality already is shifting day-to-day. He argues that effort should be placed on "giving them [people with dementia] meaningful lives in the present, rather than trying to keep them in nostalgic themes from the past" (qtd. in MacFarquhar 52). Gerontologist Anne Basting also does not like the quarantine aspect of places like Hogewey since she thinks that "separation hurts us as human beings," and that we should do more to integrate people with dementia into our "real" communities and not "pretend ones" (personal interview and unpublished letter). Other researchers in dementia, however, have supported the "past world" village initiatives and recent technological innovations that create simulations of traveling through former neighborhoods by bus and bike (Schuetze). Dr. Habib Chuadhury, a specialist in architectural design for people who have dementia, is one of the advocates since he believes that having different places for engagement can have positive outcomes: "These villages have the potential to simulate the daily life of people from when they were younger, through various activities in the home and neighborhood. Villages can provide a much wider range of movement compared to a typical dementia care unit" (qtd. in Fagan 31). Rather than feeling like "patients," then, residents are encouraged to feel more like "neighbors."

A contrasting example of how environment impacts those with dementia comes from an essay by age scholar Margaret Cruikshank, who befriended octogenarian Frieda Walter when Cruikshank ran a course at a senior center called "All about Aging." Frieda displayed signs of severe dementia at times (e.g., walking around with IRS forms, showing them to people, and telling stories of a wealthy man who was coming to give her money), but other times, she was able to tell detailed stories of her family's experiences living in Nazi Germany. A cousin, who became the conservator for Frieda, and a social worker decided that she needed to be in an institution and was placed on an Alzheimer's floor. Cruikshank saw that once placed in a "dementia ward, by people who hadn't the time or interest or skill to determine the real condition of her mental processes," the "deterioration" became obvious and sadly, rationalized her "placement" there (*Fierce* 144). She went from being a non-medicated person who loved to dance and have "friendly exchanges with people she encountered" as she walked the city to someone highly medicated at the facility, depressed, and greatly limited by her surroundings (144).

The Variability of Memory Loss

Cruikshank's experiences with Frieda and others during her time at the senior center influenced her belief, echoed by other notable gerontologists, that "each person who has dementia is unique" (*Fierce* 142). The surveys also supported this point by revealing widely different experiences with dementia—some people were treated by loved ones at home for years; others needed higher levels of care in facilities. Hence, it is not always useful to draw generalizations about cognitive loss, though the tendency to do so is common and the generalizations are almost always all negative. Margaret Gullette, in *Ending Ageism, or How Not to Shoot Old*

People, describes the variations in different people's experiences with dementia. She writes, "People with Alzheimer's disease can have memory loss one day and remember sharply etched details on another. We are misled if we think the course of any case of Alzheimer's disease is like another" (120). Effective evidence for this variance of Alzheimer's appears in qualitative studies such as Renee Beard's *Living with Alzheimer's: Managing Memory Loss, Identity, and Illness* (2016). Through her observations of nearly one hundred seniors who were going through the process of cognitive evaluation and diagnosis, differences in acceptance, understanding, and progression of the disease were strikingly apparent. The problem with a general misperception about Alzheimer's—that it always presents itself in a predictable pattern with a worst case scenario being inevitable—is individuals' lives will not be valued as they should. This, in turn, can foster a dangerous notion of a "duty to die" (Gullette, *Ending* 162). Gullette points to a number of well-regarded films, such as *Poetry*, a 2010 South Korean film that received an Academy Award nomination for Best Foreign Film, and *Amour*, a 2012 film that won an Academy award for Best Foreign Film, which seem to send a message that a life in which one does not have one's full mental faculties is a life not worth living.

A film that is generally regarded as a better representative of dementia as unique to each person and not something that should universally signal an end to life is director Sarah Polley's *Away from Her* (2006), based on Alice Munro's short story, "The Bear Came over the Mountain." The story centers on Fiona, the wife in an older couple, who experiences memory loss as she ages and eventually goes to a facility, where she becomes attached to another patient named Aubrey, much to her serial philandering husband's dismay. Ambiguity takes center stage in the film and story as Munro leaves many questions open for interpretation. Even in her mentally compromised state, is Fiona seeking vengeance for her husband's past liaisons, or does her memory impairment liberate her from the social conventions of matrimony and allow her to become involved with Aubrey out of true desire? The question of Fiona's agency is further exacerbated by descriptions of Fiona's "trickster" personality (Goldman and Powell 91). Her husband, Grant, explains that the "mystique" that surrounds Fiona leaves him unsure of how to interpret her actions: "Trying to figure out Fiona had always been frustrating. It could be like following a mirage. No—like living in a mirage" (Munro 304). The effect of so much uncertainty surrounding Fiona's behavior is that readers are disarmed from their notions that Alzheimer's, which is never even named in the story but is in the film, will be a pathway to full mental collapse. As in the case of Frieda in Cruikshank's account, whose actions some of the time indicated dementia but who at other times exhibited lucidity and mental sharpness, the character of Fiona reminds us that "dementia" is not always "all-defining"; those affected do not go over "some line into a shadow world" and remain there (Cruikshank, *Fierce* 142–143). When Grant wonders if his wife can remember him, Kristy, a nurse at the facility, responds, "She might not. Not today. Then tomorrow— you never know, do you? Things change back and forth all the time and there's nothing you can do about it" (Munro 282). For some, this unpredictability of a serious mental impairment might be terrifying, but for others, there can be a broadening of under-standing memory loss such that it does not entail the mitigation of a person's whole identity.

Not everyone appreciated the film version of Munro's story, *Away from Her*, which may have received extra scrutiny since it was an age-themed movie written and directed by twenty-seven-year-old Sarah Polley. She encountered the story on a plane ride and wanted to make a film out of it that "painstakingly honored the story" she "loved" (qtd. in McGill 102). Perhaps more signifi-cant to critics than Polley's age were the bold changes to the orig-inal story that she made in the film. One added scene has Fiona saying "ugly baby" to a family in the waiting room as she and Grant walk out of the doctor's office after her first appointment for eval-uation. In another, Fiona initiates sex with Grant right before he has to leave her at the facility, Meadowlake. Also added is a short scene of a young woman visiting a relative at Meadowlake, who calls the place "fucking depressing." Agnes Berthin-Scaillet, in a

2012 essay on the adaptation, complains that these changes detract from the subtlety of Munro's story with their "overstatement" and tendency to draw out "pathos" (11). A more positive position is held by José Rodriquez Herrera who appreciates that Polley's adaptation is "not merely mimetic but creative" in its ability to "reproduce Munro's story in a new medium without making it subordinate to the original" (118). And most of Polley's changes do in fact retain the ambiguity of the story and of Alzheimer's itself—evidence of variability even in those who have been given a diagnosis. As scholars Marlene Goldman and Sarah Powell note in their 2015 article "Alzheimer's, Ambiguity, and Irony: Alice Munro's 'The Bear Came over the Mountain' and Sarah Polley's *Away from Her*," for some, there are even questions about "whether Alzheimer's is even a disease or a part of the process of aging" (85). Given the possible ambiguity of the disease, when Fiona comments on the "ugly baby," one could say that Alzheimer's has altered her ability to know what is socially acceptable to say, but since Fiona in the story and film is shown to have a great sense of fun and play, one might ask whether her comment is mental slippage or just mean jesting. The sex scene likewise adds to the ambiguity of the story since it further complicates our understanding of the couple's relationship and her degree of anger at or acceptance of Grant's libidinous past. Even the "fucking depressing" comment by the teenager, which appears lacking in any nuance, still contributes to the uncertainties dramatized in "The Bear Came over the Mountain" since the facility that she is criticizing is both home to Fiona's late-in-life romance with Aubrey and perhaps, depending on how one interprets the ambiguous ending of the work, a reconciliation between husband and wife. The result of these changes, then, can be seen overall as furthering Munro's accomplishment in the story by showing Alzheimer's and the people who have it as not deserving to be pigeon-holed as damaged and worthless. That "The Bear Came over the Mountain" alludes to and changes the children's song "The Bear Went over the Mountain" is a reminder that even when something looks similar, like the wording of a song title, one needs to recognize difference. Whereas the children's song uses the past tense of "go," Munro uses the past tense of "come": one can be a declaration of abandonment ("go"), the other a beckoning, "come." Her story and Polley's adaptation invite people to "come" and, as the song goes, "see what they can see"—in other words, view a person diagnosed with Alzheimer's with open eyes and an open mind to the individuality of those confronted with this challenge.

Defying Expectations

To show just how much of a need there is to widen our perspective on dementia, a 2010 study of people with dementia evaluated "their quality of life better than their caregivers" did (Leland 142). This research also points to the fact that much of our understanding of memory loss and how it affects people is derived from caregivers who might view "quality of life" differently from the person who has the disease. Caregivers, who are often family members, likely focus on the losses and difficulties, whereas those persons with dementia tend to focus on what they can still do. Richard Taylor, a retired psychologist diagnosed with "dementia, probably of the Alzheimer's type" when he was fifty-eight, addresses these diverging perspectives in *Alzheimer's from the Inside Out* (2006), a collection of essays based on his experiences, which is intended to improve general understanding of dementia. Noting how it "is increasingly difficult" for those looking after him to "understand" what he is experiencing and how their "tears, anger, and frustration" signal the hurdles they face in assisting him, Taylor describes life with Alzheimer's in a much more complex and dynamic way (130). In a chapter called "What Is It Like to Have Alzheimer's Disease?" he describes his experiences as "looking at the world" through his grandmother's "lace curtains": "From time to time, a gentle wind blows the curtains and changes the patterns through which I see the world. There are large knots in the curtains and I cannot see through them. There is a web of lace connecting the knots to each other, around which I can sometimes see. However, this entire filter keeps shifting unpredictably in the wind.

Sometimes I am clear in my vision and my memory . . . and other times I am completely unaware of what lies on the other side of the knots (16). This description from someone living with an Alzheimer's diagnosis illustrates that the perception that Alzheimer's involves one defining list of behaviors and abilities is not accurate and that the disease is unpredictable. In addition, Taylor's ability to find the apt metaphor of lace curtains to describe his shifting perception signals his creative cognition is still operating and effective. Another informative and creative reimagining of the disease from someone experiencing it directly is Christine Bryden's 2018 book, *Will I Still Be Me?*. Among the many insights Bryden shares is her problem with the term "memory loss" when referring to dementia. She prefers the term "recall dysfunction" since her "memories remain" inside of her; they are just difficult to access without prompting (66).

Marvin Bonowitz was also an example of a person with Alzheimer's who defied expectations of what that diagnosis may portend. Bonowitz was a registered nurse for most of his working life, but he also had a lifetime passion for music. As a nurse, he knew that he was experiencing cognitive changes that resulted in his giving up driving, and later he was diagnosed with Alzheimer's. At ninety, Bonowitz was still living at home with his wife, Anne, but, according to his son Abraham, did not recognize his family members, including his wife, whom he repeatedly asked for: "Where's my wife?" Despite these problems with recognition, when Bonowitz went to the piano, his artistry continued to be on display. Since it became hard for him to read music, he played by memory countless songs by his favorite composers such as George Gershwin. Videos show not only his ability to play songs based on suggestions, but also to end the songs with a dramatic flourish of his hands, remembering the showmanship associated with his musical gifts. When asked in one video whose birthday is coming up, he does not remember that it is his own, but he plays the song "Happy Birthday" with fervor and virtuosity. Those who believe that Alzheimer's is only a simple and sorrowful story of loss must reconcile the narratives of those who continue to draw upon

Photographs of Marvin Bonowitz, undated. (Courtesy of the Bonowitz family.)

essential characteristics of their personhood that are not always snuffed out when dementia sets in.

Creativity and Dementia

Both Richard Taylor's and Marvin Bonowitz's experiences of maintaining their tie to creativity even with impaired memories speaks to the initiatives put forth by MacArthur Genius Award–winning author Anne Basting, whose conclusion of *Forget Memory* asks that we "insist on complex stories of dementia" (155). A theater professor by training, Basting has developed an international program called "TimeSlips," in which people with dementia at all stages participate in active storytelling that relies more on imagination than memory. Before observing a TimeSlips session at the Ovation Jewish Home in Milwaukee, I spoke with Joan Williamson, training coordinator for the program, which takes place in many different types of care facilities. The sessions are often facilitated by college students and other volunteers who have gone through the three-to-four hour training, which can now be done online as well. Williamson pointed out that TimeSlips developed from Basting's background in improvisation, with its mantra of "validate everything" and the idea of "performance" being possible for people with all different types of abilities and disabilities.

The session I observed in October 2017 was preceded by a visit from seventh and eighth graders from a religious school, Hillel Academy. While the middle schoolers chatted one-on-one with the assembled group of TimeSlips participants (most of whom were part of an adult day treatment program), there was much hand-holding, and I was struck with the importance of touch to create a bridge. Since Alzheimer's disease is such a source of terror and concern, people who have been diagnosed with it can be viewed by some as pariahs, so it was reassuring to see the physical connectedness between the students and the participants. Next, the college students from University of Wisconsin-Milwaukee initiated the official TimeSlips session. They began with a series of engaging questions, such as "Are you excited?" and "Are you ready?" They also used the participants' names regularly and frequently made comments during the introductions of "good to see you again." After a review of the picture and story that were created the week before, each person was given a copy of different pictures that they were going to select to inspire a new storytelling session. Once these were decided on by consensus, the facilitators asked the participants open-ended questions about the picture, and wrote the responses on an over-sized sketch pad that everyone could see. The story was put together with all of the group's responses, including sounds, and was often repeated back while it was being constructed. One story involved birds being shot at by a gun, another was about a child stepping into a dryer, and the third was about a cat and a small boy. Most of the group members contributed something to the story, which integrated their imaginative speculations (e.g., naming the characters, coming up with what is going on in the pictures and what happens next, titling the stories, and so on). The moments of levity contrast sharply with typical expectations of severe dementia. For example, when one of the facilitators asked how many mice the cat caught in the third story, one participant said, "I don't know. I don't follow them around," to the amusement of many. Even when participants made comments that did not seem to fit with the story that was being developed (e.g., someone offered, "I remember that from seventy years ago"), the contribution was affirmed: "You have a good memory."

Being able to witness a TimeSlips session and going through the training myself reinforced the many positive facets of what Basting has developed. Some of the early research on TimeSlips has shown that not only do people who have dementia become more socially engaged and gain improved communication skills through participating, but staff, working with these individuals who are present during the sessions, develop better attitudes. According to information provided in the training, creativity has the ability to "challenge" individuals' "minds," minimize stress, and give opportunities for "meaning and purpose." In a 2018 interview that I conducted with Basting, she also discussed how creativity allows people to take on a "new role"; it is "generative," so that an individual with a diagnosis of dementia does not have to be "only sick." Some of the stories created from TimeSlips sessions have been dramatized and performed by the storytelling creators, which has been a source of pride for those involved in the performances and also for families, many of whom expected mostly negative outcomes from a diagnosis of Alzheimer's. This change of perception seems to be at the heart of Basting's ground-breaking work. She wants to minimize the "paralyzing stigma" surrounding dementia by recognizing that the individuality of the "self" not only remains even after dementia sets in, but can be engaged in creative pursuits that bring people together and make them feel valued (*Forget* 3, 156). This should not just be "individual engagement," Basting concluded in her interview, but should involve institutions "building creative communities with care."

Minimizing Stigma

Minimizing the stigma of dementia also seems to be at the heart of Michael Zadoorian's 2009 novel *The Leisure Seeker*, made into a film by the same name in 2017. Despite the fact that John Robina, one of the main characters, has Alzheimer's, he hits the road with his wife Ella in the family's recreational vehicle for a cross-country trip. In *Forget Memory* Basting mentions that those with dementia often view no longer being able to drive as a "catastrophic" loss, and many personal accounts discuss not being able to navigate to certain locations as a telltale sign that normal mental functioning has become impaired (9). However, in *The Leisure Seeker*, with Ella's guidance, John is still a capable driver and gets them to their destinations with few incidents that are his fault. Besides being able to hold on to his driving skills, John's humor and humanity are also present in scenes, which show that those qualities have not been eradicated by the disease. When Ella reaches for a Pepsi can between his legs, John amusingly responds, "Hey, watch out what you're grabbing there, young lady" (100). In one of the later scenes, the couple has sex after Ella finds he has an erection when changing his soiled boxer shorts. The sexual interlude that follows affirms that his dementia does not render him an invalid; it is described as "something the body doesn't forget."

The novel and the film do a good job of showing aspects of John's character that remain intact (e.g., like his long-term memory in identifying people in the slide shows they view on the trip), while also depicting the changes. Throughout both works John asks, "Is this home?" showing that he is disoriented by being outside of his familiar surroundings. He also knows that his memory fails him at times and curses the loss; in other instances, he wanders off without being able to find his way back, and Ella addresses needing to hide the gun they keep in the camper from him since he has showed uncharacteristic and impulsive violent moments after developing Alzheimer's. One potential problem with the portrayal, however, is John's series of comments that he will want to kill himself if senility hits. Too often in literary works and casual conversations, this suggestion of preferring death rather than dementia is articulated. The 2018 Broadway revival of Kenneth Lonergan's play *The Waverly Gallery*, for example, has Ellen, the psychiatrist daughter of a woman in her eighties with memory problems, instruct her son to "put a bullet through my head" if senility ever occurs (99). The message is repeated in the final chapter of *The Leisure Seeker*. After recounting how a good friend of the couple with severe dementia at the end of his life was in a nursing home, John tells Ella, "I will shoot myself before I end up like that. . . . Ella, promise me, *promise* me that you will never put me in a place like that." Since these words may influence the controversial ending of the book, they could be seen as potentially dangerous, reinforcing the dualistic thinking that only a life with full mental cognition is worth living, which most of the novel and film successfully challenge.

Fiction and Nonfiction about Dementia

Skeptics may argue that a fictional work's information on a given subject should be regarded with some distrust due to a writer's creative license, in contrast to nonfiction with its emphasis on concrete facts and evidence. However, fiction can integrate useful knowledge people might be resistant to learning about elsewhere, especially on topics fraught with fear and anxiety such as dementia. *The Wide Circumference of Love* demonstrates this idea of facts-in-fiction in a scene where Gregory talks to his brother, Bruce, a physician, about the difficulty of early screening for Alzheimer's, the limitations of the medications on the market for it, and the fact that African Americans have a 50–70 percent greater chance of developing Alzheimer's due to higher rates of diabetes, high blood pressure, and high cholesterol (104–105). Fictional works can also be powerful and, at times, even more influential in changing readers' mindset than fact-based works. The Pulitzer Prize–winning 2018 novel *The Overstory* by Richard Powers on the centrality of trees to humankind's existence makes the claim that creative works are the most persuasive medium: "The best arguments in the world won't change a person's mind. The only thing that can do that is a good story" (168). One should, then, worry about imaginative works that are too suggestive about living with dementia being worse than death.

There are other instances, however, when fiction and nonfiction send the same useful messages about dementia. This is the case with the difficulty of diagnosing forms of dementia without doing an autopsy on the brain. Gullette makes this point convincingly in *Ending Ageism* by bringing in experts who explain how PET scans, MRIs, and spinal fluid do not have much "predictive power" in terms of how a person may "function" (126). The novel *Goodbye, Vitamin* reiterates similar information, which explains why there is much confusion and misunderstanding surrounding dementia: "There is, presently, no single test or scan that can diagnose dementia with complete accuracy. It's only after the person is dead that you can cut his or her brain open and look for telltale plaques and tangles. For now, it's [a] process of elimination. What we have are tests that rule out other possible causes of memory loss. In diagnosing Alzheimer's, doctors can only tell you everything that it isn't" (4). If doctors are unable to make definitive diagnoses, it stands to reason that the public would be worried if they or their loved ones could be future candidates for the disease. Medical researchers also have noted that even if amyloid plaque in the brain is detected, 30 percent of those over seventy who have that will not develop the disease, perhaps due to a brain nerve-growth factor (BDNF) that may act as a "cognitive reserve" (Park 82, 85). Despite the questionable outcome of finding plaque, older adults more often are turning to PET scans to look for amyloid plaque, even though Medicare does not cover the high cost of the procedure ($5,000–$7,000) due to the questionable "health benefits" (Span, "A Scan" D3). New areas that are being investigated for better testing down the road include a possible smell test since "diminished ability to identify odors" is often found in people who show signs of Alzheimer's. Another area of testing involves how thick the nerves are behind eyes since participants in tests with "thinner nerves" did "worse on cognitive tests ("Alzheimer's Disease" 5). In addition, scientists at Washington University have come up with a blood test to predict whether someone will develop plaque in the brain, but it is in the early stages of development.

Hope?

The medical side of dementia is not treated very often in creative works, which tend to focus more on how relationships are affected and what abilities remain and disappear. The consensus among scientists right now is that it is unlikely that a wonder drug will come along to prevent or reverse symptoms. Bredesen's popular *The End of Alzheimer's* cites the Alzheimer's Association's statement that there has not been FDA approval of a "genuinely new Alzheimer's drug" since 2003, and most medications on the market "are ineffective in stopping or slowing the course of the disease" (3). Bredesen believes that part of the problem is that people develop Alzheimer's in a variety of ways (e.g., inflammation, genes—carrying the ApoE4 gene—and toxicity), in addition to vascular dementia; therefore, it will be nearly impossible to find one medication or even vaccine to ward off cognitive decline.

Instead, he has developed a protocol that thwarts inroads that can lead to the disease. Besides advocating a Ketoflex diet, which requires a twelve-hour fast from the last meal in the evening to the first meal the next day, he, along with most doctors, strongly promotes exercise since it can increase the size of the hippocampus, which is important for memory, help reduce stress that creates "toxic" cortisol, and aid "vascular function" (191). So far, a few small independent studies have indicated a "reversal of cognitive decline" in those who followed the protocol he calls ReCode, but clearly, more investigation is still needed. Most of the neurological research has indicated that it is easier to address damage in the brain the sooner it is found, but some promising studies with mice have revealed the ability to reverse damage to neurons in the brain that most thought was impossible (Park 80).

Besides early detection, the medical community also advocates prevention steps to build up a cognitive reserve that can stave off or at least delay full-blown manifestation of the disease. Even if people have the APOE4 gene, which increases the chances they will have Alzheimer's one day, lifestyle factors have been shown in studies to affect the outcome. Ian Brown's *Sixty: A Diary of My Sixty-First Year* (2016) includes this research in his memoir as he tries to reconcile what brain changes are inevitable and what can be controlled. Brown writes that certain mental declines can be challenged "depending how much you exercise, how healthfully you eat, how much you don't drink, and even how much you have sex" (234). Studies have been able to verify this exercise claim, including a 2006 *Annals of Internal Medicine* report on 1,700 seniors over sixty-five, which found that those who exercised "three or more times a week had a 30–40% lower risk" of developing dementia compared with those who did not (Larson and DeClaire 94). Even brain shrinkage, which most think is inevitable with age, has been shown to be reversed through exercise, which makes regions of the brain such as the hippocampus grow and thus results in cognitive growth (Oaklander 43). Support for Brown's alcohol claim can be found in a 2018 study of a million people that was published in *The Lancet Public Health*, which concludes that "heavy drinking was the biggest modifiable risk factor for dementia" (Oaklander 60). Consumption of red meat has been studied as a risk factor as well, not only because of the trace metals that can be found in it, which can do oxidative damage to neural cells, but also because grilling, broiling, and frying meat increase advanced glycation end products (AGES), which are often found in the brains of those with Alzheimer's ("Will Limiting Red Meat" 6). Evidence for the link between sexuality and lower dementia risk is not as extensive, but certainly evidence exists that having a stimulating partner (perhaps mentally and physically) does contribute to maintaining higher mental functioning (Cruikshank, *Learning* 78; Macmillan 62). Something not mentioned by Brown but present in most medical research on Alzheimer's is the effect of sleep. Larson, who has run one of the longest-running studies in Adult Changes in Thought (ACT) at the University of Washington, points out that sleep deprivation creates a risk for dementia (Larson and DeClaire 99). Apparently, sleeping allows an opportunity for the body to get rid of harmful toxins and dangerous bodily elements, such as the amyloid proteins that create plaque in the brain. Less time sleeping translates to less opportunity for this important work to be done. Other new areas of research include the effects of hearing loss on developing dementia and the role of anticholinergic drugs, often used to treat incontinence, depression, and epilepsy, which studies have shown to increase the risk for dementia significantly, especially if taken daily for a three-year period (Wolfgang 22; Coupland et al. 1089, 1091).

Caregiving

Besides all of the studies looking at what may or may not prevent dementia from running its course, research also has focused on the effects of caring for a loved one with the disease. Many are managing this responsibility with incredible dedication and commitment, which the survey responses and interviews also demonstrated. Whether in a care facility or at home, countless families have prioritized the well-being of the family member dealing with dementia and are providing daily support. Although a study in *Journal of American Geriatrics Society* reports some "verbal mistreatment" of family members with dementia, likely due to the emotional and difficult interactions with the person, more often, their own self-sacrifice can take its toll on the caregiver (Schreiber 54). A 2016 Alzheimer's Association special report found that one in five family caregivers cut back on their own medical needs and even meals, while a three-decade study from Ohio State and the National Institute of Aging found that the "chronic stress of Alzheimer's caregiving can shorten lives 4–8 years" (Schreiber 35, 104). To combat the stress, strain, and isolation that caregiving for someone with dementia can bring about, Alzheimer's cafes have been introduced in communities to create social opportunities for people with dementia and their families to spend time with others sharing similar experiences. According to retired psychology professor Susan McFadden, a research and development consultant for the Fox Valley Memory Project in Wisconsin, these cafes, often housed in public libraries, allow individuals to seek company "without any shame" (Kritz 8). Some of this shame stems from the fact that dementia still has "stigma" surrounding it. Bryden, who writes of her own experience with Alzheimer's in *Will I Still Be Me?*, explains the stigma is likely due to the possible "embarrassing behaviors" of those with dementia, which makes people feel uncomfortable being around them (122). The cafes, on the other hand, offer a judgment-free "safe space" for everyone to feel comfortable without critical scrutiny.

A benefit of the creative works on dementia is the up-close view they bring to the myriad of complicated emotions involved in caregiving. In *The Wide Circumference of Love*, for example, Gregory's wife describes the mixed emotions she feels every day on the front lines of her husband's struggles with Alzheimer's. She explains, "I still see flashes of who he used to be sometimes. But I feel caught in a permanent state of grieving. I've suffered a loss. It's like a hurricane every day. I've lost my husband, and I still don't know what that will mean for me going forward" (166). Even the idea of putting him in assisted living brings no relief to her since she feels guilt and remorse, although eventually she does relent. Still, the sentiment that stays with her is "I owe him too much" (167). This statement expresses the conundrum of the Alzheimer's family caregiver of never knowing if what he or she is doing is enough.

Throughout different cultures there are a variety ways that age-related memory loss is treated. Members of the indigenous Anishinaabe in Minnesota sometimes will have a funeral for a parent who has Alzheimer's, since they regard that person as no longer "here" (Marshall, *Age Becomes* 65). Other tribes see losing mental capacity with age and returning to a more childlike state as part of the "circle of life," not a psychological disorder (Morales). In fact, according to a study done by J. Neil Henderson and L. Carson Henderson, many Native Americans do not see dementia as negative and instead consider it a "window into the unknown" and a view into the "other side," a "supernatural world inhabited by the spirits of the dead" (Browne et al.). Recognizing that memory impairment may be seen through a spiritual lens expands our understanding of dementia as not always being "loss." Research on First Nation elders examined the Secwepemc Nation in Canada who emphasize prevention rather than memory loss; their key principle is to perpetuate "minds always going." For the Sec-wepemc, storytelling is not only an important continuation of "oral history," but a way of "keeping minds healthy" (Hulko et al. 336). The stories, too, can act as a form of "resistance," breaking down conventional narratives of old age and the idea of senility and instead transferring cultural knowledge from one generation to the next (Beard 134). We desperately need a reimagined understanding of dementia as not complete diminishment. There can still be much appreciation of the person who remains, despite less cognitive function. As Gregory's son in *The Wide Circumference of Love* is wisely advised, "Your father isn't gone. Love what's left" (37).

5

Intimacy

"Love Is All You Need"?

Lust doesn't die to spare the sensitivities of the grossed-out young
who prefer not to think of wrinkly couplings, and—this is really cruel—
carnal feelings are among the very last to check out.
—Allison Pearson, *How Hard Can It Be?*

Mature love is compelling to the extent that people bring to it their past,
the vicissitudes of their lengthy lives, and a sense of both comedy and
tragedy that comes from constant awareness of the past.
—Martha Nussbaum, *Aging Thoughtfully*

How was it that some people lost interest in companionship
in old age, while others made it the center of their lives?
—John Leland, *Happiness Is a Choice You Make*

It's never too late.
—Michael Chabon, *Moonglow*

The film *Book Club*, released in 2018 with an all-star cast of Jane
Fonda, Diane Keaton, Mary Steenburgen, and Candice Bergen
(fourteen Academy Award nominations among them) generated a
great deal of excitement that Hollywood was finally utilizing the

talent of its mature female stars. The film centers on four friends who have met to discuss books for over forty years, usually of a highbrow variety, but they decide to read E. L. James' racy *Fifty Shades of Grey* series instead. Despite decent ticket sales, reviewers were not universally enthusiastic about *Book Club*, citing the predictability of the standard Viagra gag in films that feature older couples, the cloying faithfulness to the romantic comedy genre, and the overall lack of opportunities in the script for these women to display their craft. Although these complaints are legitimate, *Book Club* must be applauded for its boldness in putting the subject of sex front and center in a film with a cast of women who are all in their senior years. While some may complain that the movie was not audacious enough in actually depicting sexuality, credit is still due to director Bill Holderman for using James's novel, which features the somewhat sadomasochistic relationship of a much younger couple, to highlight the topic of sex in relation to people over sixty-five, something the public typically chooses to ignore or ridicule.

Making Fun of Senior Sexuality

Mockery of older sexuality takes different forms. Often in popular culture, characters late in life are portrayed as female nymphomaniacs or dirty old men. The character of Blanche Deveraux on NBC's long-running *Golden Girls* is an example. In nearly every episode, Blanche's insatiable sexual appetite is apparent, either in her own comments (e.g., "It's been four days since I enjoyed the company of a man") or those of other characters (e.g., "You're not a terrible person, you're just horny all the time"). While Rue McClanahan exaggerated Blanche's sexual exploits in the series, fellow *Golden Girls* actress Betty White, who played naïve Rose Nylund, has taken on Blanche's persona in interviews and other roles like Elka Ostrovky in *Hot in Cleveland*, in which she boasts of having more men than the younger women in the house for which she is the caretaker. Russell Meeuf in *Rebellious Bodies: Stardom, Citizenship and the New Body Politic* observes that Betty White's comedy is "rooted in the perceived contradictions of aging women and sex." He writes, "White's sex jokes are funny because of the idea of an elderly woman enjoying an active sex life is so implausible in a youth-obsessed culture such as ours" (149). Some may view McClanahan's and White's willingness to declare themselves sexually active into their senior years as ground-breaking, but the comedic and exaggerated elements in their performances prevent a serious reflection on the issue.

Another comic treatment of sex and age, in which the sexuality of older people is presented as ridiculous, is more blatantly hostile and likely has more long-lasting negative effects. Shows such as Seth MacFarlane's popular *Family Guy*, on the air since 1999, has included several episodes that make fun of seniors' sexuality. A season eight episode "Brian's Got a Brand New Bag" has the anthropomorphic dog, Brian, dating an "older woman" named Rita, and the jokes are endless—everything from characters asking about ancient pottery in her vagina and drooping breasts to the culminating moment when Rita breaks her hip during intercourse. In a culture that already seems incapable of regarding older individuals as life-long sexual beings, this episode further incites age bias and misinformation. As does another episode, "Mom's the Word," in which the main character, Peter, meets Evelyn, a friend of his deceased mother. In a montage of scenes, Evelyn does a faux Marilyn Monroe, flipping up her skirt and revealing veiny legs that look almost Neanderthal, to which Peter responds by projectile vomiting. Later she apologizes for her promiscuous behavior by blaming it on her medicine. When the two have a reconciliatory hug at the end, Evelyn dies from Peter breaking her spine by accident. The overall message from portrayals like these are that seniors are extremely fragile (i.e., both sustain injuries during affectionate moments), repulsive, and laughable, especially in the realm of intimacy.

The Call for Media Improvements

Given such problematic representations, it is not too surprising that there has been an outcry for better portrayals of older adults' romantic lives. A 2011 United Kingdom Film Council survey of over 4,300 people ages fifty to seventy-four indicated that 61 percent reported dissatisfaction with the representation of older women on the screen (Snapes). With films such as Jeff Tremaine's *Bad Grandpa* (2013) featuring a forty-two-year old Johnny Knoxville playing an eighty-six-year-old whose unappealing prosthetic scrotum emerges from his underwear during a striptease, one could say this statistic could apply to male roles as well, even if older male actors have more sexual opportunities on the screen, where they are often being paired with much younger female actresses—think Bond, James Bond. The objections to older adults' erotic possibilities being undermined through visual culture can be understood by sexual script theory—the idea that people learn what is acceptable and appropriate by examining the actions of others, particularly in the media. If seniors' sexuality is shown in an unflattering light, the perceived message is that those who reach a "certain age" must not think of themselves in sexual terms. For example, a popular trope in creative works is the man who has a heart attack during sex. This scenario plays out on *The Golden Girls* when White's character, Rose, withdraws from intimacy because two men in her life died from heart attacks in the middle of intercourse. Whereas the message from this trope is that sex is dangerous and even deadly, research indicates that there is less than a 1 percent chance of this happening, the same risk as having a heart attack from merely getting out of bed (Block and Baker 5).

Scholars also have lamented the problem of media depicting older adults' sexuality at the polar extremes of rabid nymphomania or extreme celibacy, when it is portrayed at all. Communication professor Kathleen Turner, in the essay "The Betty White Moment: The Rhetoric of Constructing Aging and Sexuality," notes that both "academic and popular discourses" concentrate more on "illness" than investigating "sexuality and aging in adults over fifty" despite evidence that adults in this demographic "still have sex and still have sexual drives" (218). She also observes that the infrequency of seeing older characters in their eighties or nineties in "romantic or sexual relationships on television or films, particularly in dramatic roles," shows that our "cultural consciousness" is reluctant to break this barrier. Leni Marshall and Aagje Swinnen in "'Let's Do It like Grown-Ups': A Filmic *Ménage* of Age, Gender, and Sexuality" also call for a "new aesthetics of old age" that configures "aged bodies with erotic desire" (167). They hope for future media to "portray late life intimacy for an increasingly diverse range of sexually active, gendered, aging bodies" (168). The well-regarded documentary *Still Doing It: Intimate Lives of Women over 65* by Deidre Fishel is a step in the right direction in that it features women of different ages, races, and sexual orientations who share why sex is an "energizer" in their lives despite societal pressure to repress their bodily needs and pleasures.

Sexual Statistics and Surveys

Statistics are unclear about how many seniors over sixty-five are engaged in sexual activity. The English Longitudinal Study on Aging (ELSA) reported that of the 6,200 people ages fifty to ninety in the study, two-thirds of men and almost two-thirds of women thought that sexual satisfaction was important to a strong long-term relationship (Pidd). Research from the United States indicates that 40 percent of people aged sixty-five to eighty are sexually active (Snapes; Saline 32). When the demographics are broken down further, the numbers still show a high percentage of individuals who are in their later years and consider themselves sexually active: 73 percent of those aged 57–64, 53 percent of those aged 65–74, and 26 percent of those aged 75–85 (Brody, "After a Partner Dies" D7). Other studies have shown a gap between men and women in terms of sexual activity in later years and find a partial explanation in the fact that women live longer than men and therefore have fewer potential sexual partners. Lynn Segal in her book *Out of Time* cites a study of 27,000 people over forty in which one-fourth of the women and half of the men reported having had sexual contact in the last year. Segal, however, asks readers to exercise caution when confronting numbers from "self-reports" regarding sexual topics since respondents might want to conform to social "expectations" of what is regarded as a cultural norm (115).

I would like to believe that these concerns over the accuracy of survey responses on sexual topics were the reason that I did not include anything in my twenty-five question survey on the subject, but that is probably not the case. There was some worry about prying too much into the private domains of seniors' lives and needing to respect some boundaries. As is, more than one person responded "none of your business" to different questions on the survey. But I may have been guilty, like other researchers before me, of not delving into the topic due to some lingering discomfort, having also been socialized to believe that older people and sex are mutually exclusive. Fortunately, respondents to the survey found ways to include the topic in their answers. Several noted my omission and took me to task for it. In the final question that asks what else "regarding aging . . . would you like me to know?" one person suggested that I include "questions regarding sexuality as we age." Others commented in that section that sex changed over time and became more painful, which regretfully resulted in having sexual relations less often. Another question that brought out comments on sexual topics was "What would you describe as the secret to a happy life?" An eighty-four-year-old man commented, "Maybe sex is less often, but do it!" A man in his seventies, who has been married forty years, included his wife's thoughts on the question: "Good sex! Just because you're old, that's not a reason to give it up!" Although the survey responses did not yield a significant quantity of information on the topic of sex, they did discuss other aspects of relationships into the seniors years (marriage, divorce, dating, being alone) in great detail, much of which will appear later in this chapter.

Intimacy in Literature

Unlike the visual media that provide too few or too negative depictions of elders' intimate experiences, literature (both fiction and nonfiction) offers better examples that encourage deep exploration of the subject. This is not to say one can escape the "man having a heart attack during intercourse narrative" completely. In "Night Call" from Arlene Heyman's 2016 collection of stories *Scary Old Sex*, published when Heyman was in her seventies, a son awakens to news that his father dies of cardiac arrest at the home of his receptionist, with whom he is having an affair. The woman asks the son, "Do you think if we hadn't been—do you think if we stayed watching television?—this wouldn't have happened?" (148). As indicated previously, there is a 1 percent risk of having a heart attack during sex, though 70 percent of those instances do occur during "extra-marital" relations (Block and Baker 5). Beyond predictable story threads like that, however, surprising and honest portraits reside elsewhere in literary works that are eye-opening and important. One such example comes from poet and essayist Donald Hall, who followed his 2014 *Essays after Eighty* with a 2018 collection, *Carnival of Losses: Notes Nearing Ninety*. In that collection, between homey reflections on "An Old Hermit Named Garrison" and candid anecdotes about Ezra Pound and T. S. Eliot, comes a piece somewhat shockingly called "Fucking." The title might be off-putting for some, but its content is revelatory and original. He writes that "sex is best-best, not because of secrecy or shock or crime or numbers," but because it "requires no adventure, no variety, no betrayal, no vanity." He instead believes that it is the "invariable ecstasy of habitual double orgasm" of a "couple who've been together for years, as familiar as laundry soap" who are not thinking about "love or wickedness or how many times does this make but about rubbing, licking, sticking something into something, or being stuck by something—until the KA-BOOM and the magnificent respondent KA-BOOM." Hall's words and even integration of onomatopoeia to represent the double climactic moment challenge much of what we are led to believe about erotic pleasure. The surrounding culture constantly feeds images of sexual encounters being sexy because they are based on the unfamiliarity of a new partner, and yet, Hall, close to ninety, defies that message by demonstrating that "familiar" does not have to lead to monotony. Instead, it can be magnificent due to the seasoned veterans who know how to provide mutual pleasure. Hall ends that passage by suggesting that afterward, "happily the fuckers chat about Tuesday and the grandkids and oatmeal and contract bridge" (181). This ending solidifies the message that long-term relationships recognize that the mundane daily activities are part and parcel of an entwined life that celebrates bodily contact along with what to have for breakfast.

Writing almost fifty years before Hall on the subject of sex between long-partnered couples, Simone de Beauvoir in *The Coming of Age* at first seems to provide a very different picture of intimate relations in the later years. She writes that "monotony kills . . . desire" and goes on to describe how "elderly men" in particular are in the habit of "changing their old partner for a new and generally younger one" in order to "recover their sexual vigor" (322). While this idea certainly can be supported through literary and real-life examples, it should not overshadow another point that Beauvoir makes shortly thereafter to explain why some relationships sustain passion until the very end: "The happier and richer sexual life has been, the longer it goes on. . . . If his sexual activities have been spontaneous and happy[,] he will be strongly inclined to carry them on as long as his strength lasts" (323). The point here is significant since there is much debate in literature and gerontology research about whether old age signals a freedom from the demands of the body or whether the body continues to desire with no expiration date, albeit with modifications of its execution.

Freedom at Last?

Perhaps the most famous claims for women feeling liberated from sexual passion over time comes from Germaine Greer whose book *The Change* (1991) suggests that after menopause "aging is a welcome retirement from the career of sexuality," or in other words, "to be unwanted is to be free" (qtd. in Woodward, "Against Wisdom" 186; qtd. in Segal 91). The idea behind this train of thought may be that women spend most of their lives overly conscious of their body image, especially in a society that puts a premium on physical appearance and regards it as highly important in securing a mate. One pleasure, then, of becoming older is not having to maintain this same vigilant scrutiny of one's physical exterior by disregarding the priority of always being desirable to another. The psychologist Mary Pipher writes about this release in a 2019 *New York Times* piece on "The Joy of Being a Woman in Her 70s." For Pipher, not having to contend with the "male gaze" and "catcalls" any longer, in addition to the pleasure of trading in "nylons" and "business suits" for "yoga pants," signifies liberation from the "tyranny of worrying about our looks" (10). Literature shows plenty of examples of women taking this stand as well. Elizabeth Strout's *Olive Kitteridge* (2008) includes a story titled "Starving" in which the wife, Bonnie, tells Harmon, her husband of many years, "I think I'm just done with that stuff [sex]" (82). Shortly before that scene, Harmon notes that Bonnie does not wear jewelry any longer and has cut her now gray hair "as short as a man's" (81). He does not complain about these physical changes, not even her additional weight "around the middle," but he does see them as possible clues to figuring out why his wife no longer is interested in conjugal relations—how the changes on one level might reveal insight about changes on another. A more recent example that makes a similar claim about women moving "beyond sex" can be seen in Allison Pearson's novel *How Hard Can It Be?*, which features two old friends talking with one another at their class reunion. Roz, one of the friends, tells the main character, Kate, "Thank heavens that's all over!" When asked to explain what she means, Roz says that she "couldn't be more thrilled" that "making love" is not in her future: "I shut up shop years ago" (211). Since Roz does not go into great detail, readers are left to speculate exactly what she means when revealing it was "never quite my thing"—the sex act itself or all of the mating rituals and expectations that typically go along with romantic relationships (211).

Commentary on this subject from a male perspective dates back to an early Roman text entitled *How to Grow Old* by Marcus Tullius Cicero. Cicero includes a famous response from Sophocles when asked if he still enjoyed sex in his later years: "Good gods, no! . . . I have gladly escaped that cruel and savage master" (100–101). Ancient commentary like this on the joys of celibacy in later life have staying power and even resurface in contemporary works. In his fictional works, Philip Roth, famous chronicler of aging's less savory aspects (i.e., it isn't a "battle," but a "massacre") also candidly represents changes in sexuality that males can experience over time and famously depicts older men in *Exit Ghost* (2007) as having a "useless 'spigot of wrinkled flesh' between their legs" (qtd. in Segal 84). Roth, who died in 2018, is in some ways brought back to life in the 2018 novel *Asymmetry* by Lisa Halliday, who based the character of Ezra Blazer on him, according to many sources, since they had an intimate relationship when she was in her twenties and he was in his sixties. At the end of the novel, an interviewer asks Ezra about his choice to be celibate. To defend his position that "celibacy is the greatest pleasure," he brings in Socrates and a conversation from *The Republic* in which Socrates compares celibacy to "being unstrapped from the back of a wild horse" (Halliday 265). While the reference is somewhat imprecise (it is Cephalus who tells Socrates of Sophocles' response when asked if he can still have intercourse with a woman—repeated by Cicero above—and horses are not involved), the idea that men, too, have celebrated the idea of being liberated from sexual desire shows a long trajectory from classic texts through the present.

Despite these strong claims from men and women that age can bring a welcome respite from sexual experience, others have written passionately that they distrust that sentiment and believe that loss of opportunity is more significant than loss of desire. For women, the discrepancy between the numbers of older women and available men hampers chances for partnership and leads women to preemptively decide to "close up shop." Susan Jacoby, in her chapter "Women: Eventually the Only Sex" in *Never Say Die*, explains, "Without a sexual partner, the easiest thing to do is pretend that sex does not matter" (148). Men, who are more likely to experience physical changes that make intercourse harder to perform, may not feel desirable any longer due to erectile unreliability and, hence, become undesiring. Jacoby believes that individuals should challenge the notion that giving up physical intimacy is noble in any way. While she understands that some older women may, out of necessity, "have to do without," she argues that "to give up what was once a vital part of . . . your humanity" is not "good, or virtuous, or pleasurable" (152). Jacoby does not mention the possibility for self-pleasuring—masturbation—which is discussed in the documentary *Still Doing It*. One woman in the film describes the act as a way of showing love for herself and quotes the slogan for Rocket vibrators: "We put more women in orbit in a day than men do in a year."

Benefits and Barriers

Sexuality does have benefits for people as they age, which may be sufficient reason to examine the barriers more closely. Among the benefits cited in a *British Medical Journal* study were a stronger immune system due to the endorphins released, increased levels of white blood cells, improved cardiovascular health, and relief of mild pain. Other research has focused on the benefits of sexual activity for "vaginal health" by bringing blood flow to the area and strengthening muscles (Block and Baker 227; Saline 33). These positive physical outcomes are not widely publicized and deserve greater awareness. Caution, though, should be used in touting these advantages too much as older bodies could find some of the physical demands of intercourse challenging, and it would be undesirable to feed into the "successful aging" mystique by adding a vibrant sexual life as a requirement for aging well. Barbara Marshall in "Sexualizing the Third Age" warns of such a possibility, fearing that "sexual capacities that were once associated with 'normal' bodily aging" may be "pathologized as sexual dysfunctions" and "sexiness" could become an "important means of distinguishing oneself as *not* old" (170–171). A better approach may be to expand our definition of sexuality to recognize the various avenues that can gratify one's body beyond traditional intercourse. Doctor and researcher Jonathan Huber supports this idea when he suggests that "unlearning is the most important part of remaining sexually vital in later life" (qtd. in Steinke 141). His suggestion for older couples to creatively adapt and reimagine intimacy, based on studies of seniors who are highly satisfied with their sex lives, helps to give perspective when challenges do arise.

The barriers to late-life sexuality seem to be physical, psychological, and cultural. Bodily changes for women include thinning of vaginal tissue and less natural lubrication, which can result in intercourse being more painful and increase the chance of receiving a sexually transmitted infection. Apparently, half of all women after menopause experience "vaginal dryness" and, as a result, "painful intercourse" (Epstein D4). In a 2017 study, 62 percent of the women who described sex as painful cited it as the reason they no longer wanted to be "sexually active" (Norman 189). One survey respondent mentioned this change in a section that asked for anything else regarding aging that was important to discuss. She explained that sex is more painful now, which has affected the frequency of sexual encounters with her husband and resulted in feelings of loss: "[It] was such a large part of our lives for so many years, I morn [sic] its passing as does he." While literature does not frequently depict these physical changes for women, it is interesting that Kent Haruf's novel *Our Souls at Night*, featuring widow and widower neighbors spending evenings together for companionship and eventually sex, uses the metaphor of not being "dried up" (147). The reference could allude to the fact that the lack of natural moisture in the vaginal area may lead people to believe they are "dried up." However, it is a problem that can be addressed with lubricants and hormone treatments. In a 2016 essay entitled "The Coming of Age: Sex 102," Sarah Critchton humorously describes her friends, referred to as the "Sisterhood of the Still Sexually Active," as supplying her with various remedies to help resolve the issue (e.g., "spare sticks of Vagifem," a low-level estrogen to combat vaginal thinness) (96). Even though there likely will be changes to the vagina over time, women should be cautious about doctors who pathologize these changes for commercial profit by promoting "vaginal makeovers" and machines to "rejuvenate the vagina"; research shows that "low sexual desire" often comes from "depression and exhaustion," not from female anatomy showing signs of aging (Steinke 130, 170).

Erectile Dysfunction?

Much more cultural attention has been focused on men's biological changes as they age. Most notable, of course, is the reduced blood flow to the penis, which affects the "reliability" of erections. Memoirist Ian Brown describes the experience in *Sixty: A Diary of My Sixty-First Year* using a relatable car metaphor to add levity to a situation many think is dire: "I am talking about the first time you have a dead battery. That's a shocker. I was fifty-seven the first time it happened to me. . . . It's a mechanical issue. I think the engine's turning over, but the alternator won't catch" (79). Despite the widespread awareness that erections are harder to attain and maintain as men age, information on the subject is often inaccurate and misleading. The prevalence of Viagra-induced gags in many films with older male stars (e.g., *Little Fockers*) creates a false hysteria that erection problems are "inevitable," even though, according to the National Institute of Health, only 15–25 percent of men over sixty-five are affected (Block and Baker 3–4). Often, in fact, the situation is not caused by "age" itself but by other medical conditions (e.g., diabetes, hypertension, side effects of medication) or alcohol abuse (Saline 33).

Drugs such as Viagra are of interest to some men who may miss the regularity of erections from their younger days. An AARP survey on sexuality found that 20 percent of men over fifty had tried a "potency-enhancing drug" and that 68 percent reported increased sexual satisfaction, in addition to women commenting that their "pleasure" was increased as well (Jacoby 150–151). Still, not everyone is convinced. A number of different problems are associated with the drugs, beginning with the fact that pharmaceutical companies have created the medical condition "erectile dysfunction" (ED), which not only further exacerbates fears of bodily breakdown, but does so in a way that profits those companies that sell the drugs.

Evolutionary biologist Richard Bribiescas does point out, though, that ED has appeared not just in the United States but also "across populations and cultures," where various natural remedies from "root vegetables" to garlic are used to counter symptoms (123).

Another concern surrounding these sexual-performance drugs was raised by retired sex therapist Andrea Shrednick, who, in a 2017 interview, observed that increased reliance on drugs like Viagra ignore "biological cues" and is tantamount to "fiddling with nature." She mentioned specifically that the type of erections created by these types of drugs (e.g., lasting for several hours) does not match up well with older women's thinning vaginal condition. In her words, this is a "bad combination." Another critique, from University of Canterbury Gender Studies professor Annie Potts, is that some men do "not lik[e] the mechanical feel of drug-assisted erections" and instead appreciate other types of "nonpenetrative sexual activities," which can be more satisfying for the couple overall (qtd. in Wentzell 71). This attitude is also on display in research done by anthropologist Emily Wentzell in Mexico, where erectile dysfunction drugs were being heavily promoted in advertisements. Rather than heeding the ads' appeal to a revived sexual machismo, most men in the study embraced a new state of marriage marked by "emotional tenderness and physical closeness, without penetration" (78). This type of activity even has a name: "outercourse." As Anna Woloski-Wruble, who runs sexual health clinics at Hadassah Hospital in Jerusalem, reminds people, "Penetration is only one expression of sexual activity. . . . The largest sex organ is our skin, and the most active organ is our mind" (qtd. in Saline 34). Another term for "arousing physical contact" without "penetration" is "frottage," which literary critic Susan Gubar uses to describe the "nongenital eroticism" of seniors in novels such as *Love in the Time of Cholera* (129).

The Fight to Stay Sexual

Some literary works include not only Viagra but also sexual enhancement drugs for women (e.g., Intrinsa) and show both the positive and negative aspects of these kinds of medical interventions. The inherent complexity of fictional texts creates the possibility to see strengths and weaknesses simultaneously without one side necessarily trumping the other. In the first story of Heyman's *Scary Old Sex*, "The Loves of her Life," Marianne, sixty-five, describes the rituals she must go through with her second husband, seventy-year-old Stu, before they make love—not only his Viagra but also a dose of clomipramine to minimize some of the impact of the Viagra and masturbating ten hours before to help his erection last longer. This process is described as similar to "running a war": "Plans had to be drawn up, equipment in tiptop condition, troops deployed and coordinated meticulously, there was no room for maverick actions lest the country end up defeated and at each other's throats" (40). From the passage, readers see that spontaneity is replaced by careful planning in order to ensure that execution of this bodily pleasure can be successful, which is probably not ideal but is shown to be worthwhile as the couple continues the ritual with weekly regularity. The last story in the collection—almost like a bookend for the first—describes another older couple who must get past obstacles in order to enjoy each other sexually, which confirms that seniors continue to try. Even though "aged flesh" contains "excrescences: papules, papillomas, skin tags, moles" and thinning hair, "underarm and pubic," the partners in the story want to stay sexually active with one another since their "lovemaking grafts them to one another, commingles them" and still remains a "reliable pleasure" (214). Thus, the lovemaking serves both the relationship and the self: "You do it with regularity to show you are a human being, that you are alive and civilized and can still become ecstatic" (214). Gubar in her 2019 memoir, *Late-Life Love*, affirms this ideal when she writes that "passion sustains older people" and their "desires" (295).

These motivations are strong and embolden older individuals to fight against the psychological and cultural messages that equate age with a lack of vitality and desirability. Many sources attest to the reality that it is easy to lose one's confidence and feelings of attractiveness given the combination of physical changes and challenges of aging and a society that mocks the notion that seniors may remain sexual beings until the end of their lives. One survey respondent complained that although she is given deference for being older, she misses being seen as a sexual being. Another commented on societal messages that "older women are not to be sexual or desirable in any way." The person noted that "if an older woman is sexual or grandpa is buff, it is usually parody and doesn't reflect older individuals as human beings of deep depth of feelings as complex as any other age." These same sentiments appear in the works of memoirists who write honestly about the challenges of maintaining a sexual identity in their later years. Diane Athill's memoir *Somewhere towards the End*, written when she was ninety, describes the same feeling of the first respondent, missing that absent part of her identity. She explains, "I might not look, or even feel, all that old, but I had ceased to be a sexual being . . . which had always seemed central to my existence" (15). Later, she does eventually meet someone unexpectedly and shares that "to be urgently wanted at a time when I no longer expected it cheered me up and brought me alive again—no small gift" (31). Still, Brown in *Sixty: A Diary of My Sixty-First Year* reiterates the other survey comments on the difficulty of even envisioning oneself as a sexual being when society does not. He questions how one is supposed to have "desire beyond the age of sixty," when expectations are that people at that point in life should be an "insensate stone, or at best, cuddly, grandfatherly and cute" (69).

An answer to Brown's question comes from sociologist Dr. Pepper Schwartz, who aside from being a University of Washington professor and author of over twenty books on sexuality, provides counsel on intimate matters for AARP, often bringing in her own experiences as a sexually active person in her seventies. In a *New York Times* podcast called *Dear Sugars*, Schwartz was interviewed by writers Steven Almond and Cheryl Strayed, who were responding to letters that were sent in by older individuals who did not think sexual activity was for them any longer. Her advice was clear and direct: "Fight like hell to keep it." The advice may be eye-opening for some but challenging for others, especially those who are not in long-term relationships. It raises the interesting question of whether married people have greater opportunities for physically satisfying relationships in their later years. Beauvoir addresses the topic in *The Coming of Age* when she argues that "married life" ignites "erotic stimulus." Other works show the negative aspects of a long married life that would impede physical desire. Meg Wolitzer's 2003 novel *The Wife*, for example, which was adapted into a 2017 film, depicts the demise of a marriage between famous writer Joe Castelman and his long-suffering spouse, Joan, who loses sexual desire for Joe despite living in proximity to him "season upon season," the years together being "like bricks spread thick with sloppy mortar," making a "marriage wall" (82).

Long-Married Couples

Unhappy relationships, like the Castelmans', showed up in responses to the surveys, but they were fewer than comments from happily connected partners. One respondent indicated her biggest regret was not leaving her bad marriage sooner, before the damage was done. Many more people talked about relying upon the spouse for emotional well-being and their concern over the possibility of anything bad befalling the partner. Research does reveal that couples who stay together for a long time indicate that their marriages get better over time as they learn to be "more tolerant of small disagreements" and become "slower to fight" and "more ready to forgive afterward"; they are also said to live longer (Leland 72, 77). In relationships that do endure, sexuality may change in frequency and form, but often there remains deep affection and closeness from shared experiences, bodily and otherwise. In his memoir, Brown beautifully describes what exists between his wife and himself that takes the place of traditional sex: "Our companionship gets greener and wider, more forgiving. We seem to think we have some duty to stay together—not for the children, but for the idea of being together. Because we can make each other laugh reliably, and because we have a past together that we don't want to throw away. It will mean very little once we are dead, but while we're alive it helps us believe we accomplished something" (99). A little later in the book Brown also describes his wife as a "good person to face darkness beside" since the longer one lives, the more deeply a person has encountered the "pain" of how "horrible" the world can be (123). Both of these passages display the reward for staying with a loved partner, despite inevitable difficulties, in order to use the strength of that bond to maintain pleasure amid hardship.

Death of a Spouse

For those with marriages like Brown's, the loss of a spouse is tragic, and for some, there is no recovery. A seventy-six-year-old man in the surveys talked about the pain of his wife's death from a car accident as the "hardest thing" he ever had to deal with. In fact, evidence shows that widowers fare worse than widows perhaps due to women being more likely to have a social network in place (Leland 77). Still, anyone who must continue on in life without the presence of a constant companion experiences change that can be painful and feel unnatural. Penelope Lively describes those absences in the memoir she wrote nearing eighty, *Dancing Fish and Ammonites* (2013). Commenting on the death of her husband, Lively writes, "It is an entirely changed life, for anyone who has been in a long marriage . . . alone in bed, alone most of the time, without that presence towards which you turned for advice, reassurance and with whom you shared the good news and the bad . . . no one to defuse anxieties" (42). The experiences Lively shares are likely familiar to most people who have suffered the loss of a companion on whom they have relied for emotional support, often for many decades. Less talked about but equally hard for many is the realization that the physical intimacy the couple shared is gone as well. Neuropsychologist Alice Radosh and her co-author Linda Simkin refer to this as "sexual bereavement," a grief for the loss of physical relations, which is made more difficult because it is socially unacceptable to discuss even with close family and friends (Brody, "After a Partner Dies" D7).

Lively's description of desolation might lead one to believe that those who survive the death of a spouse might seek the companionship of another mate in time. However, that does not seem to be the case. In a 2017 Aging and Society Conference talk entitled "After the Frogs and Princes are Gone: Widows and the Uncertainty in Current American Society" sociologist Regina Kenen indicated that in her detailed interviews with twenty widows, none expressed a desire to remarry. Survey responses for this book also echoed this sentiment ("I am lonely, but I would never consider marriage again"), as does other research, such as John Leland's in-depth year-long interviews with seniors for his *New York Times* series on aging and his book, *Happiness Is a Choice You Make*. One might assume that this disavowal of marrying again may be brought on by the imbalance of partner possibilities, for women in particular, since there is a great disparity between the number of widows and widowers (11.64 million widows compared with 3.28 widowers), but many forgo another lifetime partner for other reasons as well ("Marital Status"). A different explanation is that if individuals lived through an "emotionally draining death," they are reluctant to put themselves in that situation again, with perhaps less emotional energy and fewer resources to address the needs of a future ailing partner (Leland 67). Even if living alone can be lonely, one who has lost a spouse might prefer the predictability of life on one's own to the unknown elements that come when connecting lives with another. Philosopher Martha Nussbaum in *Aging Thoughtfully* explains that one facet of "mature love," which she thinks is not explored enough by philosophers, is that prospective partners are likely to have a good deal of history they bring to the relationship and not everyone may be keen to investigate what that "baggage" is (162). The film *Forty-Five Years* shows how even a couple who has been married for almost five decades can have issues from their past rise up and create discord. In the case of *Forty-Five Years*, the wife finds out about the husband's relationship with a woman prior to their marriage, and previously untold secrets from long ago threaten the security of their lengthy marriage.

Increasingly, some couples choose to cohabitate rather than marry again, and statistics for this demographic are on the rise. A Pew Research Center report in 2017 noted that there was a 75 percent increase between 2006 and 2017 in people over fifty living with someone outside of marriage. The total is around 4 million, with 900,000 being those over sixty-five (Span, "More Seniors Shun Marriage" D3). Besides the psychological reasons individuals may have for not wanting to marry again, some very practical ones exist as well. When older adults marry again, their benefits can be affected. Social Security survivor benefits can be discontinued upon remarriage, and qualification for Medicaid can be altered as well. Even finding partners with whom to cohabitate can pose challenges, despite technology-assisted dating sites providing opportunities to meet others at every age, including the senior years. Several survey respondents referred to the unpleasantness of online dating, also displayed in a scene from *Book Club* when Candice Bergen's character sees the difference between the profiles people post and the reality of meeting those individuals in person. Seventy-nine-year-old cartoonist Nicole Hollander, creator of the syndicated *Sylvia* comic, shares some of her online dating frustrations in the memoir *Tales of Graceful Aging from the Planet Denial* (2007); these include being rejected by an online dating service (Big-Brain Dating.com) because the colleges she attended were not deemed prestigious enough. She also complains of the "utter silence" that greeted her on Match.com, where profiles are arranged by age (162–163). In addition, seniors can become targets of "swindlers," who prey upon older adults, believing them to be easily manipulated out of their financial resources with romantic attention (Olson, "Swindlers"). Not wanting to be vulnerable to any of these machinations, a woman in the survey wrote that the secret to a happy life is not to go on dating sites.

Living Single

Those who maintain a "solo" life can be quite content with that arrangement. Stewart O'Nan's 2011 novel, *Emily, Alone*, follows the everyday activities of Emily Maxwell (first appearing in his 2002 book, *Wish You Were Here*, and reappearing in the 2019 novel *Henry, Himself*), who lives by herself after her husband, Henry, dies and her grown-up children have moved away. Readers expecting a depressing account of loss and bleakness will be surprised. Emily does attend a significant number of funerals of friends and mentions missing her husband and dear friend Louise, but she fills her days purposefully, lavishing much attention on her dog, Rufus, spending quality time with her sister-in-law, Arlene, and eventually finding a renewed sense of independence in buying herself a car. Occasionally, she reflects on Henry's absence such as in a passage when spring comes and she wakes early to the noises of animal-life outside: "These were the hours she missed Henry keenly, the bulk and warmth of him against her reassuring. They spooned, his arm hooked around her like a fallen branch, his knees tucked behind her, then, without a word, they both rolled to face the other way, and she held him, kissed his back. In the morning he prodded her, wanting, and while she kept luxurious memories of those trysts, what she missed most was the smell of his skin" (207). While this passage evokes longing and pathos for a past that can be visited only in reverie, it stands out for its singularity in the novel. In most of the narrative, in fact, Emily is not looking back but looking forward to making the most of her remaining years.

In the novel, part of Emily's acceptance of being "alone" can be explained by the ongoing communication she has with her adult children and grandchildren, which provides important familial connection in her life. Unfortunately, many seniors living alone do not have that resource to draw upon. They are often referred to as "elder orphans" or "solo agers." According to Sara Zeff Gerber, a presenter at the 2017 Age and Society Conference and author of the 2018 book, *Essential Retirement Planning for Solo Agers: A Retirement and Aging Roadmap for Single and Childless Adults*, 20 percent of baby boomers do not have children, many of them having chosen not to earlier in life. The numbers are expected to increase from 12 percent of people aged eighty to eighty-four in 2010 to an estimated 16 percent in 2030 (Garland 5). As a result of aging without a spouse or children, "solo agers" must take care of financial arrangements, medical assistance, and emotional support on their own. They are apt to create "small networks of siblings and friends" that fill the role children take on (Loe, *Aging Our Way* 181). Many take advantage of housing situations that provide built-in company (e.g., senior co-housing or NORCs), but still, some recommend that a lawyer specializing in elder affairs be consulted to set up trusts if needed and create documents that spell out a decision-making process if the elder person becomes incapacitated. Technology is also helping those living alone; the EyeOn app, for example, that will contact several designated people if the solo ager does not respond to alerts. Lyft, Uber, and GoGoGrandparent, which will facilitate rides without a smartphone and notify emergency contacts, can help with transportation needs while even Amazon's Alexa can provide memory assistance and some form of companionship (Garland 5).

Despite the assistance provided by these innovations, as Jacoby noted in her "Women: Eventually the Only Sex?" chapter, we undoubtedly live in a "coupled society." One solo ager explained in an interview how this reality affects her in a very practical way. She explained that the "status of being two" affects even buying groceries in that she "can't buy a half a loaf of bread" (Shrednick). Friends with spouses are busy "managing lives" that give them less opportunity for socializing with those without a partner. For the 12 million adults over sixty-five who are living alone in the United States, estimates are that 35 percent may be experiencing loneliness, which can affect longevity more than air pollution, obesity, and alcohol, according to a recent study of 100,000 people ("By the Numbers"; M. Johnson, "Solo" 1A). In fact, a former U.S. surgeon general, Vivek Murthy, compares the effects of loneliness and isolation on lifespan to be the equivalent of "smoking 15 cigarettes a day" (qtd. in Davis 26). Those who have studied the most effective methods to combat loneliness find that programs that include exercise are far more effective than "home-visiting" arranged by a social agency (M. Johnson, "Family" 7A). Sociologists also warn of not putting the onus of fixing the problem of senior loneliness on the "lonely themselves," as in advising them to "get a dog" or "take a class." These suggestions, while potentially helpful, ignore the larger issues contributing to isolation that many older adults feel from the "loss of social significance" (Davis 27). With this idea in mind, other recommendations look beyond one-on-one interactions to something more collective. Thus, in *The Fountain of Age*, based on extensive gerontology research and her own experience, Betty Friedan suggests that it is important "in age" to stop looking for the "perfect relationship" and recognize that older people "need a community" instead (622). The widow whom I interviewed came to the same conclusion after she found an identity for herself as a "substitute Bubbe" for members of an Orthodox Jewish organization in Southeastern Wisconsin called "Chabad." She expressed that while it is "not easy being alone, not easy aging," if a person finds a community of shared culture and history, it can be most "welcoming . . . [that] they envelop you" (Shrednick).

Second Chances

While many seniors sustain single lives by finding various strategies to address the challenges of being by themselves, others decide to make a second (or third) chance at love and enter into partnerships once again after being on their own. Television and films have been on the forefront of circulating these stories, which may increase the confidence of older individuals to adopt a "never too old to fall in love" attitude. One such television program is *Last Tango in Halifax*, which aired from 2012 to 2016 on BBC and was inspired by the real-life experiences of screenwriter Sally Wainwright's mother. The show features a couple in their late seventies, both widowed, who met when teenagers but rediscover each other through social media after their spouses' deaths. The title of the program, which won the 2013 British Academy Award for Best Drama Series, plays off the title of the classic *The Last Tango in Paris* (1972), notable for its explicit sexuality. Although this series does not break the older sexuality taboo by showing the couple naked or engaged in any overt sexual relations, critics have observed that the story of "desire" comes across as "authentic" because the characters are shown as knowing what they want due to their age and experience; they are not out to please anyone but themselves (Gorton 232–233).

The idea of a later-in-life romantic "awakening" on display in *The Last Tango in Halifax* is also present in *Grace and Frankie*, Netflix's ongoing series starring Jana Fonda as Grace and Lily Tomlin as Frankie, whose former husbands have "come out" as gay and end up marrying each other. The power of this storyline is that even though the husbands' relationship often attracts humorous derision from other characters who are resistant to accepting this change in sexual orientation, it is not just played for laughs; instead, the marriage between Sol and Robert (Sam Waterston and Martin Sheen) is taken seriously and reinforces that people may use the freedom of their later years to affirm a sexual orientation that they may have felt too much social pressure to reveal earlier. LGBT critics of the show wish that it would go even further in displaying the sexual nature of the couple's relationship, perhaps as in *Orange Is the New Black*, another successful Netflix show that breaks ageist boundaries but treats same-sex intimacy much more boldly. Still, *Grace and Frankie* opens the door to considering relationships in the senior years that break conventions of heterosexuality just as Jill Soloway's *Transparent* series on Amazon has popularized the prospect of gender transition in one's later years. Susan Faludi's 2016 memoir, *In the Darkroom*, on her father's sex reassignment surgery at seventy-six, also investigates transgender identity and the possibility of gender-affirming surgery as a senior. Since 70–80 percent of individuals identifying as LGBT live alone and do not share in the benefits of a partner for support, more representations of late-life relationships outside of conventional male-female pairing can foster acceptance and encourage pursuing companionship based on whom people truly desire (Macdonald 67; Abrahams). The documentary *Gen Silent* successfully makes the case for needing greater awareness and representation of nonheterosexual seniors so that their hard-fought campaign for recognition and rights does not dissipate in old age and lead to a "closeted" existence. June

Arnold's revolutionary novel *Sister Gin*, about a passionate lesbian relationship that develops post menopause, also makes a case for the joys of same-sex intimacy beyond youth: "I just never imagined that the delights of age would include the fact of endlessly drawnout [sic] orgasms" (129).

Mainstream films such as *Book Club* tend to stick closer to a traditional heterosexual model for these second-chance relationships. Most of these films are in the romantic comedy genre, which often precludes complexity. As Gubar notes in *Late-Life Love*, "literature" is far "superior to film" due to the superficial treatment she observes in the visual medium (277). Questions such as how does the first long-term relationship impact the later one and how do people make themselves open to "starting over" as an older adult when that can be terrifying, are not usually treated in these films. Instead, there may be a minor obstacle that must be overcome in order to become enraptured in late-life romantic bliss. Despite the formulaic aspect of these types of movies, they can be inspirational in some capacity by showing the process of starting over. Even the titles of some (*Hope Springs*, *Something's Gotta Give*, and *It's Complicated*) send the message that second chances at love are possible, though not without some compromise. The films also feature actors and actresses often in their sixties or beyond (e.g., Meryl Streep and Diane Keaton appear in several), which sends a message regarding the vitality of older adults, who should not be considered "finished" professionally or romantically.

Still, the films portraying "second-chance" relationships that are based on fictional works tend to have more depth. In *Our Souls at Night*, not only do the widowed neighbors, Addie and Louis, come together at night for companionship, they also philosophically reflect on what their relationship means. At one point when Louis must defend this new relationship to his daughter, Holly, he describes the arrangement as a "decision to be free"—in other words, to live for oneself and not be overly concerned about the opinions of others (52). This same perspective came through in the surveys for this book when respondents were asked about the advantages of old age compared to youth. Many alluded to feeling freer due to fewer "anxieties and concerns" and less "confusion over what is important." Often, respondents described the feeling as a new "confidence," one based on recognizing the "value" that "knowledge and experience" bring. This confidence is on display when Louis is able to tell his daughter, who is embarrassed that people in the community know Louis and Addie are spending their evenings together, "Well, honey, that'll have to be your problem, not mine. . . . I'm not embarrassed" (53).

The book and television adaptation of *Olive Kitteridge* also provide more insight into late-life "second-chance" relationships than is present in romantic comedy films. After Olive's husband, Henry, dies, she feels resigned to a solitary life, with just her dog for companionship. In no way does she expect romantic engagement with anyone, especially Jack Kennison, a distant acquaintance and an outsider in Crosby, Maine, where Olive resides. When Olive first sees his body slumped over on a walking trail, she asks, "Are you dead?" His glib response, "Apparently not," initiates a relationship that develops even though they appear to have almost nothing in common. He is a rich Republican who has disowned his adult daughter for coming out as gay, which Olive finds offensive, in addition to being put off by his expensive car and Ivy League education. But both learn slowly that nothing is gained by judging the other as abhorrent when the possibility for an emotional union is what they need more than anything else. Olive describes losing her husband as "drowning in . . . emptiness" that she could not quite fill with other activities such as volunteer work, since they never proved "enough." She comes to realize that Jack's needing her assistance when they first meet gave her a "place in the world" (269). Although Olive frequently makes negative comments on her "old, big, sagging" body, she comes to see that "lumpy, aged, and wrinkled bodies were as needy as . . . young firm ones" (270). Just as she needs to overcome her inherent prejudices with Jack, who is totally different from her core self, solidified over a long life, she must also overcome the self-critical reflection common to many aging individuals that their physical changes disqualify them for intimate relationships with others. The lesson that love should not be "tossed away carelessly" stands as a reminder that late-life opportunities for partnering the duration of one's lifespan can develop if people stay open to them, even as many choose to carry on without the entanglement of a new relationship.

Other literary works also focus on the struggles and satisfactions of beginning to be a new partner as an older adult. The stories in *Scary Old Sex*, like *Olive Kitteridge*, take the body to task for the changes that can make a person feel less than desirable. In the first story, "The Loves of Her Life," the main character, Marianne, jokes that people over forty should not "make love in the daytime" due to the visibility of all their bodily changes, such as sagging breasts, loose flesh, and various outgrowths on the skin. Despite what could be an obstacle for some, the characters in these stories show acceptance of nature running its course (e.g., even comparing the developments to beautiful "wild mushrooms"). As a result of coming to terms with their bodies' changes, the characters are able to move forward and continue to form new connections when they are beyond their sixties. Besides touching on the body image issue, several stories from *Scary Old Sex* treat the complication of a former spouse's presence in memory interfering with a present relationship, especially if the first relationship was a more ideal match than the second one, which might necessitate more compromises. The stories recognize that there can be a tendency to canonize the late partner—"glorifying the inaccessible"—while "denigrating what was available" (19). But despite the tendency to do this, Heyman's characters learn that glorifying the past detracts from the present by ultimately "darkening" one's current life; the take-away message reverberating in the stories evokes Stephen Stills's classic 1970 song, "Love the One You're With."

A different obstacle in these second-chance unions is presented in the 2010 novel *Major Pettigrew's Last Stand* by Helen Simonson. Like the immensely popular *A Man Called Ove* (2012) by Fredrik Backman, the work centers on a widower who seems to have accepted that his best days are behind him, especially without the company of a spouse. Both texts involve a reintegration back into a less isolated life as a result of someone outside of their familiar culture, though in *Major Pettigrew* that person, the Pakistani Mrs. Jamina Ali, is more than just a neighborly companion—she and the Major fall in love. Most of the hurdles the couple face are from people in the community who believe their backgrounds are too different (given that she is a woman of color), especially the Major's golf club members who are hostile to those they designate as outsiders. Mrs. Ali brings critical insight into this misguided thinking when she remarks, "A couple may have nothing in common but the color of their skin and the country of their ancestors, but the whole world would see them as compatible" (265). That the couple also appears to be from different classes is brought up by the Major's son, Roger, who asks, "What would Mother think about you chasing all over England after some shopgirl?," referring to the fact that Mrs. Ali works in the convenience store her deceased husband had owned. The Major curtails that line of questioning by telling his son that if he calls her a "shopgirl" again, he will punch him.

Another wise lesson included in the novel is the importance of a "spark" in order to have this late-in-life relationship work. Some might believe that a "spark" is only for the young, but here, the reader learns it is a prerequisite for the old as well. When the Major thinks Mrs. Ali has been scared off from further involvement from him after a disastrous event at the club, he turns to Grace, a loyal friend, and suggests they marry. She complains that there is no "passion" between them, which he questions as necessary for a relationship between seniors: "At our age, surely there are better things to sustain us, to sustain a marriage, than the brief flame of passion?" Grace corrects the Major by reminding him that "without it, two people living together may be lonelier than if they lived quite alone" (291). Such a passionate connection between the Major and Mrs. Ali eventually helps them stand up for the integrity of their relationship, when Mrs. Ali's family members object to their union and accuse her of "debauch[ing]" herself. The boldness of her response illustrates her new-found confidence derived from their blooming romance. She asks her aunt, "Would you like to hear how it is to be naked with a man you love and really live and breathe the sensuality of life itself?" (337). The novel, then, ultimately sends the message that these older adult second-chance-at-love connections may attract disapproval and censure from many parties close to the couple or from the wider community, but the shared sense of fulfilling one's own romantic longings can triumph over the cacophony of protests.

Clearly, not everyone is going to seek out or be able to find intimate companionship in his or her later years. One survey respondent declared that the aspect she appreciates most about growing older is not having to worry about the "lack of romance" in her life and concentrating instead on long-term friendships. Likewise, an interviewee for Leland's "oldest old" project talked about having more than his share of physical encounters during his long life and appreciating having an apartment to himself so that he does not have "to worry about getting in trouble" any longer (64, 117). However, for others, companionship in the last years of life provides meaning and delight. In the words of an older woman in Ali Smith's 2016 novel, *Autumn*, upon beginning an unexpected relationship with another woman, "It is like magic has happened. . . . who'd have guessed, it'd be love, at this late stage, that'd see me through" (238).

6

Women and Men

"Separate but Equal"?

What would happen if one woman told the truth about her life?
The world would split open.
—Muriel Rukeyser, *The Speed of Darkness*

"Not enough has been written about the treachery of middle life," the old
man mused. "Dante went to hell to escape it, and I've seen plenty
of other men do the same metaphorically speaking."
—Jennifer Egan, *Manhattan Beach*

I have found that women and men are not separated by
an unsurmountable chasm, as many people believe.
—Julia Serano, *Whipping Girl*

Who doesn't know about Nora Ephron's neck? In "I Feel Bad about
My Neck," a celebrated essay first published in *The New Yorker*,
which then became part of a 2006 collection of essays by the same
name, Ephron bemoaned how wrinkled necks are a "dead giveaway" about age. She advises, "You can put makeup on your face
and concealer under your eyes and dye on your hair, you can shoot
collagen and Botox and Restylane into your wrinkles and creases,
but short of surgery, there's not a damn thing you can do about a

neck" (5). In subsequent essays, Ephron continued to point out the physical problems of growing older. Her 2010 collection *I Remember Nothing*, for example, describes a seventy-year-old body in a disparaging way: "Your cleavage looks like a peach pit. If your elbows faced forward, you would kill yourself. You're two inches shorter than you used to be. You're ten pounds fatter and you cannot lose a pound of it to save your soul" (128).

Reactions to Ephron's humorous and candid reflections on bodily changes have been mixed. On one hand, supporters appreciate her willingness to make light of these changes to ease the private misery they may instill for some individuals. In this way, she is similar to notable food writer M.F.K. Fisher, whose comments in an interview describing her older body in a mirror as "strange, uncouth, ugly . . . with a shapeless little toad-like torso" have become celebrated as commiserating the loss of beauty from youth (qtd. in Cruikshank, *Learning* 154). Others find these "old body" complaints problematic. They can easily exacerbate some older adults' already self-conscious feelings about changes in physical appearance, and if they were not already thinking about the changes as negative, these texts by famous successful women discussing their physical flaws could propel them to do so. Given that both of these women worked productively up until the final years of their lives, one could certainly argue that fixating on changes in appearance is an undesirable offering from fertile minds who could be celebrating the creativity that many believe peaks in later years. In 2016, women between ages forty and fifty-four in the United States underwent 7.5 million cosmetic surgery treatments, a majority of which were procedures to diminish signs of aging at an estimated cost of $13 billion a year (Calhoun; Nussbaum and Levmore 95–96). Margaret Morganroth Gullette in *Agewise* (2011), however, advises caution when regarding such statistics since they tend to leave out the fact that the majority of women (80 percent) elect not to have cosmetic surgery at all (104). Still, admirers of Ephron's work have followed in her footsteps, continuing to write amusingly about the physical changes of aging with direct references to the necessity of cosmetic surgery. Sheila Nevins's 2017 *You*

Don't Look Your Age and Other Fairy Tales is one such example; in one of the essays, entitled "Facing Face-Lifts," she asserts that they will take seven years off of a women's age and confesses to looking in the mirror ten times a day to "obsess" over "every wrinkle" (11).

Physical Appearance Changes

It should not be too surprising that feminists have taken umbrage with Ephron's "neck" essay for perpetuating the burden of upholding one's looks into the senior years when others have advocated that this should be a time of freedom from those cultural expectations. In fact, one such collection in direct opposition to Ephron is entitled *I Feel Great about My Hands* (2011), edited by Shari Graydon, which has forty different women sharing more positive stories of aging acceptance. While feminists challenge the rhetoric of women's self-hate for their aging bodies, others flatly deny that this dissatisfaction is gendered at all. They argue that women are not more concerned with the changes in their physical appearances than men and believe there is too little research on the subject to perpetuate assumptions as fact. Julia Twigg in *Fashion and Age: Dress, the Body and Later Life* (2013), for example, cites a number of studies that show men actually may experience more negative feelings about their attractiveness as they age than women, whose feelings about their physical selves generally stay the same throughout their lifetimes (45). As the research of Lucie Baker and Eyal Gringart indicates, even though men were not as apt to undergo "appearance-enhancing activities," they became "increasingly dissatisfied with their physical appearance as they aged."

The surveys for this book at first might seem to confirm the popular perception that caring about one's looks later in life is more likely to be a women's preoccupation in that none of the male respondents brought up the subject at all in any of their answers whereas women commented on their physical appearance in various responses to the survey questions. Interestingly, almost none of the reflections were in a similar vein to Ephron's or Fisher's. The closest to those self-critical testimonies was a comment from a seventy-four-old-woman, who for the last question, "What haven't I asked you about regarding aging that you would like me to know?" first commented, "Appearance." She then added, "I don't like my weight and dark circles under eyes." Another woman in her seventies referenced feeling "invisible," usually a coded way to express disappointment that one's looks no longer attract attention. Professional writers also have used this term to describe their disappearing presence in the eyes of others. Emily Fox Gordon's well-circulated essay "At Sixty Five," first published in the periodical *American Scholar* and then anthologized in *Best American Essays 2014*, discusses how her being older manifests as an "invisibility to strangers." Another essay that appeared in the Australian magazine *The Monthly* pinpoints the issue of invisibility in terms of women exclusively. Helen Garner, writing of her experience being over seventy, reports, "Beyond a certain age women become invisible in public spaces. The famous erotic gaze is withdrawn. You are no longer, in the eyes of the world, a sexual being." Male writers have been less expressive on the issue, but some have indicated that the idea of "invisibility" is not the exclusive domain of women. Ian Brown in his memoir, *Sixty: A Diary of My Sixty-First Year*, reveals that he commiserates and empathizes with older women "when they say they have become invisible" but does not understand those who "prefer invisibility" in order to avoid the pressures of physical appearance (135). "Invisibility" may apply to men and women, but perhaps the terms means something different to each. For women, it could mean no longer receiving attention for one's looks, while for men "invisibility" might mean not being regarded as an important individual with status, according to Neal King and Toni Calasanti's article on manhood in later life (706).

Another type of comment in some of the survey answers from women about their appearance at first seems positive, but, on closer inspection, may not be. These responses celebrate "passing" as younger than their chronological age due to a youthful-looking appearance. This fairly common phenomenon involves people telling a story of someone being shocked to learn their real age, such as a former adult student of mine who was delighted that she was "carded" at a music festival to make sure the senior discount was applicable. Similarly, a sixty-nine-year-old taking the survey indicated that she did not experience ageism because she is often told, "I look younger than my age." Another woman in her sixties made the same claim, citing her "youthful" appearance as the reason that she does not experience ageism. Women who feel this way often deem themselves "lucky," but age scholars suggest that this type of attitude could be a form of internalized ageism; if a person believes that not revealing physical signs of aging is a cause for celebration, there is an inherent belief that aging is bad and should be hidden or circumvented somehow. Age activist Ashton Applewhite's "Working to Disarm Women's Anti-Aging Demons," published in the *New York Times*, also comments on the problem with "passing." She explains that "trying to pass for younger" is "rooted in shame over something that shouldn't be shameful." Women should not necessarily be blamed for this shame because the cultural messages reinforcing this idea are, according to Margaret Cruikshank in *Learning to Be Old*, "inescapable" (148). Still, it is important that people recognize that "passing," a term popularized in African American literature to reference light-skinned individuals evading the designation "black," is a form of self "erasure" (Andrews 77).

Better Messages

Despite the strong social indoctrination that older women's bodies should elicit shame and scorn (e.g., feminist Barbara Macdonald used the cartoon example of the Wizard of Id's wife being drawn with sparse hair and a singular balloon body), literature and women in real life provide counter examples that challenge these negative prescriptive messages to show that an older appearance does not have to come with critical self-scrutiny. In the novel *Our Souls at Night* by Kent Haruf, for example, two neighbors whose spouses have long since died come together in the evenings for companionship and intimacy. In a poignant scene toward the end of the book Addie Moore is lying in bed naked waiting for Louis Waters to join her. She momentarily feels self-conscious and tells him not to look at her, especially since she assumes her "old body" is too "heavy around the hips and stomach." Louis dispels that notion by telling her that she appears "lovely." He further contradicts the idea that a women's body is supposed to remain ageless: "'You're just right. You're how you're supposed to look. You're not supposed to be some thirteen-year-old girl without any breasts and hips" (152). One might find fault that Addie does not have the confidence to believe these self-affirming ideas on her own and must, therefore, rely on a partner to substantiate them. Regardless, the book and the subsequent film adaptation offer an alternative to women feeling as if they must disguise their age or strive to appear as they did in youth.

For those who might think that this interlude of realistic age acceptance is more fiction than truth, corroboration that some women not only accept the physical changes of their bodies as they age but, in fact, feel better about their appearance as they age can be found in numerous survey responses. An example of this attitude comes from a seventy-year-old woman who shared her feelings on the subject when asked about the "distinct advantages of old age over youth" in the survey. This woman wrote, "Well, we are not as concerned with our looks [smile emoji]—yes, we still make an effort but we don't feel it's as important as we once did." She added that part of what people should be doing as they age is learning to be true to themselves, which contrasts sharply with those who harshly judge themselves for not fitting into an idealized image of self or even a former self. A sixty-six-year-old woman also indicated that caring less about appearance was an advantage of age, but she framed it less as embracing one's "true" self and more about figuring out what "superficial things" should no longer be sources for worry—"appearance" and "wealth" being two of them. One individual who felt that her looks have improved as she aged (now that she is seventy) was particularly notable since even early feminist scholars such as Simone de Beauvoir described her aging self with self-deprecating and almost cruel language. Beauvoir disappointingly seems to warn her readers, "I loathe my appearance now: the eyebrows slipping down toward the eyes, the bags underneath, the excessive fullness of the cheeks, and the air of sadness around the mouth that wrinkles always bring" (qtd. in Bouson 4). These words uttered by Beauvoir when she was only fifty-one would not inspire others to embrace their older appearances, but today, at least, there is more dialogue about alternative approaches to the subject. Abigail Brooks' 2017 book *The Ways Women Age*, based on interviews with women in their late forties to seventies, contains whole chapters devoted to women who have a positive attitude about their aging selves. One sixty-two-year-old woman named Lucy talked about how much "better looking" she appears with gray hair, which she found more flattering than her earlier dark hair (74). Celebrity Jane Fonda, the subject of much debate due to her acknowledged plastic surgery, also sends a hopeful message of acceptance for a future healthier self. In recent interviews Fonda, now in her eighties, wishes that she did not feel a "need to alter" herself—that she could have been "braver," and not given in to Hollywood's pressure for women to look younger than they are. She acknowledges the sexism and ageism of the film industry, but also encourages others to put the "voices" of "inadequacy" to the side and not allow them to be the "governing voices" (Cagle 57; Brooks 198). Her experience creates opportunities for more people to follow the lead of the previously quoted seventy-year old who "feels great" about how she looks. Another example of this type of alternative self-evaluation narrative from older women on their appearance appears in a 2016 essay by publisher Sarah Crichton entitled "The Coming of Age: Sex 102." While gazing at her body of "six-decades," she sees an amalgamation of "young and old," and despite the "wear . . . [that] is inescapable," she muses that if someone were to see her walking down a beach, it would be hard not to "marvel, 'Look at that attractive older woman, so comfortable in her own skin'" (94).

Do Appearance Changes Matter to Men?

There is so much attention on older women's relationship with their changing appearance as they age that one wonders to what extent men share these concerns. As mentioned previously, Brown in his memoir *Sixty* is one of the most outspoken male writers on the subject of men's bodily changes in the later years. Brown's candid treatment of the subject is memorable in that he not only discusses familiar changes, such as hair loss, but also touches on changes in skin elasticity that often only appear in women's writing. He reports that two-thirds of all men have "significant baldness by the time they are sixty" and even acknowledges knowing men who use shoe polish as a way to cover up missing patches of hair (192). His willingness to share his concerns about the wrinkles he is discovering all over his body and the "bags" under his eyes fosters an awareness that feeling self-conscious about new and unwelcome changes in appearances is not solely the domain of women, even if their complaints are more publicized. In an ideal world, neither men nor women would judge themselves harshly for their bodies' transformation with age, but more men coming forth with their discomfort at losing the façade of their youth will make women feel less targeted as vain and superficial.

A film that draws attention to men's body insecurity, especially as they age, is Nicole Holofcener's 2013 *Enough Said*, starring Julia Louis-Dreyfus as Eva, a masseuse, who becomes romantically involved with Albert, a museum curator, played by James Gandolfini. The subject of physical appearance comes up frequently in the dialogue between the middle-aged main characters, both of whom are very aware that the body can change over time in often undesirable ways. Besides comparing teeth (e.g., Albert is missing one), breasts (e.g., Eva says hers are "real"), and hands, much of the focus is on Albert's weight. Not only does Eva describe him as "kind of fat" with a "big belly" early in the film, but his ex-wife, Marianne, whom Eva takes on as a client before realizing her connection to Albert, also chastises him for his weight, which, she says, "repulsed" her. With so much negative attention on his physique, it is not surprising that Albert is extremely self-conscious about his body, especially during intimate moments with a new partner, not unlike Addie in *Our Souls at Night*. During one encounter Albert asks for the "truth" if Eva can breathe when he is on top of her during sex and then brings up his desire to lose weight in the future. The film depicts honestly how men may be equally dissatisfied with their physical appearance as they age and how sensitive they can be about the topic. When Eva starts feeling conflicted about Albert after hearing his ex-wife's complaints, she mockingly makes weight jokes (e.g., suggesting buying him a calorie book for a gift), which he later reveals left him heart-broken. Not many cultural works show men's insecurity about their bodies' being in disrepair, so the film stands out in this regard. The fact that at least one reviewer described the Gandolfini character's undesirable body as making him unfit for a romantic entanglement with Dreyfus's Eva shows that judgment against imperfect bodies can be applied to men and women, which, in turn, feeds the cycle of self-criticism (LaSalle, "Enough").

Advertisements versus Art

Feelings of disappointment in later-life appearance for both men and women may come from within if an individual struggles with how a younger identity based on looks no longer fits an older model. But messages from the everyday imagery around us also can be influential, especially advertising, which Germaine Greer, in her afterword to the 2017 book *Aging Women in Literature and Visual Culture*, argues is "the most pervasive and persuasive form of visual culture" (322). Martha Holstein, an expert on feminism and aging, also points to the potentially destructive effects of advertising, which "reinforces the belief that our 'natural' appearance is inherently flawed and inadequate" (56). Both men and women in the surveys complained that the advertising directed at seniors is mostly medical-related, reinforcing the idea that age connotes decrepitude and decline. A seventy-two-year-old woman, for example, explained, "I get tired of ads for remedies for illnesses common in old age," while a seventy-three-year-old man also mentioned that the advertising he sees is "mostly related to drugs," which he believes will probably will do more harm than good. Gerontologists, such as Stephen Katz and Barbara Marshall, note that some advertisers are making improvements in being less age-ist and embracing a more "positive senior," but this is difficult to accomplish without succumbing to the "successful aging" ideology by portraying older people with few physical signs of aging beyond gray hair (Meeuf 154). Whatever improvements are being made, no one can deny the continued onslaught of negative age messages that seep into our televisions, magazine advertisements, and even email. I recently helped someone find an apartment in a residence for those fifty-five and older through an Internet search. The very next day, my inbox was bombarded with advertisements promoting the "unexpected miracle" of being able to "look ten to fifteen years younger," in addition to "maximum strength male enhancement" and other wonders from Groupon to help me "erase time." Even if some of the content of these types of ads and promotions are better than they were in the past, the methods to reach potential targets for their wares seem more insidious than ever.

A far better venue to show the physical changes of the body without caving in to a wholly negative or too rosy projection is visual art. The benefit of depicting older people in art is outlined in a chapter on photography in Margaret Gullette's *Ending Ageism, or How Not to Shoot Old People*. In the realm of art, Gullette argues, there are great opportunities to show individuals in their later years as "interesting, fascinating and appealing," which is important for society at large to see (24). Another cultural scholar who has made important contributions to understanding how the presentation of older bodies in art can initiate a richer appreciation of aging is Joanne Frueh, whose essay "Visible Difference: Women Artists and Aging" is, at least partly, applicable to men as well. The article proposes two tenets that illuminate the role of art, especially done by older artists themselves: "action and prophecy," both of which aid in the "creation of a possible world" (200). The artist's "action" is representing a fuller picture of what aging looks like in a way that will have future useful effects for others—hence, the "prophecy." Frueh's goal is to demonstrate that the "aging . . . body can become an object of love" for older people (212).

Kathleen Woodward also has done ground-breaking work examining age and art. Besides editing *Figuring Age: Women, Bodies, Generations* (1999), she authored the 2006 article "Performing Age, Performing Gender," which introduces the provocative work of three women artists—Louise Bourgeois, Rachel Rosenthal, and Nettie Harris, all seniors themselves—to show how their creations are meditations on art that go beyond a surface understanding of chronological age. Woodward analyzes a photo of Bourgeois, a nonagenarian who worked until the last weeks before her death in 2010 at age ninety-eight, wearing a body sculpture, called *Confrontation* (1978), which the artist wore to a fashion show. The sculpture consists of a tunic that has different body-like shapes resembling breasts and genitals all over it. It has been interpreted as mimicking eggs coming out of an ovary, which Woodward sees as repudiating the idea that fertility (and perhaps creativity) belong only to young women prior to menopause (170). While Woodward is captivated by this photograph of Bourgeois defying age demarcation, Gullette in *Ending Ageism* singles out a different photograph taken by Annie Leibowitz in 1997 for commentary that shows the artist's unabashed old age. Gullette points out that the photograph could have been taken in a way to not accentuate the wrinkles on her face or hand; instead, the "shot intentionally stresses old age" and showcases her hand, which continues to be the essential tool for her trade (42).

These photographs are powerful and do challenge stereotypical views of aging women in particular as "barren" or "ashamed" of their appearance; thus, they are emblematic of the diverse attitudes one can and likely should possess about the later years of life. However, it is also worthwhile to examine Bourgeois's art itself, especially some of the last work she did in her late nineties. In a 2008 Rizzoli publication on Bourgeois's art, critic Linda Nochlin has an essay called "Old-Age Style: Late Louise Bourgeois." Nochlin is interested in the contrast between the "bodies, soft and stuffed," that Bourgeois creates in the early 2000s (such as *Femme Couteau*) and the "hard, cold and empty" works, such as *The Institute* (2002), which is made out of silver. These contrasting projects are linked to prior works in that both are connected to memories and utilize found objects (190–196). Since these two projects use themes and techniques from earlier phases, they seem less intimate and surprising when compared with *I Go to Pieces: My Inner Life*, one of the final series Bourgeois worked on in the last years of her life. Each of the large-scale etchings features a prominently displayed woman, naked in most, with long hair in shades of pink and red. The text is embroidered in one and in Bourgeois's own unsteady penmanship in others, which gives the works a personal reverberation alluding to her advanced age. While the message in the untitled #6 gives a list of what is lost, presumably over time—mind, footing, memory, consciousness, sight—which at first reads as a litany of loss, the final line, "I can not control everything for ever [sic]," and the beautiful red-pink coloring signaling birth or rebirth diminish the pessimism of the early statement. One of the other images simply has the sentence, "I give everything away," which has a liberating message, especially since the image is of a nude woman with long flowing hair—both the nudity and the long hair being unspoken taboos for the aging woman. The image functions as an antidote to Cruikshank's concern for the omnipresent "judgment" that "old women's bodies are unattractive" and the "absence" of naked images of bodies by older women leading to "deprivations . . . both aesthetic and psychological" (*Learning to Be Old*, 148, 151). Bourgeois remedies this cultural void with these prints that do not hold back from revealing an imperfect, yet resolutely lovely female form. The prints in *I Go to Pieces* are filled with signs of aging and youth, thereby eliminating the bifurcation that tends to polarize these stages of life.

The contemporary photographer Cindy Sherman, in her sixties, also continues to make thought-provoking art involving women and age. Her 2008 project consisting of society portraits features women "of a certain age" in giant photographs that reveal subtle imperfections beneath the heavily made-up and dressed-up wealthy socialites. These images remind viewers that art asks people to remember "that there's something more below the surface that you

Louise Bourgeois, *I Give Everything Away*, 2010. Etching and mixed media on paper, six panels. Panel 1: 59 7/8 × 71"; 152.1 × 180.3 cm. (Photo: Christopher Burke © The Easton Foundation/ VAGA at Artists Rights Society (ARS), New York.)

can't really see" (qtd. in Respini 46–47). Sherman also challenges people's expectations of age in her latest Instagram photographs. Going beyond simply using this social media platform, which is generally regarded as the province of the young, Sherman also demonstrates the ability to manipulate the medium in order to examine what presenting images of oneself means in today's world. Historically always her own model—a trademark—she integrates more extreme and graphic manipulation in these images to make herself appear young, old, male, female, and of an undeterminable gender, usually with strange exaggerated features. The Instagram works show the extremes that people can go to present a "face" for the public to view; however, it also calls attention to how much of that appearance is a "mask" that gives little of the true self away. For older people too fixated on outer changes to their appearance,

Louise Bourgeois, *I Go to Pieces: My Inner Life (#6)*, 2010. Etching, watercolor, gouache, ink, pencil and colored pencil on paper with fabric relief and embroidered fabric on panel. 61 5/8 × 89"; 156.5 × 226.1 cm. (Photo: Ben Shiff. © The Easton Foundation / VAGA at Artists Rights Society (ARS), New York.)

Cindy Sherman, *Untitled #465*, 2008. (Courtesy of the artist and Metro Pictures, New York.)

Sherman's Instagram photos mock an obsession with one's "outer" self and suggest that being noticed (as opposed to being "invisible") is not always desirable. Critics are ultimately not sure exactly what message on "getting older" this project makes, but the variations of self that appear on the screen are a reminder that we are often many selves at once and cannot be defined by a chronological age (Sehgal 97).

A male artist famous for portraits that likewise defied traditional standards of beauty is Lucian Freud, who painted late into his eighties. Known for presenting the physical form in vivid detail

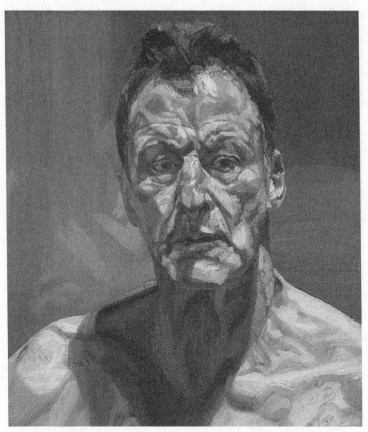

Lucian Freud, *Reflection*, 1985. (Courtesy of Private Collection © The Lucian Freud Archive/Bridgeman Images.)

and often naked, Freud, like Sherman, asks viewers to accept a self that is almost more interesting due to its imperfections. *Reflection* (1985), one of his most famous self-portraits, painted when he was sixty-three, makes no effort to hide wrinkles and blemishes all over his face and neck. The hairline is receding and the eyes seem set-back and almost watery. Despite an appearance that shows the years' wear and tear on his visage, the posture is one of confidence, and the bare shoulders also reveal a sense of bravado; he is not going to kowtow to anyone's expectations of what a formal por-trait should or should not be. There also appears to be great acceptance of age's effect on his physical self, though, one could argue he appears more handsome than some of his other subjects, including the controversial portrait of Queen Elizabeth done in 2000–2001. That portrait, which she sat for until the length of time required by Freud necessitated a model be used instead, is not universally praised, partly because the queen could be regarded as portrayed in an unflattering light. Did some of the criticism stem from the expectation that Freud should have improved the appearance of the queen, perhaps making her look less old, or were the objections launched because at least one art historian, Simon Abrahams, argued that Freud's portrait of the queen was really another portrait of himself (Salter)? Others argue, though, that by depicting her without the fixed smile often required by her public role, Freud's presentation of Queen Elizabeth was refreshing as he freed her portrait from outside pressure that an older woman should look grandmotherly and content. Whatever one's opinion on the Queen Elizabeth portrait, few can deny that the oeuvre of Freud offers a welcome relief in portraying "bodily reality . . . without flinching" and instills a positive message of body acceptance at any age (J. Harris 456).

Freud also painted David Hockney, a fellow British artist still working in his eighties, who turned down an opportunity to paint a portrait of the queen and made her a stained glass window for Westminster Abbey instead. Hockney's late art has been celebrated for his maintaining its trademark color while adapting to his old age. Penelope Lively in her memoir *Dancing Fish and Ammonites* celebrates a Hockney exhibit when he was seventy-five for its "singing color" and "exuberance." She particularly appreciated how he took the "old accustomed world" and "invested [it] with fresh significance" (53). A different take on Hockney's late art appears in Brown's memoir *Sixty* as he admires how the artist shifted his painting style (e.g., reverse perspective paintings) as his hearing loss became pronounced starting at fifty, which, Hockney felt, resulted in strengthening his other senses. Brown also appreciates Hockney's "confidence" in his art work as he ages and his seeming not to rely upon the praise and approval of others. This aspect of his art is a reminder of the freedom that older artists have to be bold and not fear criticism. Beauvoir celebrates this idea in *The Coming of Age* in a section on what artists can do near the end of their careers: "Towards the end of his life every creator is less afraid of public opinion and he has more self-assurance. The idea that he will be praised whatever he does may lead him into facility and blunt his critical sense; but if he does not yield to this temptation it is a great advantage for him to be able to work accordingly to his own personal standards, without troubling about whether people like what he does or not" (406).

Perhaps this shared belief in themselves allows these older artists at the end of their long careers to innovate and explore age as a theme in their art, particularly how physical form is represented. The gift they bring is a complex look at the body and appearance beyond what popular media feed the public as prescribed expectations for women and men. With galleries such as Carter Burden in New York showing the work of artists sixty or older exclusively, even more artists are likely to have a chance to give their late-life vision to the world (Barron A20).

Differences in Longevity

If men and women actually share some of the same anxiety about appearance as they age, they show significant biological differences. The most striking and highly publicized difference is life expectancy. Currently, life expectancy in the United States is 81.2 for women and 76.4 for men (Kinsley 53). Further evidence that there is a notable difference in male and female longevity comes from the fact that the majority of centenarians are women, with estimates being as high as 80 percent (Tavernise). A number of theories have been put forth to understand the disparity without any one explanation taking dominance over the others. Cruikshank in *Learning to Be Old* notes that in the United States, women are "twice as likely as men to seek medical help," which could explain why they may be able to prevent some ailments from getting worse and receive testing for other problems that might be forestalled by early intervention (104). Another idea suggested by Cruikshank draws on research by Lois Verbrugge, which shows that women generally demonstrate "greater intrinsic (genetic or hormonal) robustness" than men and that this allows them to bounce back more readily from illnesses. Thus, evolutionary biologists point to the female hormone estradiol, which is a natural immune booster. While men have some estradiol as well, women have significantly more of it, which may explain why they are able to resist infections or recover more quickly from them.

Other factors that might affect men's longevity are their greater likelihood of being exposed to "occupational hazards" throughout their lifetimes and their tendency to more often "engage in risky health-related behaviors" when compared with women, including drug use, violence, and sexual practices (Loe, *Aging Our Way* 83; King and Calasanti 704). The combination of taking more risks that can lead to early death or illnesses and being less likely to seek medical attention at least partly contribute to the disparity in life expectancy. Studies also believe that the social networks that women maintain could contribute to protecting their health in their later years. When the author Dan Buettner did research on geographic regions that are home to citizens who have long lives with little chronic disease, called "blue zones," in areas as diverse as Okinawa, Japan, and the Nicoya Peninsula in Costa Rica, he found that besides eating a mostly plant-based diet and having exercise as part of daily life, another shared element was having a strong social network. In Okinawa, home to women who live longer than anywhere else in the world, the groups are called "moais," meaning a circle of friends who have stayed connected over their lifetimes. If social isolation is a deterrent for a long, healthy life, it would make sense that having a community of trusted friends would have positive results on longevity, and research has supported this linkage (Buettner 258).

Taking a more social science approach, Betty Friedan devotes an entire chapter in *The Fountain of Age* to the question of "Why Do Women Age Longer and Better than Men?" The chapter is filled with a number of different theories on the subject, but a recurring explanation is that women's ability to adapt to change in the various roles that they perform in the course of their lives sets them up well for vicissitudes that come over time, leaving them better able to weather any kind of circumstances that come their way. In the chapter, Friedan contrasts the trajectory of most men, who work for the majority of their adult lives (often in one profession) and the physical and psychological effects retirement can bring about when this decades-old pattern is disrupted. Women, on the other hand, especially those who have children, do not always follow such a straight career path. Friedan argues, then, that this learned flexibility due to circumstances and the ability to shift one's identity as needed help women cope with illness and the "adoption of new roles" as they age (150). My mom, Joanne, is a perfect example of Friedan's ever-changing woman as over the course of her eighty-three years, she has been a stay-at-home-mom, an adult undergraduate and graduate student, a family and marital therapist, a public lecturer, a paid and unpaid caregiver, an active volunteer for nonprofits, and currently, a trainee with a state agency for elder adults who want to pursue advanced business skills. In the course of undergoing multiple orthopedic surgeries, which have been increasingly difficult with her hemophilia, arthritis, and most recently, a congestive heart diagnosis, she repeatedly asked her doctors at the hospital when she could go back to her training program. She saw the "patient" role in the hospital as impermanent and envisioned returning to a more active and meaningful role that provides greater chances for fulfillment for her and others.

Women's Health Challenges

While the reality that women generally live longer than men in most countries throughout the world (though the actual amount of years varies greatly) has received wide attention, a statistic about the quality of women's later years versus men's may be less well-known. According to Mara Dusenbery's 2018 book on gender inequity in medical treatment, *Doing Harm*, if one looks at "active life expectancy," defined as "the number of years living free from significant limitations that prevent [individuals] . . . from doing everyday tasks," men fare better than women (20). Put another way, women today appear to live longer, but very often those extra years involve disability or at least poor health (Wallace and Villa 13). While three-fourths of all people experience some degree of back pain in their lives, many of the female chronic health issues involve joints and bones (Friedan 423). Arthritis, an inflammation of the joints that can be caused either by an autoimmune disorder or wear and tear over time on cartilage connecting the joints, appears to affect women more than men in that one-third of women in the United States experience it between the ages of forty-five and sixty-four and over 55 percent do after age sixty-five (Bouson 102).

Several women in the surveys discussed the health challenges posed by their arthritis. A sixty-nine-year-old described how her severe osteoarthritis has led to three total joint replacements while rheumatoid arthritis now requires a shoulder replacement, which doctors refuse to perform due to her poor health; she is also unable to afford a stem-cell procedure that would help strengthen that area of the body. Another woman who also has had several surgeries due to osteoarthritis talked about the constant presence of her joint pain, though she commented that she does not let it deter her from volunteering at a free clinic where she uses her nursing skills. Men mentioned arthritis as well when asked about "health challenges," but their descriptions did not involve surgical procedures the way that the women's answers did. For example, a seventy-five-year-old man called his arthritis just part of "normal ageing," but he did not mention how severe or debilitating his might be.

A Mixture of Views on Menopause

Most people explain the bone loss that affects women more than men as a result of hormonal shifts that occur after menopause, including, in particular, the loss of estrogen. A few respondents mentioned menopause directly in their survey responses, and those responses mirror the polarized nature of the literature on the subject—menopause as a positive demarcation in a women's life or one that is associated with many negative experiences. A typical positive response came from a sixty-nine-year-old woman who mentioned that one of the "distinct advantages of old age over youth" was "being a post-menopausal woman" who "no longer" had to deal with a "menstrual cycle." In contrast, a sixty-five year old described all the negative changes she believes were brought on through menopause, including "hot flashes" and "personality change," none of which, she says, could be rectified through hormones due to her having a history of breast cancer.

Between these two camps is a small minority who have almost no opinion on menopause since it was a nonevent in their lives. The American short story writer Grace Paley, for example, famously wrote, "I can't remember my menopause or, remembering it, haven't thought to write much about it. . . . I've asked some of my age mates, old friends, and they feel pretty much the same way. We were busy" (qtd. in Segal 221). Gullette offers an in-depth theoretical approach to this position in her chapter on "Menopause as Magic Marker" in *Declining to Decline* (1977). She explains that the movement to make menopause a "major life event" medicalized the physiological changes and opened the door for physicians to promote hormone replacement therapy, which turned out to have negative health outcomes for a significant number of women with its increased risks of vascular disease and cancer (98). In other words, menopause was made a "magic marker" for the medical community to financially benefit from that time in life, which may have otherwise passed rather uneventfully for a majority of women. Support for the theory that menopause has a cultural basis rather than a strictly biological one comes from anthropological research revealing that women in some countries like Japan rarely report symptoms common to American women, such as hot flashes and emotional changes (King 135). Such information raises questions as to how much of the public's perception of the menopause experience has created certain expectations that are far from universal. Certainly, the medical propaganda for hormone replacement therapy begun in the 1960s, led by gynecologist Robert A. Wilson, who published one of the first scholarly articles on the subject with his wife, Thelma, helped to create a haze of misinformation, which made women believe they needed to do *something* when menopause happened.

Apart from such scare tactics, women writers have taken up the topic themselves, each carving out a unique stand on the issue. *The Madwoman in the Volvo* (2014) by Sandra Tsing Loh, one of the most well-known menopause memoirs, which was adapted into a stage performance in 2016, puts forth the idea that menopause is indeed a "marker" for women's lives, but a positive one that allows them to be liberated from taking care of others and begin taking care of themselves. She reasons that reproductive hormones change women's base identity to make them more nurturing in order to fulfill a motherly role, and menopause allows women to return to their former selves. Her "bible" in coming to these conclusions is Christiane Northrup's *The Wisdom of Menopause*, which argues that the symptoms experienced leading up to menopause (perimenopause) are the "labor pain necessary for rebirth into happy, healthy, fulfilled" individuals soon thereafter (qtd. in Loh 241). Not everyone, though, is taken with Northrup's reasoning. Marina Benjamin, for one, in her 2016 narrative, *The Middlepause: On Life after Youth*, finds Northrup to be "too free with her generalizations"; as an example, she questions Northrup's advice for deep facial skin peels as a path to "rebirth" (27). The perspective that Northrup propagates on menopause being a kind of "rebirth" actually has its roots in an unlikely source—namely, science fiction and fantasy writer Ursula Le Guin's 1976 essay called "The Space Crone." In this work, Le Guin argues that women should celebrate the fact that they are masters of "change" and that menopause is a woman giving birth to her "third self" in "old age" (the first self being a virgin; the second, her reproductive self). To become a "crone," for Le Guin, is a "rite of passage" that she believes should be celebrated, rather than thinking no change is happening and "pretend[ing]" one is a "man" (73). The final argument in Le Guin's essay makes a case for why an "old woman, over sixty" working at Woolworth's (a general-merchandise chain) is the best representative if beings from "space" requested one person who is "exemplary . . . of the race." Le Guin explains thoughtfully how menopause wizens individuals who go through it, making this older woman a perfect candidate: "We want her to go because only a person who has experienced, accepted, and acted the entire human condition—the essential quality of which is Change—can fairly represent humanity" (74).

Compared with the rosy perspective that Loh, Northrup, and Le Guin put forth, not everyone celebrates menopause as a positive rite of passage, as noted earlier. In literary works, characters often make passing negative comments about it. This is the case in Elizabeth Strout's *Olive Kitteridge*, when Olive refers to her added weight gain late in life as a result of menopause. Research does show that decreases in the estradiol hormone can change "fat metabolism," though this could be a convenient culprit on which to lay blame (Benjamin 12). A different indictment of menopause comes in *The Optimist's Guide to Letting Go*, a 2018 novel by Amy Reichert, in which sisters Victoria and Gina seek to explain their mother's "crazy and bitter" attitude as a result of her late-life hormonal changes. One of the sisters remarks, "I'm rooting for a fast-acting cancer or a falling meteor rather than waiting for menopause to do its worst" (9).

Since those examples appear infrequently in literary works, they may have limited impact on readers who may not even remember the fleeting mention that corroborates the pervasive cultural view that menopause is something for women to dread. A fictional treatment of the subject that is far more hard-hitting and central to the narrative appears in Allison Pearson's *How Hard Can It Be?* From almost the beginning of the novel the main character, Kate Reddy, starts identifying her symptoms of perimenopause, which she likens to a band, Perry and the Menopauses, obliterating all the "happy hormones" from her body. Besides not sleeping well, Kate feel as though she is "strapped to a dying animal" and wants nothing more than to have her "old self back" (16). When she googles the symptoms of perimenopause, the list is long and brutal, bordering on hopeless; while readers are instructed not to do the google search, it is included in the novel despite the fact that many women may not have any of these experiences (e.g., increase in facial hair, feelings of apprehension and doom). Kate's contends with her "symptoms," which she blames on menopause (despite a problematic marriage, career problems, and difficult caretaking for elderly family members), until she takes a friend's advice and seeks hormone replacement therapy from "Dr. Libido." Hormone therapy, for Kate, is a "fountain of youth" that allows her to regain some of her former self, but the novel does not seem to confront any of the drug route's problematic history. Despite physicians prescribing it to 75–95 percent of menopausal women at one time, studies have confirmed that it increases the risk of cardiovascular disease and breast and endometrial cancer, while reaping great profits for drug makers such as Pfizer, who produce the popular drug Premarin (Benjamin 38, 47; Cruikshank, *Learning* 106; Gullette, *Declining* 104, 112; Larson and DeClaire 37). Women today apparently take the hormone replacement drugs in smaller and safer dosages, but the fact that the novel makes menopause symptoms out to be so bad and the relief through a drug regiment to be so good certainly seems to send misinformation to readers that menopause is a medical problem that can only be remedied by modern medicine; this point of view harkens back to a less enlightened past that resulted in tunnel vision on the subject. A new book on the subject, *Flash Count Diary: Menopause and the Vindication of Natural Life* (2019) by Darcey Steinke, takes an original approach by looking at whales that also go through menopause. Steinke describes how post-menopausal whales are leaders who guide all the other whales on journeys, and how women can also use this time in life to lead and not follow. In addition, she provides an important history lesson on the problems with hormone supplements. Besides describing how Premarin, an estrogen supplement, derives from "pregnant horses," Steinke offers cautionary information on the cancer connection with hormone therapy and her shock over books such as *Hot Topic* (2016) that contain warnings from a doctor, "Once you lose your hormones . . . you are nothing more than roadkill" (qtd. in Steinke 63, 66).

An interesting moment in *How Hard Can It Be?* comes when Kate wonders if her husband, Rich, is "having his own manopause," when he makes abrupt changes, such as quitting his job (291). Others have wondered as well if men experience something akin to menopause, though it is not often discussed in gerontology research. In her chapter "Menopause as Magic Marker" Gullette argues that men's aging process must be discussed more openly since it is essentially "taboo." She describes how several of the symptoms that women go through during menopause are shared by men, most notably hot flashes and loss of bone mass (110). Benjamin in *The Middlepause* explores the subject in greater depth, but she does not believe there is an equivalent to menopause (or "andopause") for men. While it is true male testosterone levels decrease around 2 percent a year after age thirty and that this can alter some typical masculine behavior (e.g., physical fighting), this loss does not seem to have the same impact on men's sense of self. Still, prescriptions for testosterone, backed by heavy advertising, are on the rise, doubling between 2011 and 2013 to 2.2 million in 2013, even though early research has shown that it may increase plaque in the arteries of the heart (Rabin D4). Benjamin brings up another important facet of men and menopause when she argues that it may be harder for men to *not* have a "clear physical culprit" to blame for a "midlife" evaluation that generates disappointment and/or regret. On the other hand, she believes most men do not experience "mental menopause" since they are more likely to have a secure "social standing" with more stability in their "public roles" (11).

This apparent dearth of research on the possibility of male menopause in comparison with the thousands of articles on the subject relating to women gives a false impression on how much science has looked into male and female health in their later years. One must remember that is was only in 1993 that Congress passed the National Institutes of Health Revitalization Act mandating that women and minorities be included in National Institute of

Health (NIH) research, meaning that most of the studies done before that time used mostly male participants even though we now know that there are significant "differences between men and women" in relation to how they respond to drugs and "risk factors for various diseases" (Dusenbery 3; Norman 147–48). Due to decades of excluding women as subjects in medical studies, resulting in limited and biased data, there is still a lot of information that has yet to be unearthed. In the words of Dr. Janine Austin-Clayton, the associate director for Women's Health Research at the NIH, "We literally knew less about every aspect of female biology compared to male biology" (qtd. in Dusenbery 11). Researchers have learned, however, that women are given less pain medicine after surgery; their symptoms are taken less seriously and often reasoned away as being caused by stress, weight, or menopause; in addition, their wait times in the emergency room and for information back from tests are longer (Norman 198; Dusenbery 4). Since medical research is now more inclusive of minorities than they were in the past, a clearer picture is emerging of how race, ethnicity, and gender create different outcomes in late-life health. Despite outliers such as Asian American women in wealthy communities, evidence shows that older women who belong to minority groups are the "most likely to have chronic illness" (Cruikshank, *Learning* 96). Part of the explanation is that certain minority groups are less likely to seek out medical treatment either due to cost, accessibility of health facilities, the insufficient number of minority health professionals who could put people at ease, or the possibility of language barriers. The situation also can be seen through the lens of "intersecting inequalities over the life course," according to Toni Calasanti and Sadie Giles, who point out that the lower income and different types of employment that many minority women have often limit their health-care options for years. Therefore, some of these minority groups "enter old age in poorer health" (72). Holstein provides additional research that "gender, race, and class" often affect individuals' development of chronic illnesses and their ability to secure proper treatment (121). One can only hope that in the future, statistics like African American women dying more often from "heart disease, stroke, and breast cancer" become obsolete as society finds better ways to make health care equitable for all (Cruikshank, *Learning* 39). Some steps that can help to make this reality happen include making sure good affordable health care is available to everyone and not only those with jobs that provide decent benefits. In addition, training medical professionals on stereotypes and bias regarding minorities and access to translation services can contribute to reducing the racial and ethnic disparities in the sicknesses people face as they age.

The Struggles of Men (and Women?)

Although older women, especially minorities, appear to fare worse in terms of chronic health conditions, men are not without their own struggles. As Richard Bribiescas in *How Men Age* notes, "During our evolutionary past and arguably up to the present, men and women have faced challenges that are unique to their sex" (5). Men, for example, are more likely to have heart disease and cancer. In fact, they are twice as likely to have a heart attack when compared with women, and it remains the leading cause of death for men in nearly all racial and ethnic groups (Loe, *Aging Our Way* 13; "Men and Heart Disease"). A statistic that illustrates another unique "challenge" affecting men more than women is the suicide rate of older men. Over 85 percent of elderly suicides in the United States are by men, most often by white males who are sixty-five or older (Friedan 559; Segal 82). Equally troubling are the numbers that indicate they are "far more likely to die" from the suicide attempt: "one out of four senior citizens" succeed in committing suicide "compared to one out of two hundred attempts for young adults" (Simon). No one seems to know for absolute certainty why this demographic may be so vulnerable to suicide risk, especially when they are most likely to have economic security compared with other women of the same age and with minority groups. Depression is often mentioned as a factor, as is the idea that loss of status and power that can come with aging are harder for men to reconcile, along with the absence of traditional household labor division that can come with retirement (Meadows and Davidson 295, 309). Another possible factor is noted in Meika Loe's *The Rise of Viagra* (2004), which includes interviews with older men who talk about how not having full erectile function has made them feel "incomplete" since our commercial culture celebrates virile manhood as the ideal (79).

Perhaps a global explanation could be that men may have a more difficult time expressing their emotions on this series of life changes. In her book *Out of Time* Lynne Segal makes the claim based on male and female writers that perhaps women generally are more "cheerful" about the aging process (90). Segal uses a variety of male writers to support her premise, giving special attention to Martin Amis and his series of novels portraying old age to be like "starring in a horror film" (87). Certainly, besides Segal's examples, other male authors have written extremely negative treatises on how unbearable getting older is for them, and some, such as Brown in *Sixty*, suggest suicide as an option. In that memoir, Brown describes himself as the "turd in the living room that everyone would like to disappear" at one point and uses the analogy of a "dried pepper" later on, since he feels mostly decorative like those peppers, "old and flakey and hung in a corner," which he describes as "depressing." These metaphors clearly indicate a less than positive state of mind, but it is the references to suicide that are even more worrisome. He writes about wondering some days where he could "buy a bottle of arsenic" and regularly thinking that if his writing powers fail him, he will have to kill himself (120, 271). Since his tone at times is quasi-humorous, it is hard to ascertain whether what is being said is for exaggerated comical effect or it is an expression of genuine deep-seated dissatisfaction. This is also the case for law professor William Ian Miller, who, though in his sixties and healthy, describes aging in his 2011 memoir *Losing It* as "slow inexorable decay" and takes down those who might see it more positively as "culpably moronic" (3; 249). The *Hendrik Groen Diary* books, featuring a male protagonist written by a male author using a pseudonym, follow this pattern as well by taking a wry but dark look at aging most of the time ("When you're as old as the hills, you've got nothing left to strive for") and dangling self-inflicted death as an option the characters discuss frequently.

These male authors on the surface seem to support Segal's claim that men might have a harder time accepting growing older, but there are women writers who project an equally brutal vision. Garner's essay "The Insults of Age" complains of how patronizing people are to those who are older. She writes that too many believe seniors are "weak, deaf, helpless, ignorant, and stupid" with "no opinions" or "standards of behavior." In fiction, authors such as Margaret Drabble in *The Dark Flood Rises* (2016) create a number of older characters who have positive and negative traits, but even within this complex treatment of the subject, the main character Fran asserts, "Old age . . . it's a fucking disaster" (218). Similarly, Erica Jong's 2015 *Fear of Dying* has central protagonist Vanessa Wonderman describe the aging process in no less harsh terms, indistinguishable from the male writers who decry its dehumanizing power. Vanessa notes that her optimism is harder to sustain as she ages: "I hate getting older. I don't see anything good about it. The downward slope of life is full of rocks. Your skis are blunt and there are these patches of black ice everywhere, ready to slip you up. They may have been there before but you never noticed them. Now they are lying in wait for you on every slope" (41).

Although these literary examples by women authors do not touch on suicide as an option to escape the indignities of old age they describe, other works do, thereby, raising questions if indeed men have a bleaker outlook on the topic than women. The feminist scholar and pseudonymous mystery writer Carolyn Heilbrun mentions the prospect of suicide almost at the beginning of her memoir *The Last Gift of Time: Life beyond Sixty* (1997). She writes in the preface that at seventy, suicide should be an "option" to consider (7). The subtitle "Life beyond Sixty" indicates that she chose *not* to pursue that "option," which she reiterates in the text as well. Nevertheless, Heilbrun did choose to end her life in 2003, which left many wondering what prompted this dire action. Those who knew her well suggest that she worried about becoming a "useless person" and that "to be inconsequential, for Heilbrun, was to die" (Grigoriadis). Gullette devotes a chapter to Heilbrun's suicide in *Agewise* and reasons that the revered scholar might have attributed "her creative, professional, and emotional losses to aging" and seen them as "unavoidable . . . like an incurable illness" when "ageism" instead might have caused the losses in status that proved unacceptable (47). Suicide is also integral to the novel *Olive Kitteridge* in that Olive lives with the legacy of her father's suicide and contemplates it herself, especially when she is widowed and estranged from her son. The realization that she could end her life at any point if living becomes unbearable gives Olive quiet satisfaction until called out by her neighbor Louise during a visit who remarks, "You've probably thought of killing yourself" (154). After this uncomfortable moment, when Louise almost reads the dark corridors of her mind, suicide resurfaces most significantly in the last connected story that comprises the novel when Olive chooses life over death. With the unlikely companionship of Jack Kennison, Olive sees more reason to stay alive. The final words of the novel highlight her choice: "It baffled her, the world. She did not want to leave it" (270). Strout apparently saw many more new "chapters" for Olive's late years, besides this romantic relationship, since a sequel, *Olive Again*, was released in late 2019.

Closely comparing these works by male and female authors indicates that even though there may be an impression that men struggle with aging worse than women, it is not borne out by the writing. Yes, Philip Roth's famous quote, "Old age is not a battle. Old age is a massacre" likely will live on, reinforcing the stereotypic idea that men cannot handle the difficulties that age may bring. But despite the greater number of older adult men committing suicide, there is widespread evidence that the majority of men and women cope with these changes remarkably well. When asked on the survey about "general mood most days," my sample showed no distinguishable differences in their answers. A few respondents of each gender occasionally commented on feeling lonely, tired, or angry with the direction the country is heading, but the majority indicated that they were "generally positive," "upbeat," and "optimistic." Though most people gave no further explanation in their answers, a few did, which could be revealing of sentiments others might share. One person wrote, "Very lucky and happy to be alive. Ten years ago almost died from surgery [and] that's when I became disabled. I look forward to each day. I smile and laugh often." This response, from someone without full function of her body, indicates that attitudes about aging may not be gender-specific at all, but instead can be determined by individuals' ability to accept their present self and conditions. Some of those who filled out the survey discussed the antidepressants they take, which has helped them to deal with failing health. An example of one of these responses shows that even with the drug boost to help dark moods, those who are adapting well to becoming old have shifted their perspective and thinking, which is not a trait unique to gender. Referring to his mood, the person wrote, "Most days it is good. I have taken an antidepressant for over two years. As a result, I don't fixate as heavily on things that worry me as I did when I was younger. I also had some counseling for a number of years. I believe I understand myself better and how I react to things, and can handle my emotional life better." Older women and men may not approach this path of self-acceptance in the exact same way, but they both have equal ability to do so.

7

Money, Work, and Retirement

"Are We There Yet?"

It's expensive, getting old.
—Margaret Drabble, *The Dark Flood Rises*

Work is happiness, to make you live longer.
—Ping Wong from *Happiness Is a Choice You Make* (John Leland)

It's not a good strategy to think you're never going to retire.
—Jacquelyn James, "Longer and Better" (qtd. in John Hanc)

Any source of optimism in old age requires a platform
of economic security and wellbeing.
—Lynn Segal, *Out of Time*

When film critic Mick LaSalle called the 2018 film *Where Is Kyra?* "poverty porn," he gave two reasons for his characterization. The first is that viewers will consider themselves to be "caring people" for being "willing" to endure the main character's economic demise on the screen, and the second is that audience members will see themselves as "better off than the title character." LaSalle demonstrates his distance from the subject matter of desperate poverty through this commentary, which fails to recognize how common economic insecurity is for people as they age, especially women. A recent poll, for example, revealed that as people age, they are more concerned about not having enough money to live on than they are about dying (Jordan and Sullivan). *Where Is Kyra?* is, then, actually a very important and realistic portrayal of people who find themselves in mid-life without the comfort of a financial safety net.

Research has confirmed that perhaps the most significant difference between men and women in later life is their economic status. In almost every category, women fare a lot worse than men. According to the nonprofit National Institute on Retirement Security, women after retirement are "80 percent more likely" to be impoverished due to "lower lifetime earnings, less money in savings, and lower Social Security benefits" (Sommer BU4). Statistics from 2015 show that women in their senior years had a median income of $18,250 versus $31,372 for men (Gonyea and Melekis 47). Women in the surveys for this book provided examples of their finances being affected by taking time away from work to raise children, thereby reducing their Social Security benefits as well. Women who worked also mentioned day-care costs as affecting their ability to save. Besides the statistics that reflect women often having taken time off from paid employment for caregiving or working only part-time, other financial problems older women have include the greater likelihood of age discrimination if they try to reenter the workforce, with sexism and ageism creating a barrier as impenetrable as the famed "glass ceiling" (Holstein 75). Too often, women's "attractiveness" is used as employment criteria, and they are disparaged more harshly than men as they age in this regard (Calasanti and Slevin, *Gender* 126). Divorce also tends to leave women poorer since they do not qualify for Social Security benefits from their spouse if the marriage lasted under ten years, even if the wife took time away from her career to raise their children. It is projected that by 2020 women who divorced or never married will be 25 percent of the population over seventy-five, and their poverty rate will be "double . . . [that of] the elderly population as a whole" (Jacoby 131).

The Poverty of Older Women in Film

A notable feature of *Where Is Kyra?* is that director Andrew Dosunmu filmed almost the entire movie with very little light—a strategy that can represent how most individuals are "in the dark" about the realities of poverty, for women in particular as they age. One has to look hard at the screen in order to make out, from the shadows, what is happening, which partly explains the title since often it is hard to identify the title character, Kyra, who is played by Michelle Pfeiffer. She is hard to locate, not only due to the cinematic darkness, but because she is portrayed as someone who has lost her identity. Having been divorced, she is no longer someone's wife, and when her mother dies, she is no longer a caregiver. The result is a struggle for both identity and a source of income since it has been two years since Kyra was laid off from her job. The film does not shield viewers from the humiliation Kyra faces trying desperately to find any kind of work again after she is no longer needed to care for her mother. While no one makes direct comments about her age during her job searches, she herself explains the difficulty when forced to ask her ex-husband for money to help her get by. "I am no spring chicken," she vaguely offers, which shows that her being older has made it harder to be considered for opportunities. Viewers see evidence of her struggle in that Kyra is not even asked back to work after one day of passing out flyers on the street. Later, as Kyra decides to "become" her mother in order to keep cashing her mother's Social Security checks after her death—donning a wig, make-up, and an older person's clothing—one cannot help but to think of the cycle of female poverty in age. The mother lived in a tiny crowded apartment, likely using only her monthly Social Security to survive, and now her daughter cannot break the pattern and desperately needs those checks, too, even before she actually qualifies for them.

The "dark" *Where Is Kyra?* shares much in common with a film that also represents female poverty in later life, Woody Allen's 2013 *Blue Jasmine*, with Cate Blanchett in the title role. Allen's tribute to *Streetcar Named Desire* by Tennessee Williams, as many critics have noted, can be observed in the shared storyline of a wealthy woman having to lower her standards, in this case by taking residence in the small apartment of her sibling once she becomes destitute. But unlike *Streetcar*, *Blue Jasmine* focuses on the difficulty of "starting over" to attempt financial independence after divorce and being out of the work force. Jasmine arrives in San Francisco from New York penniless (but with Louis Vuitton luggage from her former life) and must figure out how to support herself. When much younger, she married her money-manager husband, Hal, left her degree in anthropology unfinished, and did not develop many marketable skills during her time as Hal's socialite wife. The film depicts how unprepared women can be at the dissolution of a marriage (in this case, she learns he is a serial cheater) when they do not have education or professional experience to fall back on in order to create a new life for themselves. Jasmine thinks that she would be suited for a career in interior design, but attempts to take the online degree are hampered by her lack of technological skills, which can be a barrier for older people who are trying to become employed in industries that are reliant upon computer savviness. The fact that the film does not give an easy fairy-tale ending of Jasmine finding another man as a "meal ticket" leaves the problem of how she will cope in viewers' laps, so they must recognize that women's potential money woes as they age are serious and not easily resolved. The same absence of sugar-coating women's late-life poverty appears in Paul Weitz's 2015 film, *Grandma*, starring Lily Tomlin, whose character does not have the $630 that her granddaughter needs for an abortion; representing the commonplace poverty of many women in later life, she, in fact, has only $43 in the bank, despite being a celebrated poet and former academic. Most of the film illustrates the near impossibility of securing the money one needs, despite having friends and family with means.

Financial Insecurity

Money worries in the senior years can, of course, plague men as well as women, as the survey responses revealed. A seventy-four-year-old man, married for forty-nine years, said that he is "constantly in fear of not having enough [money] to maintain a happy life." Another man in his seventies worried about the possibility of outliving his income. Even the older adults who currently felt secure within their means expressed uncertainty about how their financial future will play out, especially since medical costs are an unknown variable that makes future planning difficult. A woman in her seventies explained her uneasiness from never being sure if there will be enough money to pay bills if her husband's health declines or her health takes a turn for the worst: "We live comfortably financially. But in the back of our minds, money is always a concern. We worked all our life and tried to save money for things like catastrophic illness, but sometimes there is a little worry that if that illness ever occurs, our saving may not be enough to cover it and we do not want the resulting shortfall to fall on the shoulders of our children." That several memoirs, such as Jonathon Kozol's *The Theft of Memory*, describe scenarios similar to this woman's concern shows that the possibility of something like this happening is real and has played out for families, likely around the globe. Roz Chast devotes a few pages to the dilemma in her graphic memoir *Can't We Talk about Something More Pleasant?*, where she refers to the "astronomical amount of money" needed to keep her parents "housed, fed, safe, and comfortable" and worries if "the money would hold out till the end" or if any funds would remain for her inheritance (144).

Not all the financial anxiety expressed in the surveys was forward-looking. Many seniors divulged their current states of economic instability. A woman in her seventies said she would not have been able to afford a car if her sister had not left her a $12,000 inheritance. Another woman, sixty-nine years of age, indicated that she lives from Social Security check to Social Security check to make ends meet and lost her home due to "huge medical bills," a job loss, and divorce. While she had tried to save for retirement, in her words, "life delivers blows," including those that force people to use savings sooner than they imagined. Others described debts and mortgages that left them in a precarious state.

An eighty-year-old noted that with her "small and shrinking nest egg," she has to "live frugally," often using gift cards provided by her daughters; she commented that it is hard to not live like her friends and to have to get by with an "old car, old clothes," and a small apartment. All of these individuals would be included in the numbers of seniors who researchers predict will have "insufficient funds" to maintain their standard of living as they age, a number ranging from 41 to 50 percent (Rix 36).

The fate of older people living without sufficient means and little-to-no savings is not a recent phenomenon that can be blamed on a particular presidential administration or a steep stock market decline. Simone de Beauvoir gives in-depth historical treatment to old age poverty in her classic work *The Coming of Age*, in which she notes that in the United States, the passage of the 1935 Social Security Act still left significant portions of the population over sixty-five with "incomes far below the subsistence level" (244). She quotes economist Margaret S. Gordon, who makes a claim that still holds true today: "Poverty among the aged remains one of our most persistent and difficult problems" (244). Something that is making the situation worse, however, is that pensions, which provided a replacement income for those no longer working, are being offered much less frequently today. Whereas in 1980, 38 percent of employees in the United States had a pension connected to their jobs, the number dropped to 20 percent in 2008 and 14 percent by 2011 (Jenkins 142). The number is expected to decline further as employers turn more often to employee contribution plans, such as 401ks, which cost them less money and put the investment risk more on the employees who choose where their retirement money will go to accrue interest. Critics of this trend note that with the disappearance of pensions, employees do not feel the same sense of loyalty to the company and leave for other positions more frequently, which actually creates an economic loss for the company that must now invest in hiring and training new workers. In addition, many minorities and low-income workers do not have jobs that provide this kind of "coverage," and, according to research, they are less inclined to explore high-risk investment opportunities due to "financial inexpertise" and employment instability (Cala-santi and Slevin, *Gender* 101, 103).

The economic future of many seniors also looks bleak because few have been able to put away sufficient money in savings. Estimates vary to some degree, but roughly 30–50 percent of households with adults fifty-five or older have no savings at all; those who have some savings, generally have less than $100,000, which most agree may not last long, especially as the cost of living continues to rise (Jordan and Sullivan; Larson and DeClaire 154; Nussbaum and Levmore 190). The awareness of the need to save money throughout one's life comes out strongly in the book surveys. One question asked, "What is one piece of advice you would give your twenty-year old self?" and many responses focused on this issue. Some were general suggestions (e.g., "set aside something for a rainy day" or "save more money"), but others gave more explicit advice, such as "start saving for retirement with your first paycheck." Thoughts about saving money also appeared in a question about whether people can do something in their younger years to affect the quality of their later years. A seventy-eight-year-old part-time tax preparer brought up his shock in seeing how little money people over sixty-five have in savings. He exclaimed, "I don't know how they will live."

Still Working

The answer to this tax preparer's question of how people manage with insufficient savings is that a significant portion of them continue to work beyond the traditional retirement age, which is typically in the sixties. As of 2019, the average age of retirement in the United States, according to the Census Bureau is around sixty-three, shortly after one can begin collecting Social Security at sixty-two (Anspach). A tremendous cultural shift of working late into one's senior years has taken place recently, sometimes for financial reasons, but in other instances, for more complex emotional and psychological reasons. Thus, the Pew Research Center reported that in 2000, nearly 13 percent of Americans who were sixty-five or older worked full time or part time versus 18.9 percent in 2016, when there was a total of 9 million senior-aged workers (Hanc F4). Put another way, employment of those over seventy-five has seen a 172 percent increase since 1977 (Leland 33–34). In fact, the Bureau of Labor reports that there was more "labor force growth" in the age groups of sixty-five to seventy-four and seventy-five and older than in "any other" group (Hannon F7). Economists predict that this trend will only continue as surveys of baby-boomers between the ages of forty-five and seventy indicated that at least half plan on working into their seventies and beyond; already, there are more sixty-five year-olds employed in the United States than teenagers, which has not happened since 1948. By 2022, it is estimated that seniors will comprise 36 percent of the workforce (Jenkins 146, 159).

When asked about work and retirement, seniors in the surveys offered very divergent answers regarding their satisfaction or general feelings about each. While some people indicated that they were still working for financial reasons (e.g., a seventy-five-year-old lawyer who works part-time responded, "Lost a lot in the stock market in 2008, why else am I still working?"), many more discussed the satisfaction they derived from continuing their careers. Another attorney, this one in his eighties, said that he still works because of the "affirmation from many of the clients" he has represented over the years. An architect, also in his eighties, put no expiration on his career and indicated he will work "forever." He explained that he needs to be "creative" and that it would be a "sin to stop" since he is "at the top" of his game in terms of "experience" and "talent." Another facet of those working late into their years is a sense of purpose, which researchers have found to be a significant factor contributing to longevity. One woman in her seventies temporarily had to quit her job to take care of her ailing husband, who has now recovered, so she is returning to work. Her thoughts on the value of work aptly describe the satisfaction many derive from employment beyond the income, which, of course, helps as well: "Years ago people would typically retire at age 65. Today that is not case. More and more people are working far past age 65, assuming their health allows. True, sometimes the reason is financial, but there is also the desire to feel 'needed,' that someone depends upon that person to show up for work, that someone 'wants' that person to be part of an organization that works better because that person is there. And employers today recognize the value of the work ethic of the older employee."

What about Retirement?

Given all of these positive motivations for continuing to work, it is not surprising that many who left their jobs reported feeling a deep loss. A woman in her sixties explained that since quitting her part-time job, she does not feel "needed now" and also worries about not using her "brain." A seventy-three-year-old man echoed this idea of not feeling "valued" after he gave up working fourteen years ago; he also noted that after retiring, he felt many people were "less interested" in what he had to "offer" in terms of his "thoughts" and "deeds." Some respondents, such as a seventy-one-year-old who works in real estate and as a caregiver for seniors, even reported going back to work after retiring because she realized, "I love to work." In her book *Disrupt Aging* (2016), Jo Ann Jenkins, head of AARP, describes that practice as not "uncommon": people "retire" and, then, "unretire a year or two after" (179). Economists have noted that over one-fourth of individuals who retire later resume working and, according to a RAND corporation study from 2017, nearly 40 percent of those over sixty-five who are working today are formerly retired (Span, "When Retirement" D5).

Considering the impact of work on people's health and well-being, it is not too shocking that many workers choose to continue working beyond their sixties rather than remain retired. Physician Eric Larson's 2107 book, *Enlightened Aging*, based on his years of studying how to delay and prevent Alzheimer's disease and other declines in memory and thinking, cites research that shows depression, weight gain, and increased alcohol abuse often occur after retirement and lead to a "dramatically" higher death rate. By contrast, those "working past retirement age were happier and more satisfied with [their] health" compared to those who had retired (Larson and DeClaire 155). Studies conducted world-wide also have shown "better cognitive function" in those still employed in their later years (Larson and DeClaire 155). Betty Friedan in *The Fountain of Age* disseminates additional research on the effects of working into one's later years. She shares studies by Erdman Palmore that showed "work satisfaction" as the "best overall predictor of longevity," most likely due to the social ties it affords people and the sense of purpose it gives (204). However, Friedan does distinguish between "satisfying work," which positively affects longevity, and "unsatisfying work," which can "reduce" it (81).

Different Types of Work

This distinction is important to keep in mind as there are so many different types of work, including many which may be difficult to continue to do with the physical or mental impairments that can occur over time. And if the work that can be continued is not bringing a sense of satisfaction, it would make sense that the benefits attributed to doing so would not be found. Research has referred to people in professions that can be pursued beyond typical retirement age as "knowledge workers." Certain fields, such as business, law, and education, can offer older workers ongoing fulfilling work because "knowledge is the basis." Laura Carstensen, director of the Stanford Center on Longevity, explains, "You don't see a deficit [of that knowledge] with age" (qtd. in Hanc F4). In contrast, jobs that are more taxing and usually require less education are not as desirable for older workers. A study showed that 60 percent of seniors with college degrees who retired would want to return to the working world whereas only 40 percent who did not have degrees expressed the same interest (Span, "When Retirement" D5).

Beauvoir in *The Coming of Age* also comments on how jobs that involve physically challenging work actually age people faster and are not feasible to continue. In the conclusion of that work, she uses the example of a miner who might be "finished" working by fifty whereas someone of a different socioeconomic class could work beyond eighty (541). Members of the "exploited classes," according to Beauvoir, are apt to struggle later in life more than their wealthier peers not only because are they likely to be in less healthy physical condition due to the type of work that they performed, but because they also were unlikely to have had sufficient leisure time to cultivate hobbies and interests that could be a welcome refuge when their working life expired. Her insights on work and age are among the best sections of the book because she is aware of class differences and how they may affect not only the types of jobs that people have but also how certain jobs will impact a person's whole life—while working and beyond. She also shies away from offering simplistic solutions and easy quick fixes to work-related problems as people age. Beauvoir believes there need to be broader social remedies, especially those that can do away with the class divisions that separate people in work and life. Her challenge to readers is in a searing question she asks and then answers that goes beyond the scope of just working and age: "What should a society be, so that in his last years a man might still be a man? The answer is simple: he would always have to have been treated as a man" (542). Beauvoir, despite being an early and influential feminist, uses "man" to represent "human," but her words here clearly relate to women as much as to men.

Beyond Polarities, the Humanities Approach

Elsewhere in *The Coming of Age*, Beauvoir demonstrates her nuanced understanding that work for older adults must be studied beyond set polarities (e.g., positive or negative; higher classes versus lower classes) and instead examined from different perspectives. For example, she talks about how certain characteristics of working people can improve as they age (e.g., conscientiousness, punctuality, pleasure in work, willingness) and how others might bring challenges (e.g., losses of sight, hearing, energy, tempo, memory, adaptability) (231). By framing the issue in such a way, she provides a complex picture of seniors' work experiences, which probably involve both improvements and losses.

Other humanities texts accomplish something similar by presenting neither a too optimistic nor a too pessimistic version of work for older adults. *Olive Kitteridge*, the novel of connected stories by Elizabeth Strout, opens with Olive's husband, Henry, in the pharmacy where he works. Its centrality to his existence is shown both in the title of that story, "Pharmacy," and in the description of how his satisfaction with his work allows him to bear any "unpleasantness" outside of the store (4). In a later story entitled "Tulips," which comes after Henry retires sooner than he planned because a large chain drugstore was going to move into his building, he does not know "how to fill his days," but tries to fill the void with woodworking classes and by joining the American Civil War Society with Olive (144), who is retired from her job as a teacher. Strout describes them as "finding their way in this retirement land" (144), and the kinds of losses and gains she represents also come through in the surveys. For example, when asked about work and retirement, an eighty-five-year-old woman said that she finds retirement "fulfilling at times" but also misses work on other occasions. Another woman, who is in her seventies, said that she appreciated the "luxury" in retirement of "not having to rush to get a job done," but also wanted to keep working because of the enjoyment of being at her job and the "interaction with customers." Strout shows both of these perspectives within a single story in the book titled "A Winter Concert." Two couples, whose children used to be friends, bump into each other at a concert, and when one of the husbands, Alan Granger, is asked if he will retire, he responds, "I'll retire the day I die." Meanwhile, the other husband, Bob Houlton, comments about his retirement, "I love it" even when pressed, "Doesn't it make you crazy to be home all day"?" (132). Literature is able, then, to show both perspectives, without privileging one or the other.

This multifaceted viewpoint on work and retirement is also seen in Margaret Drabble's *The Dark Flood Rises*, which, like *Olive*

Kitteridge, features an older person, in this case the central character, Francesca Stubbs, continuing to work at her job inspecting housing for the elderly. Not only does Fran appreciate the important work that she does, but it gives her insight into others her age who also continue to work, such as the actress Maroussia Darling. She realizes that Maroussia must be rewarded by the "applause" and the fact that it is "paid work." This realization causes Francesca to muse that "work is a savior of sorts," in that it provides not only the satisfaction of being appreciated but also the "lifeline" of "honourable [sic] sums of money" making their way regularly into a bank account (193). While Fran and Maroussia continue to ply at a trade, others in the book either cannot work any longer (such as Fran's first husband who is physically incapacitated) or choose to pursue noncareer interests such as art and literature with equal delight. Again, like *Olive Kitteridge*, judgment is not made on characters' decisions or abilities to work or not work past retirement age, but their choices are revealed as being motivated by many different factors with equally satisfying outcomes.

Literature can also express nearly inexpressible feelings about working or not working into old age when those feelings are muddled and not clear. For some individuals on the subject of work or retirement, their attitudes are simple and easily reduced to one or two word responses. In the surveys, for example, respondents often said their retirement could be described as "joyful" or bliss," whereas those who missed the engagement and element of unpredictability of work repeatedly referred to their post-work life as "boring" or "okay." In contrast to these succinct but not very introspective descriptions, literary works, like qualitative research, can tap deeper into psyches to illustrate a tangle of emotions and ideas that cannot easily be communicated, especially on a subject like one's working life, which often, for older individuals, comprises decades of time, longer than many romantic relationships and even friendships.

One such example of a book that does a fantastic job of digging deep into a person's often convoluted relationship with a long-held career is Domenico Starnone's 2016 novel, *Trick*, translated by Jhumpa Lahiri and shortlisted for the 2018 National Book Award. The book centers on Daniele Mallarico whose main profession has been producing drawings for various texts. Even though Daniele is past retirement age, he continues to take on commissions, including a job to illustrate Henry James's short story "The Jolly Corner," which he attempts to do while babysitting his young and mischievous grandson, Mario, when the parents are at an out-of-town conference. Since Daniele is struggling to complete his assignment while taking care of Mario, he tries to figure out why he is even continuing to work, and there is no easy answer. Daniele understands that it is "not for money" since his house is paid off and he had saved "comfortably." Instead, he reasons that work's cycle of frustrating pressure but satisfying rewards makes it hard to leave: "I was scared to think myself free from the obligations of work. For the last fifty years I'd moved from one deadline to the next, always under the gun, and the anxiety of failing to suitably tackle one then another, followed by the pleasure of successfully doing just that, was a seesaw without which—I finally confessed to myself outright—I couldn't bear to picture" (75–76). The patterns that develop from a long professional career almost seem etched into his being, so the prospect of exorcising them is unimaginable, especially without knowing what might replace them. The pull that Daniele feels between eliminating the pressure by no longer working and the desire to continue the familiar routine of his work might be difficult to articulate in standard surveys on work but can be communicated through stories in which the innermost thoughts of a person can be revealed.

Age Discrimination

If literature and real-life stories show numerous older individuals wanting to be employed into their sixties and beyond, a question that might be asked is, "Why not go ahead and take the path of nonretirement?" Are there any serious problems with or concerns about people who want to work until they "die," like the character in Strout's story "Winter Concert"? One issue that does arise is age discrimination. At first, one might think that age discrimination is not even possible with federal laws offering protection against workplace discrimination to those forty or older. The Age Discrimination in Employment Act (ADEA), passed in 1967, applies to employers with at least twenty employees, employment agencies, and government offices at the federal and state levels. States have their own laws as well, which also include workplaces that have fewer than twenty employees, and these laws are often viewed as offering greater legal protection against discriminatory practices. The ADEA, passed over fifty years ago, set forth to eliminate age discrimination when hiring and firing workers and to offer legal assurance that age should not be considered in pay, benefits, promotions, layoffs, or other aspects of employment. Critics argue, however, that this act is not effective and requires additional legislation such as the Protecting Older Workers Against Discrimination Act, which was created by a bipartisan Senate committee in 2017 to help shore up loopholes put into effect by a 2009 Supreme Court ruling that stipulated older workers had to show evidence that age discrimination was the "prime, or motivating, reason for demotions or dismissal" (Olson, "Proof" B2).

Surveys of older workers and scholars on the subject agree that age discrimination remains a hurdle that people must confront if they want to continue to work past typical retirement age; for low-income workers with little to no savings who must work, it is an outright challenge. A 2018 AARP survey revealed that 90 percent of workers over age forty-five indicated that age discrimination is common and that two-thirds "experienced it personally" ("The Last Acceptable Prejudice" 4). In addition, the U.S. Equal Employment Opportunity Commission reported a 26 percent increase in age discrimination complaints, from 16,548 in 2006 to 20,857 in 2016 ("Age Bias" 9). Discrimination can take many forms, ranging from a hostile work environment where derogatory comments or teasing about age are prevalent to layoffs that target older workers first, whereas in the past seniority might have helped workers keep their jobs longer, while newer, younger employees were let go first. Despite the fact that different media have made strides to replace the inundation of offensive stereotypical images of seniors so common in the past, some argue that ageism happens more often in the realm of work than anywhere else. According to Martha Holstein in *Women in Late Life*, "The workplace is a primary site of ageist practice" (75). Research shows, too, that older women face more age discrimination in hiring than men, something that had been suspected but now is supported by evidence based on a large-scale study by economists (Rikleen). The idea that ageist practices thwart seniors' abilities to obtain and sustain viable employment showed up in the survey responses as well, in particular on a question about whether respondents had experienced ageism. One person, for example, noted that she knew of people not being able to find jobs due to their ages while someone else pointed out that asking when a person graduated high school is a giveaway to steer employers away from older individuals. Another survey respondent who was gainfully employed wrote about not being able to reveal her age at her job and having to "pass" for being in her fifties due to rampant ageism at work.

Allison Pearson's 2017 novel, *How Hard Can It Be?*, provides additional examples of how age still is looked down upon by many employers in work environments. Even though the protagonist, Kate Reddy, is a fifty-year-old "returner" (coming back from the "Mommy Track"), she encounters much scrutiny because of her age and eventually makes herself younger on paper when applying for positions in order to increase her chances of finding a job. She rationalizes this decision by pointing to a newspaper article in which the British "Government Tsar of Older Workers" recommends that people should "fudge" when they took their exams when filling out applications "so employers can't figure out" that they are "ancient persons of forty-three or over." The article also states that those with "old-style qualifications" are likely to "suffer discrimination" (191). If Pearson is addressing the difficulty of those fifty or older finding work due to age alone, one can imagine how increasingly challenging this could become as people "show" their years not only in terms of dates on applications and resumes but in terms of physical appearance (e.g., gray hair, liver spots, etc.), which makes them often choose "cosmetic interventions" to lessen that factor (Holstein 75).

A question that arises about age discrimination is "why"? Besides the general "othering" of individuals outside of the mainstream or norm, are there particular concerns about older people as workers that surface and is there evidence to support or challenge these notions? Beauvoir claims that "society turns away from the aged worker as though he belonged to another species" (542). In terms of employment, Jenkins thinks that part of the problem is employers see "older workers as more of a liability than an asset" (160). Some of the complaints from employers include high salaries and health care costs for people who have been with a company for a long time and questions about their stamina and willingness to innovate and adapt to new technology. A large over-reaching issue is ultimately whether an older person is going to be as productive as a younger co-worker (Jenkins 161; Hannon F7). Both Beauvoir and Jenkins, who devote multiple chapters in their books on age and employment, cite numerous studies that show not only are older workers as productive as their younger counterparts, but in many cases, they are more so. Jenkins, for example, cites a University of Michigan study looking at age in relation to the economy and technology that concluded as "the average age of the workforce increases, the overall workforce is more productive" (162).

Countering Stereotypes in Film

While conventional wisdom might dictate the more negative view of older workers, regardless of the University of Michigan study's conclusions, cultural works have the power to break those long-accepted notions and offer striking counter-examples, which often can be truer to life. A powerful example of a work that can alter the public's view on seniors' potential in a workplace environment is Nancy Meyers's 2015 film, *The Intern*, with Robert De Niro and Anne Hathaway. In the film De Niro's character is seventy-year-old Ben Whittaker, a former executive, who, after retirement, becomes a "senior citizen intern" at a fashion startup company, run by Hathaway's character, Jules Ostin. At first glance, *The Intern* might not seem to offer valuable commentary on elders in the work place since the main character is, as the title suggests, an unpaid intern who takes on this opportunity to fill his time in a meaningful way and supplement some of his other retirement activities, such as doing tai chi in the park. However, as the film progresses, viewers see not only why Ben needs this job for his sense of fulfillment and purpose, but also why his presence and experience help everyone he comes in contact with at work.

The movie opens with a voiceover explaining why retirement offered only temporary "novelty" for Ben, and how he needed to be a "part of something" since there was a "hole" in this life that he needed to "fill." A flyer for a new initiative at About the Fit, a fashion e-commerce site, to hire senior citizens as interns, piques his interest, despite the application process involving uploading a personal video since cover letters are viewed as too "old school" by the company. Right away, the film takes on the technology question that is often thought to be a potential barrier for older individuals at work. Although Ben does not have vast tech knowledge (i.e., his former job was working at a white pages company before the advent of computers), he is shown as capable of learning. This possibility is illustrated right from the onset as Ben states in his application video that he will need to "figure out" the technology part of the job, even if that involves asking his grandchildren for help. When Ben receives the position, he is hired along with a more traditional-age intern, Davis, and as they set out their "tools" for the day in front of them, we see the contrast: Davis has his smart phone, ear buds, flash drive, and tablet while Ben pulls out of his briefcase a calculator, pens, a small clock, and his glasses case. Though the contrast between the more technically savvy young person is visually developed in the scene and Ben at first does not know how to turn on the high-tech computer in front of him, with some guidance he is able to learn, which is confirmed later on, when Jules helps him to set up his first Facebook account.

These scenes reinforce the message to employers and potential older workers themselves that technical skills can be developed and that their lack should not be feared as a barrier. In fact, this type of training is taking place presently through an AARP Foundation program called Mentor Up, which has young people volunteer to instruct older individuals in various forms of new technology. Companies such as General Electric have used this type of mentoring and have seen the mutual benefits as the more seasoned workers share their wealth of knowledge with the individuals who have helped them with computer assistance (Jenkins 176). Another important question raised about older workers is whether they will be able to adjust to having someone younger than they are in a position of authority. The movie and real-life mentoring show that intergenerational cooperation can thrive and the different generations can assist each other, rather than being in conflict.

The fact that the younger generation can benefit from co-workers who have decades of valuable experience is really at the heart of *The Intern*; this is a message that cannot be reinforced enough since suspicion of and bias against the older worker is so great. Some businesses already recognize this potential asset and have created initiatives either to keep their long-term employees longer or to lure them out of retirement. AT&T, for example, offers large computer monitors that make it easier for older employees to read text on their screens, while other companies provide flexible schedules or reassign physically challenging tasks in order to meet the needs of workers in their later years. CVS pharmacies also made changes to retain employees by developing a program called "Talent Is Ageless," which increased the workforce numbers of those over fifty from 9 percent to 24 percent in the last ten years ("More Businesses" 6). A facet of this program is that CVS hires "snowbird" pharmacists who spend winters in a warmer climate (Jenkins 169). Other companies boast even greater numbers of typical retirement-aged employees who choose to keep working. For example, Huntington Ingalls Industries, which is involved in shipbuilding, has no age limits in its Apprentice School and values anyone who has knowledge of the industry. Another company with large numbers of senior workers is Silvercup Studios, a film and television production facility, which touts that over 50 percent of its workers are over fifty. The Executive Vice President of Silvercup explains that there are "distinct advantages" to hiring employees in later years. "They're more settled. . . . There's more sense of loyalty. And it costs more to bring in new staff than it costs to retain people" (qtd. in Hannon F7).

De Niro's character, Ben, perfectly represents this sense of loyalty throughout *The Intern*. In one scene, an employee asks him for inside information on what is happening with the company head, Jules, since Ben has been observed in her office when potential CEOs are being interviewed. He keeps what he knows confidential in this and other situations, and further shows his loyalty by refusing to go home until Jules does, explaining, "I can't leave before the boss leaves." It is not surprising, then, that while Jules at first ignores him completely and gives him little to no actual work to do, she comes to consider him someone "you can count on." Another component of his character that makes a positive impression about workers with experience is that he shows respect for himself and for others. Much is made of Ben's impeccable formal dress, compared with the millennial men he works beside who at first never even tuck in their shirts but gradually improve their professional appearance as a result of his modeling. Equally significant, Jules's assistant Becky is rarely shown much recognition and appreciation by her boss (despite having an economics degree from the University of Pennsylvania); however, when Jules praises Ben, he makes sure to credit Becky with assisting him, showing the importance of acknowledging others for their contributions and not being overly focused on oneself.

Critics of *The Intern* argue that Ben comes off a little too perfect compared to all the imperfect characters around him and that he is not given enough real work to do. He does seem to spend a disproportionate amount of his time chauffeuring Jules around, once he earns her trust, leading one film reviewer to offer the alternative title, "Driving Miss Texty" (Phillips). The film also seems to get a little lost in Jules's messy personal life—philandering stay-at-home husband and a testy mother—but that does not over-shadow the fact that it remains a strong reminder that people do not become less valuable workers as they age, and, in fact, can become more valuable. Ben meaningfully fills the voids from widowhood and retirement by engaging in an exciting work environment that needs his way of leading by example and subtly suggesting how confidence can be achieved by bringing one's best self to the office each and every day. As one of his younger co-workers remarks, "Gray is the new green."

When Is Retirement Right?

With so many positive aspects of continuing work deep into one's mature years, it seems reasonable to ask about retirement. When is retirement a desirable option, or, in the words of this chapter title, how do people know if they are "there yet"? *The Intern* provided one litmus test when Ben, in his video application, mentions that musicians retire when there is no more music in them; he counters that he still had "music" inside him, which is why he is not ready for a life of leisure. This subjective test may or may not work for others, but everyone must decide for themselves now that a mandatory retirement age has been abolished for most professions by the 1986 amendments to the Age Discrimination in Employment Act. Exceptions include the military and federal law enforcement, as well as pilots and air traffic controllers, due to the physical and mental demands of the duties associated with those high-risk occupations. Research has shown that people working in certain jobs that are strenuous (e.g., health aides, bus drivers, fast food workers) are understandably much more anxious to retire compared to individuals doing less "arduous" work (Rix 38). With retirement being voluntary, as opposed to "compulsory," workers can be free from "society's psychological pressure" that a chronological age is the sole determination of a person's fitness to work (Nussbaum and Levmore 59–60). Instead, health, mental well-being, and financial status determine if retirement is the right decision. Social Security, put into effect in 1935, helps make retirement more feasible and is viewed by many economists as the "most stable retirement pillar" despite ongoing debate as to whether it will be depleted with the rising numbers of aging baby boomers (Sommer B4). Another serious problem is the number of hardworking individuals whose jobs do not include Social Security, such as domestic labor. Whereas 90 percent of white men and women receive Social Security, the numbers are between 72 and 84 percent for people of color (Calasanti and Slevin, *Gender* 98). Still, the existence of Social Security reminds citizens that retirement is an "earned right that is at least in part a public responsibility"; this viewpoint is too often lost in the misperception that the elderly are "taking" something that has not been earned (Holstein 197).

It is not uncommon to hear how much retirees love the "freedom" of retirement. John Leland expressed surprise in his book *Happiness Is a Choice You Make*, based on in-depth interviews with the "oldest old," that none of his subjects talked about their "professional accomplishments"; most were "glad to retire," and longed only for the "camaraderie of the workplace" (135). Despite these projections of retirement as generally welcomed or shunned, literature on the subject explores dimensions beyond a merely positive or negative impression to reveal philosophical depth that might not easily arise in interviews and surveys. Once again, Beauvoir's *The Coming of Age* proves insightful on the subject of age and work by providing many different views of what retirement may mean for older adults. When she introduces the topic in a chapter on "Old Age in Present-Day Society," it seems that her focus will be mostly negative. Beauvoir quotes Ernest Hemingway as saying that the "worst death for anyone was the loss of what formed the center of his life and made him what he really was"; she connects this idea to retirement in that when a person relinquishes a profession, that individual is "giving up one's calling," an essential part of identity, which can be compared to death (262). Elsewhere in the chapter, Beauvoir continues the negative metaphors by comparing no longer earning money to "loss of caste" (266). While the United States, of course, does not have a formal social stratification system like

India's, the word reverberates with associations to hierarchy and exclusion that highlight how one's cessation of paid work can signal not only a loss of standing but a division between those continuing to earn money and those who do not.

At the same time, however, Beauvoir brings in a number of different studies that have inconclusive research on whether retirement is, in fact, generally disagreeable. One study of teachers, for example, indicated that 29 percent found retirement "more agreeable than they expected" and 31 percent "less agreeable." The closeness of those numbers does not reveal a lopsided majority for one side or the other. In attempting to understand this discrepancy in viewpoints, Beauvoir recognizes that the reasons people work can affect attitudes about retirement. She contrasts individuals for whom work was not a "matter of choice" and instead an "obligation" with those whose work was considered "fulfilling of oneself"; for those who tended to work out of "obligation," such as financial necessity, retirement can be a "release" and freedom from that obligation (262–263). While others have sought to explain the divergent attitudes about retirement based mostly on the overly simplistic distinction between physical and mental work, Beauvoir's analysis is original in focusing less on the nature of the work itself but more on the motivation for working. She also uses her philosophical acumen to reflect on incongruities in the nature of work itself that present themselves in varying attitudes about retirement. Work, in Beauvoir's view, generally has a "double aspect" to it in that there is very often an element of "bondage" and "drudgery" while simultaneously a "source of interest" that "helps integrate the worker with society" (262–263). Given this tension, or "ambivalence," according to Beauvoir, it should not be too surprising that people in retirement can feel pulled between feeling relief from leaving behind the "drudgery" and disappointment from no longer being an active part of the social fabric uniting all who are employed. These mixed emotions regarding work and, as a result, retirement present themselves in Joyce Farmer's graphic memoir *Special Exits*, in which the father character, Lars, meets an old acquaintance who asks about his retirement. Lars indicates that it has been seventeen years since he retired, and it was the "second best thing" that he ever did. When asked, "What was the first?" Lars mentions "to have a job to retire from!" (119). For Lars, who is based on Farmer's own father, retirement is grand but so is having a job—evidence of the tension that Beauvoir spells out as part of the complexity of work.

An Ambivalent Retirement?

A film that beautifully captures this "ambivalence" regarding retirement is Alexander Payne's 2002 comedy-drama *About Schmidt*, adapted from Louis Begley's 1996 novel of the same name. *About Schmidt* often is brought up as an example of retirement being portrayed in film due to the opening scenes featuring Warren Schmidt (Jack Nicholson) sitting in his stark office staring at the clock, waiting for the final moments of his career as an actuary. Shortly thereafter, the obligatory retirement party is shown, complete with lackluster speeches and muted emotions all around. When Schmidt sits around the house watching television trying to exchange pleasantries with his wife, the impression is one of purgatory. Like other retirees in real life who are said to watch fifty hours of television a week, Schmidt is consumed by this passive activity to the exclusion of more engaging pursuits (Pipher, *Women* 118). Even though Schmidt's work life appeared to be far from scintillating, it could not be as dull as his post-work life appears to be. What changes, though, comes from a television commercial he views that asks for money to "foster" a child in a developing country. Rather surprisingly, he commits to this plan (he does not seem to be a philanthropic person) and soon begins sending long, confessional letters to his six-year-old foster child, Ndugu. In these letters that are shared in voice overs, Schmidt expresses dissatisfaction with his wife, who dies shortly thereafter, leaving him to figure out how to spend his remaining retirement years. Since he and his wife had bought a Winnebago prior to her death, he sets out on a road trip in order to find fulfillment. One idea is to try to save his only child, Jeannie, from marrying a man who Schmidt thinks is not worthy of his daughter's affection. Plans to stop the wedding are nothing short of disastrous, which results in his returning home, feeling more defeated than ever. After expressing despairingly that his life has been devoid of purpose, he finds a letter from a nun who is looking after Ndugu in Tanzania that indicates his sponsorship has helped the boy with medical issues and includes a picture that the boy painted of a bigger stick figure and a littler one holding hands against the backdrop of a bright yellow sun. The film shows how retirement can take people out of their familiar, work-centric routine. Removed from that scripted pattern, individuals may have the chance to see something previously off of their radar and take action that could pay fulfilling dividends. Since several of Schmidt's post-retirement quests did not work out as planned (e.g., trying to help his replacement at work or convincing his daughter to move back to Nebraska to take care of him), the film does not suggest that retirement will be an easy life of alternative plans and schemes. However, it does indicate that not everything that is meaningful comes from one's job and that sometimes people must stop working to have the time and vision to find a purposeful existence.

With so many differing viewpoints on these subjects, it is reasonable to ask, how do seniors decide whether to keep working past sixty, seventy, or even eighty? Ruth Bader Ginsburg, who is in her eighties, remains a Supreme Court judge, even after broken ribs from a fall in her office and lung and pancreatic cancer surgery. Should she contemplate retirement? What is an ideal time to retire for anyone? And when they do retire, will older adults have enough money to live out the rest of their days without financial worry? These questions with no easy answers are important to pose, but often are not considered until very late in life. Research suggests that people will give more thought to the practical concerns of their old age if they can envision themselves as old. Several studies at Stanford University recognized that after viewing "progressively aged photos of themselves," people were willing to allocate greater amounts of money for retirement compared to a group that just looked at a contemporary photograph. As a result of these findings, Bank of America developed an app that "digitally ages users' portraits" in order to "motivate them to increase their retirement savings" and provides an estimate of "cost-of-living increases" (Jenkins 138–139). "Aging Booth," another app that applies a similar technique of aging a contemporary photograph, is also being utilized by human resources departments, along with competitive computer games, to pique employees' interest in their future selves and the myriad financial decisions that will need to be made (E. Harris).

Whether these forward-thinking strategies will bring results that will have a long-term impact on how younger generations plan for their old age remains to be seen. Less technologically savvy, but perhaps equally instructive, can be the examples of family members' experiences—how they fared in their later years monetarily and what lessons they learned. My mother continues to pursue work in her eighties, for a variety of reasons, but mostly because she is a happier person when working and does not like to waste her time. She might have made different financial decisions along the way if she had known more about Social Security, pensions, and the necessity of retirement savings, but she has been lucky to be healthy enough to stay employed part time and to find agencies that appreciate her assets and do not discriminate against her age. After fifty-nine years of practicing law, my father recently retired at eighty-four, following his father's example of late-life retirement, since my grandfather practiced dentistry into his eighties. This family tradition of continuing to work disregarding age-based constraints sends a message that being employed is meaningful and not to be given up without strong justification. That idea is conveyed as well in the words of Kathy Thomas, who told her life story of being a domestic worker from the time she was sixteen into her senior years, in a 2016 essay "Dirty Work": "Work saved me. It gave me power and pride at times when I had none. It still does. So even though it's getting harder, I can't imagine stopping" (75).

8

Death

"The Final Frontier"?

Endings matter, not just for the person but, perhaps
even more for the ones left behind.
—Atul Gawande, *Being Mortal*

I want Death to find me planting my cabbages, neither worrying
about it nor the unfinished garden.
—Michel de Montaigne, from Sallie Tisdale, *Advice for Future Corpses*

At some point in my seventies, death stopped being interesting.
—Donald Hall, *Essays after Eighty*

I try to imagine a way our story can end without a magician.
—Elaine Feinstein, *Talking to the Dead*

The art of dying is the art of living.
—Sherwin Nuland, *How We Die*

An unspoken rule these days, when making a television show about
people in their later years, seems to be that death has to be integrated as a theme even if the program is a comedy. Fox's 2018
attempt to revisit *The Golden Girls'* type of humor with an ensemble

cast, *The Cool Kids*, begins with a dying member of a male clique at retirement home "Shady Meadows" leaving behind his dining companions-friends who must plan an appropriate farewell while fending off intrusive newcomer Margaret (Vicki Lawrence), coveting the empty spot at their table. Critics' reactions to the show have been lukewarm to hyper-critical (Matthew Gilbert of *The Boston Globe* called it the "worst sitcom on TV"), but it is not inconceivable that some viewers might enjoy the antics of this group of friends, who celebrate their departed compatriot with alcohol and debauchery while the facility they live in wants to keep the theatrics down to a minimum.

A much more profound treatment of the subject appears in another 2018 series that mixes comedy and drama, *The Kominsky Method*, starring Michael Douglas and Alan Arkin, on Netflix. That show centers on the forty-year relationship between acting teacher Sandy Kominsky (Douglas) and his agent and friend, Norman Newlander (Arkin). One of the most moving moments in the eight-episode first season comes in the sixth episode, "A Daughter Detoxes," in which the two men take a road trip to bring Norman's daughter to a rehab facility. Norman is depressed by the recent loss of his wife, and when asked by Sandy what he is thinking, he offers, "Suicide." Norman explains that his "continued existence is pointless." Sandy argues that Norman still has "a lot to live for," but is put on the spot to come up with specifics. When he finally comes up with the fact that Norman is "beloved," that does not move his friend, but a few moments later, Sandy does not hold back, "I need you . . . for my continual well-being." Jokes ensue, but a serious question remains on the table: How do people view death as they age, especially in relation to the changes that come about from loss? What continues to make life purposeful, and what do people do when life no longer feels worth living?

Literature offers myriad perspectives on every aspect of death from classical times through today. The ancient Greek philosopher Epicurus argued that people should not fear death because death is not bad for the living, who are not yet dead, and it is not bad for those who have died since they have no consciousness of being dead. Just as we should not mourn the period of time before we are born, we should not mourn the time we are no longer among the living. Contemporary writers have noted that most literary works actually show more of a fascination with death than a fear of it. Don DeLillo in *White Noise*, for example, comments that "all plots tend to move deathward," and several of his other fictional works focus directly on death, such as the 2017 novel *Zero K*, about a man who wants to preserve the bodies of loved ones for a time when human life can be revived after death (26). Margaret Atwood in a lecture delivered at Cambridge University entitled "Negotiating with the Dead" also acknowledges that "all writing of the narrative kind, and perhaps all writing, is motivated deep down" by a preoccupation with "mortality . . . the risky trip to the Underworld" (qtd. in Danticat 154–155).

Euthanasia Literature?

One genre of death literature concerning older individuals has sparked controversy for its subtle (but sometimes overt) messages that people of a certain age should either kill themselves or be killed for the good of society as a whole. With euthanasia presently a hotly debated topic, one might assume that the books portraying this idea might be fairly recent. However, British writer Anthony Trollope's 1882 futuristic novel *The Fixed Period* was one of the first. It depicts a fictional island near New Zealand that adopts a social experiment to take away the negative experiences of aging by having citizens at sixty-seven enjoy one last year of pleasure at Necropolis before being put to death. The difficulty in interpreting "elderly euthanasia" works such as Trollope's, published when he was sixty-seven—the year he died—is that readers cannot absolutely determine if the central idea of weeding out old people as they approach a certain age is satire or a serious solution to problems connected with aging. The ambiguity also appears in other novels. William Nolan and George Clayton Johnson's *Logan's Run* (1967), which eventually was turned into a television series and a 1976 film by the same name, also projects a dystopian society concerned about population control and resources, in which people must die by the much earlier age of twenty-one.

More recent novels resort back to the old-age death plots. Christopher Buckley's 2007 novel, *Boomsday*, features incentives for baby boomers to commit suicide at seventy, an idea that becomes widely popular among citizens when people become worried about the economic repercussions of mass retirement. While Buckley is a political satirist and *Boomsday* could be interpreted as making fun of those prognosticators who predict a "gray tsunami" and other disastrous outcomes when baby boomers will require their Social Security benefits and potentially expensive health care resources, the 2010 young adult novel *Matched* by Ally Condie has the older generation killed off at eighty with a less clear societal benefit. In this popular dystopian novel (part of a trilogy), the government controls most of people's important decisions, such as who they will be "matched" with as a life partner in marriage, where they will work, and how long they will live, the cut-off age being eighty. Again, an author is offering a literary work suggesting an expiration date for citizens and demonstrating the logistics of how to make that happen—in this case, slowly poisoning individuals who are seventy-nine. *Matched* differs significantly from some of these other literary works that have old-age euthanasia at their center in that one of the characters, the grandfather to the protagonist, Cassie Reyes, rebels against blindly following the dictates of the Society. The Society not only decides to cull citizens who live too long, but also opts to pare down cultural artifacts, deciding that only one hundred of everything (paintings, poems, etc.) need to be saved. Cassie's grandfather smuggles her a poem outside of the government's selections that will provoke her to challenge all of the choices that have been designated for her. The poem is none other than Dylan Thomas's "Do Not Go Gentle into That Good Night," which urges Cassie to resist passivity but also can be applied to her grandfather's imposed death sentence; he, too, will not "go gentle" with others' decision that eighty is a long enough life. While he does not have the physical strength to resist the mandatory death sentence, providing his granddaughter with the tools to fight a totalitarian state's draconian rule on longevity is in itself a form of rebellion.

Life Expectancy

These various literary texts toying around with different age limits for its elders raise an important question: How long do most people want to live? Furthermore, what does research show about how long it is possible to live? Several respondents to the surveys for this book had ambitious expectations for how long they planned on living. For example, a woman who was seventy-three shared that she intends to reach a 111 and based that on longevity running in her family. Many people assume that longevity is an inherited trait, but those in scientific fields note that parents' longevity influences only 3 percent of an offspring's life expectancy (compared to 90 percent for height), although others put the genetic inheritance for life expectancy closer to 25 percent (Gawande 33; Leland 202). A ninety-two-year-old man also imagined himself becoming a centenarian; he indicated that his health and mood are "fine" as he is still living in a house with his wife of sixty-seven years. Perhaps this goal is not completely far-fetched. His survey responses also indicated that his humor is still intact—a helpful quality to weather unexpected and unpleasant challenges through the years—as his final comment about what is important to know about aging is that the "first hundred years are the worst." Not everyone taking the survey expressed a desire to live into their nineties and beyond; several individuals said that they sincerely hope not to live to that age due to the likelihood of decline. One woman in her late sixties explained that living with and taking care of her ninety-six-year-old mother, who is "waiting to die," has been "depressing" and has affected her feelings about living deep into her later years.

Despite our preferences and expectations, most of us will not be able to control how long we will live. With the exception of a few remarkable cases of people living past 110 (e.g., Jeanne Calment appears to be the oldest confirmed person at 122), doctors see 100 to 110 as the limit to human lives. Sherwin Nuland, who wrote a best-selling and critically acclaimed book on dying, explains that even if scientists find medical breakthroughs for "every disease," the "maximum" will not change very much (84–85). According to Nuland, most deaths of older individuals can be attributed to seven main diseases, singly or in combination: "atherosclerosis, hypertension, adult-onset diabetes, obesity . . . Alzheimer's and other dementias, cancer and a decreased resistance to infection" (78). But even as evidence mounts that the body naturally breaks down from disease and wear, a committed group of individuals is trying to push medical boundaries to extend life beyond traditional limits. Fueled by extraordinary wealth, individuals like Peter Thiel, co-founder of Pay Pal, Larry Ellison, co-founder of Oracle, and Sergey Brin, co-founder of Google, are pouring millions of dollars into antiaging research to see if science can "cure death" (qtd. in Ehrenreich 80). Research aimed at initiating a "war on age" is happening in places such as the SENS Research Foundation, led by biogerontologist and chief science officer, Aubrey de Grey. His approach is to target "categories of damage" and find solutions for each. An example would be cell loss. Over time, the body does not replace cells that are dying, which can speed up the aging process. Grey believes that stem-cell therapy can improve this situation and is working to see if putting different cells into a body can cause them to replace themselves again, which could help cure diseases such as Parkinson's, caused by cell loss in the brain (Illing). Supporters of this kind of research point to success thus far in increasing the lifespan of "nematode worms, fruit flies and mice," and project eventually adding "twenty to sixty" years to the "human lifespan" as "cellular senescence" is further explored (Davis 24). Other new techniques involve transferring the blood of young people into older bodies through transfusions, but this is in its beginning stages and has raised ethical questions among scientists, as it was started by an entrepreneur without a medical background (Aronson, *Elderhood* 91; Maxmen).

Critical commentary on facilities such as the SENS Research Foundation that are trying to defy the aging process appears in a literary work ironically titled *The Immortalists* (2018) by Chloe

Benjamin. The novel centers on the four Gold siblings living in New York, all of whom one day visit a fortune teller offering the date each will die. The oldest sibling, Varya, eventually becomes a researcher into longevity, which she explains to a reporter, is not called "antiaging" because that evokes the misperception of "science fiction cryonics"; instead, the laboratory promotes that it will "enhance life span" by doing experiments, often involving animals, to cure cancer, Parkinson's, and heart disease (271). The veneer, of course, sounds appealing as many enterprises seek to eliminate debilitating diseases that affect older people, but Benjamin also lifts the veil on the negative side of these practices by showing not only the harm to the animals but also to those who are working with them. One of the projects to reverse aging is severe calorie restriction in mice, which has often been touted as a possible path to living longer. Varya practices some of these same restrictions herself as part of a monastic lifestyle, but readers see how destructive they are for her well-being. The subtle message, then, is that people need to live in the present and work on building meaningful relationships, as Varya eventually does with her aging mother, rather than invest in a futuristic endeavor to escape the natural process of bodily change over time. This idea of trusting the body's natural processes without medical manipulation is also communicated in an essay from gerontologist Barbara Macdonald in the collection *Look Me in the Eye*. She writes that the body has "always had two jobs: to make sure that I live and to make sure that I die" (114). Not everyone will take comfort in this reminder, but it is useful insight about our physical selves in terms of their design and function.

Acceptance or Fear of Death

The book's survey research did show a number of people who accepted death as a natural part of life with nothing to fear. Some of these people became more philosophical about death as they aged, such as the seventy-one-year-old woman who said that she used to be "terrified of dying" but no longer is and another woman around the same age who added to the end of her survey,

"Everyone dies—no one escapes but the best is always yet to come."
These attitudes support evidence that shows that the young tend
to fear dying more than older people (Applewhite, *This Chair* 214).
Part of the reason may be the satisfaction of a fulfilling long life
or a broadened world view from much lived experience that accepts
the cycle of life. Clearly, religion is also a factor in affecting attitudes toward death. Nearly all respondents who said that they did
not fear death considered themselves devout participants in their
faith. For some, life on earth is simply "preparation for dying or
life after death," as a sixty-nine-year-old man explained. Rather
than being fearful, for him, that idea is "joy!" Others explained
that by having "faith in God," it is easier to regard "Death" as a
"normal part of life." What becomes clear from these comments
is that belief in a higher power not only gives comfort that there
may be an afterlife—taking the pressure off of having to experience everything in this world—but also takes away the worry of
having to control one's destiny and figure what is the right time to
exit. This viewpoint was vividly described by a man in his late sixties who explained his "philosophy" as "when the Big Guy gets
out his eraser, it will be time to go home. It isn't up to me and I
don't plan to do anything to advance His call." He reasoned that
while we cannot control whether the bus is going to "stop" or run
us over, we can "control" our "own happiness," which should be
the focus rather than a long lifespan.

Still, for many, the reality of death is terrifying and not easy to
confront. In fact, Michael Pollan's latest book, *How to Change Your
Mind* (2018), on the science of psychedelics discusses how New
York University researchers have been investigating psilocybin
(found in "magic mushrooms") in order to help people ease their
fear of death. Cultural works and the surveys provide a variety of
explanations for the fear of dying. While social scientists, such as
Ernest Becker in *The Denial of Death*, have investigated the fear
of death as a primal part of the "human psyche," others see the
anxiety as tied to a particular aspect of the death experience.
Repeatedly, what surfaces is not a fear of death itself, but fear of
the dying process and the various unpredictable ways that it can

happen over an indeterminate length of time. A 2018 study published in *Science* magazine supports the claim of the many unknowns surrounding dying. In the study of Medicare recipients who were given the "highest probability of dying" within a year according to doctors, half were still alive a year later—a circumstance that shows how difficult it is to determine what may be one's "final days" (Frakt B3). Fear of dying, a common mindset, is actually the title of a novel by Erica Jong. Watching her mother nearing a hundred and losing her faculties, such as speech, the main character, Vanessa Wonderman, reflects on this liminal state of being alive but severely incapacitated; her term for this is "lingering," which is said to be "worse" than death for "living creatures" (175). The noted author and editor Diana Athill, who died in 2019 at 101, discusses this same notion in her memoir *Somewhere towards the End* regarding her mother and shows how the fear of dying is established from watching loved ones' experiences and eventually becomes a part of an individual's own thinking. Athill explains that both she and her mother tended to agree with the statement, "I am not afraid of death"; however, they often followed that sentiment with, "It's the dying that I'm afraid of" (60). After her mother suffered from a bout of angina and struggled to breathe, Athill was confirmed in her view that the "process of dying" is far more terrifying than "being dead" (60).

The surveys also reinforced the fact that much of the fear that people have about death concerns the possibility that dying may be a long, drawn-out process that could include extreme pain and discomfort. This sentiment was articulated by a woman in her eighties who wrote that she does not "fear death," but only the prospect of "long suffering before death." "Suffering" before death was mentioned in multiple surveys, often times using the plural "our" to indicate married couples shared this concern and likely had spent time talking about it. Conversations in families and between partners on what could happen in the event of a prolonged death and the steps that they may or may not want to take in terms of end-of-life decision-making has motivated many people to establish advance directives, often called "living wills." These legal documents spell out individuals' "directions" to medical staff if they are not able to communicate themselves. According to a 2017 study of nearly 800,000 people, approximately one-third of Americans have an advance directive to let health professionals know what kind of life-sustaining measures they want or to do not want (such as cardiopulmonary resuscitation, artificial nutrition, or ventilators) if they are incapacitated. The number increases as people become older, with 46 percent of those over sixty-five having taken this step (Yadav et al.). Those who have not taken this step may not want to commit to specific guidelines for future care in case they change their mind over time or when faced more directly with a near-death situation.

Others may be reluctant because the topic is too depressing and something that can be put off for another day. Roz Chast illustrates this reluctance in her graphic memoir *Can't We Talk about Something More Pleasant?*, which opens with Chast trying to have a conversation with her parents about their end-of-life wishes. They refuse to offer anything on the subject, and the last panel on the page shows all three feeling at least momentary relief that they have been spared the discomfort of "that talk." Perhaps due to the difficulty of having people discuss their wishes about near-death decisions, avenues have developed to make this dialogue more possible. The award-winning journalist Ellen Goodman, for example, created an initiative called "The Conversation Project" that provides people with the tools to talk with their family members about their end-of-life wishes in order to have them respected. In a 2018 survey, The Conversation Project found that 95 percent of people actually want to have this discussion and 53 percent said they would be relieved to do so (The Conversation Project). Other initiatives include "Go Wish" cards that have thirty-six different goals on them to help advance care planning. An example might be "not being short of breath" or "maintaining my dignity," and patients are asked to sort the cards into piles of very important, important, and not important in order to initiate discussion with family and physicians. Currently, most doctors spend under six minutes talking to patients about end-of-life care issues, with the doctors doing the talking for much of that time, so this tool could be useful in bringing issues to the table (Meier et al. 9). Additionally, beginning in 2016, Medicare began reimbursing physicians for time spent with patients doing advance planning, which could increase the opportunity for longer, more meaningful discussions.

Dying Alone, Dying at Home

Besides the fear of the process of dying, another fear surrounding death that emerges from a variety of sources is a fear of dying alone. In his textbook based on a series of lectures, Yale philosopher Shelly Kagan discusses the topic at length because he feels people are preoccupied with it. Citing folk song lyrics, a children's book, and even his own family members, Kagan sets out to dismiss that fear by explaining that death is not quite as solitary as most people imagine it to be (e.g., Socrates dies, after drinking hemlock, surrounded by friends) and also by arguing that we actually do other activities alone (e.g., I am the only one digesting my lunch), suggesting that death should not be singled out as being the exception to all those other endeavors (198, 202). It is not clear how much comfort the philosophical approach may have for those deeply concerned about the solitary nature of death. Several survey respondents mentioned their fear of dying alone without elaborating details or explanation. They were all widowed, though, and living by themselves, so part of their worry may stem from the practical reality that no one might immediately register their absence from the world, if their death occurred at home. News media tend to sensationalize stories of decomposed bodies found after significant periods of time until perhaps the smell alerted authorities, so this nightmarish scenario could also fuel uneasiness.

In contrast to that ghastly image, Athill in her memoir talks about the almost universal desire elders have to be in their homes when passing with the "companionship of someone they love and trust" (54). According to research, 80 percent of Americans do express a desire to be at home when they die, likely because of the comforting presence of familiar belongings and, ideally, family members, even though 80 percent usually die in hospitals or nursing homes (Larson and DeClaire 163–164). New research from the *New England Journal of Medicine* reveals, however, the trend is changing in that for the first time in fifty years natural deaths at home, increasingly on the rise, are now surpassing hospital deaths, despite the obstacles that may entail for family caregivers (Kolata). Atul Gawande in *Being Mortal* thinks that as society talks more openly about end-of-life issues, we will not see a disconnect between what people want to happen and what actually does happen when death is near; in other words, there is hope that wanting to die home and not being alone can now be made more possible with palliative care and hospice being available outside of hospital facilities. What can also help allay fears of an isolated and/or institutionalized end is taking steps while alive to make sure that the worst fears, such as alienation from loved ones at the time of death, will not happen. The idea that in life people can secure some outcomes surrounding their death—to alleviate some fears, at least—is advocated in Nuland's *How We Die*. As a doctor, like Gawande, Nuland believes that the medical community should not be in the driver's seat when it comes to end-of-life decisions, and, he argues, they will not be if we make sure that "those who know who we are" understand our priorities and enforce them (255). For Nuland, one is not "dying alone" if those closest to the individual bring to the death decision-making process knowledge of what is most important to the person losing his or her life. This knowledge, he feels, offers "hope" that the dying person will not "be abandoned" (257).

A "Good Death"?

Nuland wrote about death not just from a physician's perspective but as someone whose life was touched by death early on. His mother, with whom he was very close, died from colon cancer when he was eleven, and strong memories of her dying impacted his childhood. Eventually, he lost his brother Harvey to colon cancer as well. In *How We Die* Nuland expresses concern about the idealization of certain kinds of death, commonly referred to as a "good death," which sends a message that there is "some preconceived image of dying right" (262). While he understands the desire for "closure" that is under one's control, more often than not, the reality may not match the wish. What exactly constitutes a "good death" is, of course, going to vary from person to person depending on individuals' priorities at the end of their lives. Dilip Jeste, director of the Sam and Rose Stein Institute for Research at the University of California–San Diego School of Medicine, surveyed articles from 1996–2015 on what people who are dying, their family members, and health professionals consider a "good death" in a 2016 article in *The American Journal of Geriatric Psychiatry*. All three groups ranked "honoring patients' preferences, staying pain free, and having emotional well-being" high, while family members were more apt to cite "quality of life," "life completion," and "dignity" more often than patients themselves (Larson and DeClaire 164). The significant findings from this research were the consistency among patients that their priorities be honored and the fact that families and medical staff did not always view a "good death" in the same way as the patients.

Obviously, a "good death" will be interpreted subjectively to some extent. In Japan, there is a term "kororo" that means "dying quickly and painlessly," part of a phrase that is used in prayer— "healthy longevity followed by a good death" (Larson and DeClaire 69). In the United States, the Institute of Medicine defines it as being "free from avoidable distress and suffering for patients, families, and caregivers; in general accord with patients' and families' wishes; and reasonably consistent with clinical, cultural, and ethical standards" (qtd. in Meier et al. 8). Implicit in this definition is the hope that the death will not be prolonged if it will bring about sustained misery for the dying person and loved ones. In practical terms, then, for many, a "good death" is a quick death. As sociologist Meika Loe observes in *Aging Our Way*, this idea of a "good death" represents "our cultural values: quickness, efficiency, [and] avoidance of dying" (248). A more clinical term for the term of minimizing the time a person may suffer when dying is "compression of morbidity." Stanford University School of Medicine professor

James Fries coined the phrase in 1980 in research published in *The New England Journal of Medicine* as a hypothesis to see if postponing "chronic infirmity" as people aged would result in a "shorter period of time" of "terminal decline" (Swartz). Not all medical professionals believe "compression of morbidity" is something that people can determine or control themselves. Gawande, for example, points out that "swift catastrophic illness is the exception" since usually "death comes only after long medical struggle with an ultimately unstoppable condition" or "just the accumulating debilities of very old age" (156–157). Perhaps because of the limited power to control the length of time of "morbidity," the fantasy of a hastened departure from this world, ideally while sleeping, permeates the mindset of many.

The surveys brought out repeated references to the desirability of dying quickly, ideally while sleeping, as a "good death." A seventy-eight-year-old man, for example wrote that he feared "dying a bad death" and hoped "to go to bed one night and never wake up." An eighty-six-year-old woman expressed the same sentiment for minimal sickness before death when she explained her desire also to die in her sleep or have a "short terminal illness." Most of the respondents recognized that this particular hope was not theirs alone, but shared widely amongst their peers. A woman in her seventies, who witnessed both of her parents endure long illnesses, shared that most people she knows would like to "just fall asleep and be done with it." Despite the widespread desire for a "compression of morbidity" and modern health care advances, geriatricians like Louise Aronson believe that progress on this front has not yet materialized (*Elderhood* 260).

John Leland's shadowing of octogenarians for his book *Happiness Is a Choice You Make: Lessons from a Year among the Oldest Old* corroborates that many seniors desire a hasty death for a mixture of reasons. For some, such as a woman named Ping, there is a desire to not have to endure pain from "bones" that "hurt . . . [her] terribly." For others whom Leland interviewed, monetary concerns were an issue as well as the potential emotional fatigue on family members that could result from a lengthy terminal illness. Another woman named Ruth offered that she wanted to "die fast" in order to not be "burden" on children. A different perspective on a quick death comes in University of Michigan law professor William Ian Miller's book *Losing It*, his diatribe on the aging process. In it, Miller argues that if he is forced to spend years without his full physical and mental faculties due to a degeneration of the body, it will cancel out the years of accomplishment. He writes, "Will I decay by degrees, enduring years of dementia, befouling myself while staring vacantly ahead and feeling no shame? Such an end would cancel out a lifetime of achievement" (211). Miller's worry here could be described as "psychic dismemberment," a concern that essential parts of his identity would be destroyed and disappear forever (Pipher, *Women* 168). Besides worrying about his legacy, he advocates that a quick "good death" (preferably during sleep) is "good because it makes no demands on our courage or any other virtue, no facing pain or fear" (254). For Miller, then, the best death scenario is one that does not mar an individual's reputation in life and does not require bravery to endure.

Complex Literary Treatments of a "Good Death"

Literary works also take up the theme of a "good death" as one that has a "compression of morbidity," but in some works, there are challenges to the perspective that *everyone* subscribes to the idea. That is not the case, however, in Joyce Farmer's *Special Exits*, based on her father's and stepmother's experiences in advanced old age. In one frame early on, the father, Lars says, almost out of the blue while feeding the cat, "Sometimes I wish I could just die suddenly" (16). Though the comment comes without explanation, the next frame has him holding his back with clear pain radiating from it, which leaves readers to believe he is in some degree of discomfort that is likely contributing to this frame of mind, even if it might be a fleeting thought. While *Special Exits* displays the older person wishing for quick death, Chast's memoir, *Can't We Talk about Something More Pleasant?*, brings out an adult child's perspective on the topic. Chast, an only child, devotes several frames to the fanciful possibility that both of her parents one day will "die at the same time in their sleep," which would mean that she would "NEVER have to deal [with the unpleasant realities of death]" (22). The illustration shows a manic Chast, whose "NEVER" in that frame hints at the fantasy mode she has slipped into, given that neither parent will "go gentle into that good night." Other works show that some people want to believe the fantasy version as a possibility for themselves. In Margaret Drabble's novel *The Dark Flood Rises*, the first husband of the protagonist, Francesca Stubbs, the former doctor Claude, remains mostly in bed with a "slowly deteriorating physical condition." Despite his limited mobility and dependence on others for assistance, he is "certain that he is going to die with ease . . . in bed, comfortably, relinquishing consciousness easily, when the time comes" (107). Though Drabble never shows us Claude's "ending," which leaves open the possibility that his inkling is correct, the novel is filled with many other seniors' deaths, some quick and unpredictable, but many the exact opposite, requiring medical intervention and prolonged discomfort.

One of the most complex literary treatments of the desire for a quick "good death" occurs in Elizabeth Strout's novel of connected stories, *Olive Kitteridge*. What makes this novel unique in its incorporation of "good death" issues is that it includes both the commonly parroted viewpoint of the advantages to dying in one's sleep *along with* a critique of that perspective. As discussed in earlier chapters, a benefit of complex topics being treated in fictional works is the possibility for seeing the issue from multiple lenses that prevents readers from taking ideas at face value and redirects them instead to further engage and scrutinize different viewpoints. In the story "Security" Olive visits her son, Christopher, his new wife, and adopted child in New York—an undertaking that requires great energy from Olive, who lives mostly sequestered in her native Maine without much change in routine, especially in her later years. In thinking about how old age has so many stages of which young people are not aware, Olive mentions that between all those stages, people "prayed to die" in their sleep, the familiar dictum seen in other literary and nonfictional sources (224). Less common, however, is an earlier reference in the book that highlights the unlikelihood of that type of death occurring. Olive, the frank realist, talks with one of her close friends, Daisy, about a grief group that Olive joins after her husband, Henry, dies. She rejects the idea from the group that anger is an appropriate reaction to death. Her explanation shows an awareness of how unlikely "compression of morbidity" is, which should mitigate any anger: "Why in the hell should I feel angry? We all know this stuff is coming. Not many are lucky enough to just drop dead in their sleep" (148). What exactly "stuff" constitutes is left unclear, but likely it is the messy side of dying—the unpredictability, the often stretched-out time period, all the unknowns that contrast with the "convenience" of ending life while asleep.

The subject is picked up again in the final story "River" when Olive meets Jack Kennison on a walking path after she finds him slumped over and mistakes him for being dead. In their conversation, Olive explains the appeal of a "quick" death since she saw Henry "shrivel for years in a nursing home" and even shares that she would like to "die"; subsequently, she offers no sympathy for Jack's fear about dying alone and utters a response not unlike Kagan's: "We're always alone. Born alone. Die alone. What difference does it make?" (254–255). These words show a fearlessness at the prospect of death that undermines the statement that she fears a death like Henry's. More telling than Olive's words on the subject, though, are her actions. She has contemplated suicide at different points in the novel, which would offer a "quick" death that seems so desirable to many, but Olive continues to choose life—whatever it may bring—since she is not actually ready to "leave it yet" (270). The inconsistency in Olive's statements on death and in her actions reminds us of the difficulty of knowing exactly what we may want when we talk about a "good death." Attitudes may be contradictory at times and even statements made in one context may not hold true moments later. Margaret Morganroth Gullette in *Ending Ageism, or How Not to Shoot Old People*, makes the point that statements made during "intense suffering" about a desire for death should not be interpreted as declarations of a person's intent to truly want to end their lives (138).

Hospice

For some people, the words "good death" are automatically associated with the hospice movement. Begun in London by physician Dame Cicily Saunders, hospice was born out of the recognition that terminal patients have special needs that should be accommodated. The first hospice center was built in 1967 and brought to the United Sates in 1974; later, a model was developed to bring hospice home care to dying individuals, and Medicare, as of 1983, began offering coverage of this type of palliative care as long as a physician can establish that the patient has less than six months to live. This international movement has expanded greatly over the years, and in the United States, estimates are that between 40 and 45 percent of those who die use hospice for at least three days, and 80 percent of those patients are sixty-five or older; the average amount of time in hospice care is seventeen days, a low number perhaps due to physicians' possible reluctance to give a definitive diagnosis of "terminal" when some outcomes are difficult to predict, as well as Medicare's strict rules as to who qualifies for hospice (Aronson, *Elderhood* 300; Gawande 193; Gillick xvi; Tisdale 96). Still, as of 2017, 1.49 million people used Medicare for hospice, a 4.5 percent increase from 2016 (Kolata).

That Gawande in *Being Mortal* is a staunch supporter of hospice for dying patients comes as no surprise. Since his mantra throughout the book is that "endings matter," he is understandably an advocate for an approach that is catered to the individual's needs and desires at the end of the life cycle as opposed to what a physician thinks is best for that patient. Gawande brings in research to demonstrate that in terms of quality of life, not only do terminal patients fare more poorly with medical interventions to sustain them (e.g., electrical defibrillation or chest compressions), but their family members are worse off months after the patients die

(155). This is likely the case because much of the time is devoted to the various procedures, often involving machinery, that could prevent intimate conversation, comfort, and closure. *Being Mortal* brings in additional studies as further evidence for the benefits of hospice care. One example is a 2010 Massachusetts General Hospital paper based on patients with stage-IV lung cancer, which revealed that the patients who had supplemental palliative care "experienced less suffering at the end of their lives," with some even living 2.5 times as long as those who just had typical oncology treatment. The significant difference in approach, according to Gawande, is that the primary aim of medicine is life extension, sometimes by any means possible, while hospice uses a team of professionals that includes social workers and chaplains to focus on a "best possible day" for the patient, with special attention on "freedom from pain and discomfort" (161, 247).

Despite Gawande's influence and notoriety (e.g., *Being Mortal* continues to be on the *New York Times* best-seller list and was turned into a 2015 *Frontline* documentary), his viewpoint on the efficacy of hospice care for those at the end of their lives is not without detractors. Karen Brown published a personal account of how hospice "failed" her father in the *New York Times* in 2018, entitled "Not the Death He Wanted." Brown, a reporter at New England Public Radio, describes the fiasco she experienced on behalf of her father who was dying of pancreatic cancer. When her father needed assistance due to a sharp increase in abdominal pain, she was unable to reach the necessary hospice staff, and her father died without the necessary palliative measures. Brown includes recent news reports of "3,200 complaints against hospice agencies in the past five years" and a Medicare survey showing that under 80 percent of patients surveyed felt they were "getting timely care." Critics might explain that the rise in complaints over staffing is due to the increase in for-profit hospice agencies that may be trying to stretch their personnel too thin in order to make more money. For hospice home care, for example, which is what 94 percent of Americans use, one can expect "only four hours of face-to-face care in a week" (one hour with a nurse and two visits of "up to ninety minutes" from an aide), with the majority of care being carried out by family members (Tisdale 98–99). Another issue that needs to be addressed is the disparity between hospice care for Caucasians and that for minorities. Research shows that minorities use hospice care less frequently than white Americans and that their quality of care is far inferior (Castellucci 13; Tisdale 98). Some of the distrust of hospice on the part of minorities could stem from a long history of neglect and exploitation by the medical community. But there also seem to be factors relating to insurance barriers, religious/cultural conflicts, and complaints around respect that are keeping several minority groups from availing themselves of quality palliative care. A 2018 article in *The American Journal of Hospice and Palliative Medicine*, for example, found that hospitals wait longer to refer minorities and uninsured patients to hospice as compared to Caucasians; as a result, this demographic spends longer periods of time in hospitals than may be necessary. The study did find, however, that increasing "awareness of hospice services" would help "minority populations" to access its benefits, including "quality of care" (Haines et al. 1081, 1083).

"Death with Dignity"

A final characteristic usually associated with the idea of a "good death" is dignity. People want to maintain some semblance of their self-respect and individuality, especially when time and circumstances seem to be stripping them away. The phrase "death with dignity" also now has an association with euthanasia, which literally means "good death." As momentum shifts toward people at the end of life making their own decisions about treatment and care, there is more interest than ever in the questions of whether individuals have the right to die when they feel it is their time and whether there is any ethical way to have physicians be involved with the process. A seventy-seven-year-old survey respondent, in fact, thought that the survey should have included a question on "how people feel about euthanasia." He expressed worry regarding the "lack of social acceptance of euthanasia," which prevents people from being able to decide "when they want to go" if "their desired quality of life is no longer possible." This gentleman's belief in the right to have control over his own death is shared by two-thirds of other American adults, who also agree that there are situations when a person should be able to end his or her life (Tisdale 39). A strong display of support shows itself as well in the growing list of states, along with Washington, DC, that have implemented laws allowing some form of assisted death or, by court order, will not prosecute physicians who provide fatal medication to those terminally ill; as of 2019, the list includes California, Colorado, Hawaii, Maine, Montana, New Jersey, Oregon, Vermont, and Washington.

Despite having legislation allowing assisted death under certain circumstances, not many of those requesting the drugs to end their lives actually go ahead and use them. For example, in 2017, 214 people in Oregon received "Death with Dignity" prescriptions, but only 143 used them (14 of whom used prescriptions given to them in 2016); 80.4 percent of the 143 were aged sixty-five or older (Larson and DeClaire 178). Few find these numbers terribly surprising since scholars agree that the intent behind this legalized option for those with a terminal illness is to provide them with the power to choose their fate, even if that means not using the fatal drugs. Autonomy is the key principle behind assisted death initiatives, and residents in states not allowing assisted death can struggle with not being able to make their end their own. Sarah Lyall, author of "One Last Thing for Mom," an article published in the *New York Times*, shared her frustration that there was not a way to honor her mom's repeated wish to end her life of pain from late-stage lung cancer. This situation may be more common than many of us might imagine. While the desire to end one's life is not a topic that the general public wants to talk about freely, fiction can represent this taboo perspective with unwavering clarity. The *Hendrik Groen* diaries, for example, not only include real-life statistics on issues pertaining to death (e.g., "sixty-four percent of the elderly believe in the right to end their lives in a humane manner once they've had enough" [*The Secret Diary* 249]), but the books also feature several characters who talk to their doctors and to their friends about wanting to control their "end." Hendrik's best friend, Evert, who already has suffered through an amputation and now faces a terminal diagnosis, flatly tells his friend about preparations he has made: "I'm ready for the Grim Reaper. . . . I'll die the way I want to" (*On the Bright Side* 300). A few nonfiction writers also have given utterance to this frank desire to end their lives on their own terms. May Sarton, for one, writes in *Endgame: Journal of the Seventy-Ninth Year*, "I want to die, there's no doubt about that. When you have as much pain as I have and there's no way out[,] you *do* want to die" (277).

With outspoken advocates promoting the right to die, there should be some concern that it is too fine a line between the right to die and an underlying message that the old and infirm have an obligation to die. The literary examples at the beginning of the chapter all spelled out dystopian scenarios when people of a certain age were forced to die, but in real life British writer Martin Amis called for euthanasia booths "on every corner" passing out a "martini and a medal" to deal with potential problems arising from the "silver tsunami" (qtd. in Davies). Comments like these and cultural texts that show old age infirmity as not worth living, such as Michael Haneke's Academy Award–winning film, *Amour*, are in danger of creating a climate that devalues seniors' lives and perhaps causes them to see death as a necessity, particularly for the good of others. Gullette in *Ending Ageism* raises a central question related to this problem when she asks if everyone in the future will have the "mental freedom necessary for autonomous end-of-life decision making" (159).

Complexities of "Death with Dignity" in Film

Just as *Olive Kitteridge* is able to explore the desire for "compressed morbidity" and arguments against it, so an Israeli film directed by Tal Granit and Sharon Maymon entitled *The Farewell Party* (2014) offers a challenging perspective on the "death with dignity" debate that discourages viewers from comfortably residing in either camp. Unlike the much more subdued *Amour*, which also raises questions about assisted suicide for the elderly, *The Farewell Party* starts off with a quasi-comical tone as the central character, Yehezkel (Ze'ev Revah), pretends to be the voice of God when a fellow resident of his retirement home calls to complain that her cancer is back, and she wants to die. While assuring her that she is going straight to heaven, he tells her that she will have to keep on fighting since there are "no vacancies" at the present time. The subtle joke in the opening is that Yehezkel is an inventor who will be able to create a machine whereby a person can give themselves a fatal dose of medicine if their quality of life is irreparably bad due to a terminal illness, and, thus, "plays God" in more than one way. He makes the machine for his dear friend Max (Shmuel Wolf) who is suffering and wants to die but is unable to do so. Max's wife, Yana (Aliza Rozen), solicits Yehezkel's cooperation by pleading, "They're keeping him alive as though dying is a crime." By contrast, Yehezkel's wife, Lavana, believes her husband's actions are those of a "murderer." Lavana further complicates the moral tangle by insinuating that Yana is encouraging the death of her husband "for her herself" and has "put that idea in his [Max's] head."

Rather than resolving the contentious issue of whether Yehezkel's machine to help his friend end his pain-ridden life should be commended or condemned, the film becomes even more embroiled in questions. News about the invention circulates in the retirement facility, and others want to avail themselves of it. The small team that is assembled to pull off the deaths (a veterinarian who has access to tranquilizers used for horses and a former policeman who cleans up the evidence) descends into conflict when money is secretly exchanged for a later mercy killing, which Yehezkel never would have condoned. New moral issues continue to surface once Lavana develops Alzheimer's disease and eventually asks her husband to use the machine as the disease continues to worsen. She argues, "I'm disappearing. . . . I won't be myself." They take steps to find a facility for Alzheimer's patients, but it proves unacceptable for Lavana and Yehezkel. Their inability to agree upon a workable solution for Lavana's increased desire to end her life shows how a person may not have a consistent view of assisted death, especially if it concerns a loved one. Yehezkel is able to help Max and Yana by offering his machine to end Max's life, but he is extremely resistant to use it for Lavana, who has a different diagnosis and because she is central to his life. Even Yehezkel's role as "God" is challenged, despite the mercy that his machine offers those who want to die, when a technical malfunction of the machine results in one woman changing her mind. By the conclusion of *The Farewell Party*, audience members are likely to both understand the necessity of Yehezkel's invention allowing dying individuals a chance to end their lives peacefully without implicating anyone in the action *and* see all the potential abuses of the technology and the resistance one might feel if requested to use something similar by a loved relative. If society ever does move closer to creating and legislating mechanisms to end life, it is important that these dilemmas are considered to avoid opening a Pandora's Box on assisted death.

Dealing with Loss

Much of the chapter thus far has wrestled with the issues individuals face as they confront the reality of their own mortality. Equally significant, of course, is the reality that the older people become, the more losses they are likely to endure—the death of spouses, parents, siblings, friends, and even sometimes children take their toll on the surviving person. An eighty-two-year-old woman wrote in the survey that I should have asked more questions about what it feels like "to have . . . peers passing away and watching people deal with losing spouses," something she described as "hard to watch." Insight into why these losses can be so demoralizing appears in psychiatrist Marc Agronin's book *How We Age* (2011), when a son describes his ninety-five-year-old mother's desolation that everyone she has cared about has died: "The people that defined me are gone, so who am I?" (202). Those who have written about their struggles to confront the deaths of family members, friends, and associates deal with the experience individually. Some are hesitant to make new acquaintances for fear of more likely goodbyes in the future. Others have described trying to harden their hearts and adopt a stoic attitude or a fatalistic one, such as "That is how life is." People clearly have different coping mechanisms. When she became a widow, the poet Elaine Feinstein wrote a collection of poems entitled *Talking to the Dead* (2007) with moving reflections on processing memories of her deceased husband, as in "A Pebble on Your Grave":

It's easy to love the dead.
Their voices are mild. They don't argue.
Once in the earth, they belong to us faithfully.

Feinstein is not alone in writing about how easy it is to canonize the dead and lock them forever in memory with their perfection intact. This tendency is displayed in C. S. Lewis's *A Grief Observed* (1961) on the death of his wife and more recently, Joan Didion's *Year of Magical Thinking* (2005) and Jonathan Santlofer's *A Widower's Notebook* (2018); creative minds understandably process their unthinkable losses by recreating their missing adored person in prose. Santlofer goes even one step further and not only writes about his wife who died unexpectedly after a routine knee operation, but channels his grief by reimagining her through drawings. He explains that at first he could not look at photographs of his wife due to the pain, but he found that by sketching her from the photographic images—the sketches are included in the book—he was able to keep small details of her alive and dilute some of his deep sadness.

The act of bringing back part of a loved one through a creative pursuit and healing by sharing stories also is utilized by people who are not professional writers or artists. The surveys, for example, were filled with detailed explanations of seniors sharing their lifetime of losses and how they struggled to work through that pain. Here is one man's story:

> Unfortunately, one downside to getting older is that you lose family and friends along the way. Two deaths that had the most profound impact on me were the deaths of my brother-in-law, Daniel, and my father. Daniel died the day before Thanksgiving, the victim of suicide. Our daughter was nine and our son was five. One of the hardest things I have ever had to do was tell my wife that her brother was dead. The next was, along with my wife and her other brother, telling their parents. Time, they say, heals all wounds. That wound is fainter, but it will never be healed. My father celebrated his 81st birthday with no hint of any problems. A week later, he died from issues related to his lungs. The suddenness of his death stung. He was not only my father; he was my friend, mentor, confidant and a constant. I miss him every day. I cope with these losses because I have family who shared them with me and understand the loss. I have friends who have experienced similar losses in their lives and understand. We supported and support each other. I had a father who showed me the way.

It is clear from this man's statement that he carries the wounds from those significant deaths but mollifies their impact, as much as possible, through communicating with others who understand what it means to no longer have that meaningful person or collection of people around. Sometimes a loss is so great that a person feels unable to fully recover. A woman in her seventies explained in the survey that her identity was altered after a certain family member's death: "Because of the circumstance of the last family loss, I am not the person I was and have lost part of myself that never came back. Prior to that I was always able to come back."

In *The Last Lecture*, Randy Pausch shares wisdom that he received after his video on living in the face of terminal cancer was viewed worldwide; it connects strongly with the feelings this woman expressed on managing grief. The person quoted

Krishnamurti, a spiritual leader in India, who offered counsel on the impending death of someone beloved. He said to tell the person who is dying that when he dies, a part of the friend dies as well and will travel with him "wherever he goes"; "he will not be alone" (185). Perhaps, then, losing a part of oneself when someone else dies is not necessarily bad. It is a way of recognizing that life and death both unite us with one another.

Afterword

"We're all terminal," notes a character in Luis Alberto Urrea's 2018 novel, *The House of Broken Angels*. He makes this comment to the main character, Big Angel, who is celebrating his birthday during the final weeks of his life, to show that we are all united by the inevitability of death; only our different "schedules" separate us. That reminder applies perfectly to *Gray Matters*. At some point, maybe sooner than later, the content of this book will be relevant to everyone as the boundaries between "young" and "old" shift away from being the polar opposites most people imagine. Big Angel, at the center of Urrea's larger-than-life novels, blurs these boundaries continually. In one scene he feels powerless in his "diaper" with "legs aching," but moments later he treasures his wife, Flaca, with her "earned . . . splotches and scars and moles and wrinkles," whom he desires "exactly" as she is (71). Again literature helps us see aging as a difficult experience, but, most often, one worth the effort. This profound lesson came through time and time again in the stories shared by seniors in the surveys as well.

During the summer of 2019, while I was working on the final revisions of this book, many of my friends and acquaintances on social media were projecting images of their future "old" selves via FaceApp. Over a hundred million people have used this magic mirror to see their elderly selves, a startling enthusiasm that demonstrates our continued fascination with aging even as conversations with many people about growing older revealed a deep sense of dread. The app holds no allure for me personally, but the multifaceted dimensions of later life continue to whet my researcher's appetite and guide me to better understand what it means to reach the late decades of life. How do I know this project has changed me? Who knows us better than our moms? Mine, who is in her eighties, has told me repeatedly that I have become more patient with her than I was before I started the project and generally more empathetic as well. It is hard to get back into one's former mind-set, once information has been absorbed and processed, but I do remember conversations when she told me that she did not feel useful since she was no longer a practicing therapist and her hands-on mothering days were also in the distant past. Lacking a nuanced understanding of the psychological aspects of aging, I often told her to enjoy her time without work and family responsibilities and embrace a life of reading books for pleasure. Such naïve advice! Research shows that seniors who have purpose in their lives tend to have fewer heart attacks and strokes and less chance of developing dementia (Graham 1). I now realize that feeling "valuable," what my mom was describing, is what makes waking up every day seem worthwhile.

In addition to realizing the critical importance of feeling useful to happiness in old age, I began to see older persons in a whole new way. My biggest "ah ha" moment came from a line in Margaret Cruikshank's *Learning to Be Old* regarding "survivorship." She writes that any "human who reaches eighty is a model of regeneration and adaptation." Reading those words changed the way I looked at adults in their later years, those I mingled with at the YMCA every morning, residents at my mom's apartment building, or even strangers at the grocery store. Before encountering Cruikshank's observation, I did not give much thought to the back stories of older people I randomly encountered or even relatives in their eighties and nineties. Now, I wonder about what experiences they may have gone through, what changes they have had to make or to accept; I have learned to appreciate their full lives of stories and "adaptation." Other revelations altered my perception of older adults as well. Global statistics show that people become more content as they age, contrary to all the poisonous "angry" old men and women stereotypes. Examples from the humanities in this book and from the surveys also countered the simplistic rendering of later life frequently seen in popular culture and showed complex individuals thoughtfully reasoning their way through significant life issues pertaining to their grown children, their finances and friends, their health and housing, and even mortality. As a result, I am much more aware of and opposed to ageism in any form, especially because research shows such pernicious discrimination can take years off a person's life if it is internalized. Watching one of the early Democratic presidential debates in 2019, for example, I was struck by the repeated calls for the older candidates such as Bernie Sanders to "pass the torch," a thinly disguised ageist suggestion that younger candidates should "take over" presidential leadership since the generation before them was no longer equipped to handle the job. Author Marianne Williamson, another Democratic candidate on the stage, responded to this ageism with the comment, "That someone has a younger body doesn't mean you don't have old ideas." Ironically, her defense was itself an example of the casual ageism that permeates society: "old" is being equated with "outdated." I tweeted about the exchange but was shocked that the issue was not picked up by any major media source until Sanders himself addressed the display of ageism in the debate when talking to reporters the next day. That my teenage sons now perceive ageism in television shows and commercials before I can even point it out gives me a modicum of comfort—perhaps younger generations will not use older people as punchlines and instead recognize how a society that makes fun of older adults ultimately hurts everyone by making the populace scared to death of each birthday past fifty as opposed to grateful for every one we get. I am sincerely hoping the "ok, boomer" put-down is a temporary cultural moment that swiftly exits.

This project reveals several major problems with aging in the United States that must be resolved. The huge disparity in the number of older women and older men living in poverty is profoundly unjust, especially since many women reduced their work hours to care for children and other family members, thereby losing wages, savings, and Social Security earnings. Life expectancy continues to vary by race and ethnicity: minority groups like African American and Native American males live ten to fifteen years less than white and Asian women. Some progress has occurred on this front recently, showing that inequality can be addressed, but it must be prioritized beyond just awareness of the problem. Besides issues of inequality, the conundrum of those seniors who are ready to die but are unable to end their lives is a difficult one that gerontologists need to discuss and try to resolve with input from families and people who have faced that dilemma themselves. We should not have to have random strangers on a plane ask their seatmates how to help someone die, which happened to me one day when I told a fellow passenger that I was writing about aging. He said his mother begs him every day to help her end her life due to severe pain she no longer wants to endure. There are no easy answers here, but we cannot be afraid to confront these realities in our own conversations and in movies and books that depict difficult but significant issues of later life.

My sincere hope is that young people, such as my fourth- and sixth grade nieces, will grow old not dreading the experience but seeing the possibilities and hope for this time of life. I hope they will encounter books, films, art, and television programs that show one's later years as rich and full as earlier decades, despite the many challenges inherent in growing old, and remember that age ultimately is just a number. Above all, I want them to remember that they "have what it takes to survive."

Acknowledgments

This project might never have happened if I did not stumble across Atul Gawande's *Being Mortal* several years ago. Gawande convinced me from the start that as a society we do not talk enough about end-of-life issues and how important it is for people to voice their wishes and understanding regarding their medical conditions and quality of life. He wrote in a way that spoke to people of all different backgrounds and brought in research and stories, both of which were eye-opening in revealing how much there is to learn when personal lives are altered by breakdowns in the body. His book opened the door for me to pay attention to others' stories, particularly the lives of older individuals who have not been given sufficient scholarly focus in the past.

Margaret Cruikshank's *Learning to Be Old* was another book that altered my perception of aging in an unforgettable way. She packed so much scholarship and insight into that text, which I now use in the classroom with my undergraduates. Her willingness to write the foreword to this book is an incredible honor as she continues to be one of the most respected voices in the field of cultural gerontology.

I am thankful for my Gender, Sexuality and Women's Studies students who have studied aging with me in a humanities-based course. They helped by circulating the survey that I used for this project and gave me an opportunity to receive different perspectives on many of the texts that are included in this book, especially *Olive Kitteridge* and *Can't We Talk about Something More Pleasant?* I also appreciated the work of Anne Lochner, a student whose research on nursing homes and assisted living dovetailed with my interest in those subjects.

Many people helped with the survey that brought into the open what older adults had to say in their own words. My mom, Joanne Wagner, a retired family and marital therapist, drew up the first draft and Robert Hall, an independent study student, helped adapt it and used some of the results in his own project on the subject. University of Wisconsin–Milwaukee at Waukesha psychology professor Jill Rinzel helped a tremendous amount with the survey as well—both in making the internal review board process clearer and helping me to put the survey online (and understand the data better). Waukesha YMCA Fitness Director Robyn Pearce was very kind to let me distribute the survey to her exercise classes for seniors. Many colleagues and friends helped with circulating the survey far and wide as the link was shared across the country by people who took the survey themselves or knew of seniors who would. My deepest gratitude to everyone who took the time to fill out a survey as I learned more from reading and rereading those than if I had just stuck to gerontology research. People shared their lives with me, and I hope that I have treated their offerings with due respect.

Speaking of research, I am very fortunate to have the small but mighty staff at my campus library, University of Wisconsin–Milwaukee at Waukesha, who did incredible work for this project over a two-year span. They have found me obscure sources available only through interlibrary loan; they helped me renew some books for a year and half and tracked down articles, even the day after Christmas. Scott Silet, Joyce Bell, Jane Cavanaugh, and J. P. Slater, Kelley Hinton—what would I do without you?

Much of my research took place in the fall of 2017 when I was awarded a University of Wisconsin Colleges sabbatical that helped me sift through hundreds of sources and do some important interviews. Thank you to Dan Anhalt for sharing his experiences with family members who have had Alzheimer's, Andrea Shrednick for insight on aging alone and sexual issues seniors face, and Joan

Williamson for her introduction on Timeslips. Anne Basting, the creative genius behind Timeslips, also generously gave time to answer my questions and allowed me to use an unpublished letter that she wrote to *The New Yorker*. The Bonowitz family was gracious in offering me information about and images of Marvin's piano playing in my chapter on dementia. Laraine O'Brien and Carol Cannon's senior co-housing seminar was an excellent way to learn about that alternative option, and all the lively participants provided much food for thought. During that seminar, I was delighted to meet Susan Cerletty and Joanne Hulce and to learn about intergenerational housing up close. Thank you, too, to Professor Emeritus Michael Hunt for being so responsive to emails about NORCs and for putting me in touch with Ann Albert, who shared wisdom about Elder Villages and NORCs.

As anyone who knows me will attest, I am thrilled that this book is being published by Rutgers University Press, in particular, in its Global Aging Series. The editor of that series, Sarah Lamb, has been such an inspiring advocate of the project from the beginning. Her scholarly work, along with other writers in the series, such as Margaret Morganroth Gullette, is illuminating the topic of age in exciting and original directions. Editorial Director Kimberly Guinta and especially Editorial Assistant Jasper Chang have graciously given their time and support to seeing the publication through to the end. There is not enough cheese in Wisconsin to express my gratitude. I also must thank the anonymous reviewers who made the final manuscript much stronger as a result of their excellent suggestions. Thank you as well to the individuals who helped with reproduction rights for famous art work: Andrea Mihalovic from the Artists Rights Society, Wangui Maina from Metro Pictures, and Jacob Daugherty of Bridgeman Images. You all made this intimidating task a bit less daunting. Sherman Williams from the *Journal Sentinal* was generous in providing the rights to a photograph on senior co-housing that the newspaper had featured. Greg Hyman of Westchester Publishing Services also was a fantastic help throughout the copyediting process.

When I first started researching aging, my dad, who likes to send me articles on topics that I am interested in, was not sure what exactly I was looking for. Soon, articles from *AARP Bulletin*, the *Chicago Tribune*, and even *Hadassah Magazine* were pouring in on everything from age discrimination to Zadoorian's *The Leisure Seeker*. My mother also studied sources carefully and provided good articles from *Generations*, the journal of the American Society for Aging, which were integrated here. Anita Rosenblum, an aunt who is in her nineties, made sure I was aware of articles and books in the *New York Times*, bringing the average age of my research assistants to eighty-six! Many thanks as well to several people who spent time going over these chapters to provide input. My colleagues Jon Kasparek and Tim Dunn were particularly helpful, and I appreciated the astute remarks from my husband, Trevor Huskey, and my mom who read several chapters. Bill Schneider was key to my understanding a somewhat obscure conversation between Cephalus and Socrates about sex and old age. My children, Ethan and Cole Huskey, must be credited with supplying me with *Family Guy* and *BoJack Horseman* episodes that were relevant. They probably are more aware of age-related issues than most young adults since they have let me share this project with them on a regular basis. I will always remember driving my older son back to college and his asking, "Menopause is what again?" My husband, Trevor, also made my life better by not complaining about my endless hours writing, researching, and editing leaving him to watch more *Law and Order* episodes than he may have wanted. I cannot forget my sisters, Lisa Lindenman and Holly Lem, who are always encouraging and positive about accomplishments small and large, and their children, Courtney and Brent Lindenman and Hanna and Lily Lem-Moustakas, the next generation who we can only hope inherit a world where aging is universally appreciated and better understood.

Finally, heart-felt appreciation to all the seniors in my life who made this book feel relevant: my in-laws, Ingrid and Gene Huskey, my father and his wife, Darryl and Iris Lem, and my mom, Joanne Wagner. I wanted to learn about this time in life to help understand what you and people your age may be going through in order to become more sensitive to your daily experiences and appreciate any challenges you may face. The book is dedicated to your persevering ways and your willingness to let me see the world from where you stand. You have my utmost respect and appreciation.

Works Cited

About Schmidt. Directed by Alexander Payne, New Line Cinema, 2002.

Abraham, Roshan. "NYC's Seniors Get Solid Wins in City's Budget." *City Limits Magazine*, June 2019. *EBSCOhost.*

Abrahams, Sally. "An 'LGBT-Welcoming' Place to Call Home." *AARP*, 2016, www.aarp.org/livable-communities/housing/info-2016/age-friendly -LGBT-housing.html.

Adams, Patch. Foreword. *The Senior Cohousing Handbook*, by Charles Durrett. New Society Publishers, 2009, pp. xiii–xiv.

"Age Bias in the Age of the Millennial." *Chicago Tribune*, 4 Mar. 2017, p. 9.

Agronin, Marc. *How We Age: A Doctor's Journey into the Heart of Growing Old.* De Capo Press, 2011.

Albert, Ann. Personal Interview. 20 Aug. 2019.

"All in Together: Creating Places Where Young and Old Thrive." Generations United and Eisner Foundation, 2018, www.gu.org/app/uploads /2018/06/SignatureReport-Eisner-All-In-Together.pdf.

Almond, Steve, and Cheryl Wild. "Sex and Aging with Dr. Pepper Schwartz." *Dear Sugars*, 19 May 2018, www.nytimes.com/2018/05/19 /podcasts/listen-to-dear-sugars-sex-aging-with-dr-pepper-schwartz .html.

"Alzheimer's Disease: Working to Solve the Mystery." *Icahn School of Medicine at Mount Sinai Focus on Healthy Aging*, Feb. 2017, pp. 4–5.

Amour. Directed by Michael Haneke, Les Filmes du Losange, 2012.

Anderson, Hannah, and Matt Daniels. "Film Dialogue." *The Pudding*, Apr. 2016, pudding.cool/2017/03/film-dialogue/.

Andrews, Molly. "The Seduction of Agelessness, Take 2." *Generations*, vol. 41, no. 4, Winter 2017, pp. 75–82.

Anhalt, Dan. Personal Interview. 18 Oct. 2017.

Anspach, Dana. "Average Retirement Age in the United States." *The Balance*, 12 Aug. 2019, www.thebalance.com/average-retirement-age-in -the-united-states-2388864.

Appelo, Tim. "Hollywood Report: No Progress on Diversity." *AARP*, 1 Aug. 2018, www.aarp.org/entertainment/movies-for-grownups/info -2018/hollywood-discrimination-study.html.

Applewhite, Ashton. *This Chair Rocks: A Manifesto against Ageism*. Net-worked Books, 2016.

———. "Working to Disarm Women's Anti-Aging Demon." *The New York Times*, 10 Oct. 2017, www.nytimes.com/2017/10/10/style/women-looks -ageism.html.

Arieff, Allison. "A Housing Crisis for Seniors." *The New York Times*, 29 Jan. 2017, Sunday Review, p. 6.

Armstrong, Sue. *Borrowed Time: The Science of How and Why We Age*. Bloomsbury, 2019.

Arnold, June. *Sister Gin*. 1975. The Feminist Press, 1989.

Aronson, Louise. *Elderhood: Redefining Aging, Transforming Medicine, Reimagining Life*. Bloomsbury, 2019.

———. "Old People Are Not All the Same." *The New York Times*, 13 Aug. 2017, Sunday Review, p. 6.

Athill, Diana. *Somewhere towards the End*. Norton, 2009.

Away from Her. Directed by Sarah Polley, Foundry Films, 2007.

Backman, Fredrik. *A Man Called Ove*. Simon and Schuster, 2014.

Bad Grandpa. Directed by Jeff Tremaine, MTV Films, 2013.

Baker, Beth. *With a Little Help from Our Friends: Creating Community as We Grow Older*. Vanderbilt UP, 2014.

Baker, Lucie, and Eyal Gringart. "Body Image and Self-Esteem in Older Adulthood." *Aging and Society*, vol. 29, no. 6, 2009, pp. 977–995. *EBSCOhost*, doi: 10.1017/S0144686X09008721.

Barron, James. "Age Requirement at Chelsea Art Gallery: Over 60 Only." *The New York Times*, 10 July 2017, p. A20.

Basting, Anne. *Forget Memory*. John Hopkins UP, 2009.

———. Personal interview. 5 Sept. 2018.

————. Unpublished letter to *The New Yorker*. 10 Oct. 2018.

Bayley, John. *Elegy for Iris*. St. Martin's Press, 1998.

Beard, Renee. *Living with Alzheimer's: Managing Memory Loss, Identity, and Illness*. New York UP, 2016.

Beauvoir, Simone de. *La Vieillesse (The Coming of Age)*. 1970. Translated by Patrick O'Brien. Norton, 1996.

Becker, Ernest. *The Denial of Death*. Simon & Schuster, 1973.

Benjamin, Chloe. *The Immortalists*. Putnam, 2018.

Benjamin, Marina. *The Middlepause: On Life after Youth*. Catapult, 2016.

Berthin-Scaillet, Agnes. "A Reading of *Away from Her*, Sarah Polley's Adaptation of Alice Munro's Short Story, 'The Bear Came over the Mountain.'" *Journal of the Short Story in English*, vol. 55, Autumn 2010, pp. 157–171. *EBSCOhost*.

Blaine, Bruce. *Understanding the Psychology of Diversity*. Sage, 2007.

Block, Joel, and Susan Crain Baker. *Sex over 50*. Parker Publishing, 1999.

Blue Jasmine. Directed by Woody Allen, Gravier Productions, 2013.

Bonowitz, Abraham. Personal Interview. 12 Aug. 2018.

Book Club. Directed by Bill Holderman, June Pictures, 2018.

Bouson, J. Brooks. *Shame and the Aging Woman: Confronting and Resisting Ageism in Contemporary Women's Writing*. Palgrave, 2016.

Bredesen, Dale. *The End of Alzheimer's: The First Program to Prevent and Reverse Cognitive Decline*. Penguin, 2017.

"Brian's Got a Brand New Bag." *Family Guy*, season 8, episode 4, Fox, 8 Nov. 2009.

Bribiescas, Richard. *How Men Age: What Evolution Reveals about Male Health and Mortality*. Princeton UP, 2016.

Brody, Jane. "After a Partner Dies, Mourning the Loss of Sex." *The New York Times*, 7 Mar. 2017, p. D7.

————. "How Loneliness Takes a Toll on Our Health." *The New York Times*, 12 Dec. 2017, p. D7.

Brooks, Abigail. *The Ways Women Age: Using and Refusing Cosmetic Intervention*. New York UP, 2017.

Brown, Ian. *Sixty: A Diary of My Sixty-First Year*. Random House Canada, 2016.

Brown, Karen. "Not the Death He Wanted." *The New York Times*, 7 Jan. 2018, Sunday Review, p. 10.

Browne, Collette, et al. "United States Indigenous Populations and
  Dementia: Is There a Case for Psychosocial Interventions?" *The
  Gerontologist*, vol. 57, no. 6, Dec. 2017, pp. 1011–1019. *EBSCOhost*.

Bryden, Christine. *Will I Still Be Me? Finding a Continuing Sense of Self in
  the Lived Experience of Dementia*. Jessica Kingsley Publisher, 2018.

Buckley, Christopher. *Boomsday*. Twelve, 2007.

Buettner, Dan. *Blue Zones*. National Geographic Press, 2009.

"By the Numbers: Older Adults Living Alone." *APA*, vol. 47, no. 5,
  May 2016, www.apa.org/monitor/2016/05/numbers.aspx.

Cagle, Jess. "Jane Fonda at 80: Men, Movies and My Incredible Life."
  People, 1 Oct. 2018, pp. 52–57.

Calasanti, Toni, and Sadie Giles. "The Challenge of Intersectionality."
  Generations, vol. 41, no.4, Winter 2017–2018, pp. 69–74.

Calasanti, Toni, and Kathleen Slevin, editors. *Age Matters: Realigning
  Feminist Thinking*. Routledge, 2006.

———. *Gender, Social Inequalities, and Aging*. AltaMira Press, 2001.

Calhoun, Ada. "The New Midlife Crisis." *Oprah.com*, 6 Oct. 2017, www
  .oprah.com/sp/new-midlife-crisis.html#ixzz4ukN6RTKg.

Carstensen, Laura. *A Long Bright Future*. Broadway Books, 2009.

Castellucci, Maria. "Study: Blacks and Hispanics Report Low-Quality
  Hospice Care." *Modern Healthcare*, vol. 47, no. 28, 10 July 2017, p. 13.
  EBSCOhost.

Cerletty, Susan, and Joanne Hulce. Personal Interview. 8 Jan. 2019.

Chabon, Michael. *Moonglow*. Harper, 2016.

Chast, Roz. *Can't We Talk about Something More Pleasant?* Bloomsbury, 2014.

Cicero, Marcus Tullius. *How to Grow Old*. Translated by Philip Freeman.
  Princeton UP, 2016.

Cohn, D'vera, and Jeffrey Passel. "A Record 64 Million Americans Live in
  Multigenerational Households." *Pew Research Center*, 5 Apr. 2018, www
  .pewresearch.org/fact-tank/2018/04/05/a-record-64-million-americans
  -live-in-multigenerational-households/.

Cole, Thomas, et al., editors. *A Guide to Humanistic Studies in Aging*. John
  Hopkins UP, 2010.

Columbus. Directed by Kogonada, Sundance Institute, 2017.

Condie, Ally. *Matched*. Dutton Juvenile, 2019.

The Conversation Project. 2018, theconversationproject.org.

Coupland, Carol, et al. "Anticholinergic Drug Exposure and the Risk of Dementia: A Nested Case-Control Study." *JAMA Internal Medicine*, vol. 179, no. 8, June 2019, pp. 1084–1093. *Jamanetwork*, doi: 10.1001/jamainternmed.2019.0677.

Crichton, Sarah. "The Coming of Age: Sex 102." *The Bitch Is Back: Older, Wiser, and (Getting) Happier*, edited by Cathi Hanauer. Harper Collins, 2016, pp. 91–103.

Cruikshank, Margaret. *Fierce with Reality: Literature on Aging*. Hamilton Books, 2016.

———. *Learning to Be Old: Gender, Culture, and Aging*. 3rd ed. Rowman and Littlefield, 2013.

Czerwiec, M. K. "Comics and End of Life." *Health and Media Policy*, 25 Sept. 2017, healthmediapolicy.com/2017/09/25/comics-and-end-of-life/.

D'Addario, Daniel. "The 10 Best Shows." *Time*, Dec. 18 2017, pp. 118–119.

Danticat, Edwidge. *The Art of Death: Writing the Final Story*. Graywolf Press, 2017.

"A Daughter Detoxes." *The Kominsky Method*, episode 6, 2018, Netflix.

Davies, Caroline. "Martin Amis in a New Row over 'Euthanasia Booths.'" *The Guardian*, 24 Jan. 2010, www.theguardian.com/books/2010/jan/24/martin-amis-euthanasia-booths-alzheimers.

Davis, Joseph. "No Country for Old Age." *The Hedgehog Review*, Fall 2018, pp. 18–29.

"Dear Reader: What If Youth Wasn't Wasted on the Young?" *The New York Times Magazine*, 3 Sept. 2017, p. 6.

DeLillo, Don. *White Noise*. Penguin, 1999.

———. *Zero K: A Novel*. Scribner, 2017.

"Dementia Stages and Strategies." *Icahn School of Medicine at Mount Sinai Focus on Healthy Aging*, Nov. 2017, p. 7.

Derrick, Julyne. "Relocation Stress Syndrome." *A Place for Mom*, 5 Apr. 2018, www.aplaceformom.com/blog/relocation-stress-syndrome/.

Didion, Joan. *Blue Nights*. Vintage, 2011.

———. *The Year of Magical Thinking*. Knopf, 2005.

Drabble, Margaret. *The Dark Flood Rises*. Farrar, Straus and Giroux, 2016.

Dreifus, Claudia. "Asked about Retiring, They Have Simple Answer 'Why'?" *The New York Times*, 16 Dec. 2017, www.nytimes.com/2017/12/16/business/asked-about-retiring-they-have-a-simple-answer-why.html.

Durrett, Charles. *The Senior Cohousing Handbook*. New Society Publishers, 2009.

Durrett, Charles, and Jean Nilsson. *Senior Cohousing Workshop Participant Guide*. McCamant & Durrett, 2013.

Dusenbery, Maya. *Doing Harm: The Truth about How Bad Medicine and Lazy Science Leave Women Dismissed, Misdiagnosed, and Sick*. Harper-Collins, 2018.

Egan, Jennifer. *Manhattan Beach*. Scribner's, 2017.

Ehrenreich, Barbara. *Natural Causes: An Epidemic of Wellness, the Certainty of Dying, and Killing Ourselves to Live Longer*. Hachette, 2018.

Enough Said. Directed by Nicole Holofcener, Fox Searchlight Pictures, 2013.

Ephron, Nora. *I Feel Bad about My Neck and Other Thoughts on Being a Woman*. Knopf, 2006.

———. *I Remember Nothing*. Knopf, 2010.

Epstein, Randi. "Menopausal Vaginal Monologues." *The New York Times*, 4 Sept. 2018, p. D4.

Esmonde-White, Miranda. *Aging Backwards: Reversing the Aging Process and Look Ten Years Younger in Thirty Minutes a Day*. Harper Wave, 2014.

Fagan, Frank. "The Village of Hogewey." *Canadian Nursing Home*, vol. 25, no. 2, June/July 2014, pp. 28–31.

Faludi, Susan. *In the Darkroom*. Metropolitan Books, 2016.

The Farewell Party. Directed by Tal Granit and Sharon Maymom, 2-Team Productions, 2014.

Farmer, Joyce. *Special Exits*. Fantagraphics, 2010.

Feinstein, Elaine. *Talking to the Dead*. Carcanet, 2007.

Ford, Richard. *Let Me Be Frank with You*. Harper Collins, 2014.

Forty-Five Years. Directed by Andrew Haigh, Film4 Productions, 2015.

Fox, Lauren. *Days of Awe*. Knopf, 2015.

Frakt, Austin. "With Age Comes Wisdom. Misconceptions, Too." *The New York Times*, 25 Dec. 2018, p. B3.

Freeman, Mary Wilkens. *A Humble Romance and Other Stories*. Harper, 1915.

Friedan, Betty. *The Fountain of Age*. Simon and Schuster, 1993.

Friend, Tad. "Why Ageism Never Gets Old." *The New Yorker*, 20 Nov. 2017, www.newyorker.com/magazine/2017/11/20/why-ageism-never-gets-old.

Frueh, Joanna. "Visible Difference: Women Artists and Aging." *The Other*

within Us: Feminists Explorations of Women and Aging, edited by
Marilyn Pearsall. Westview, 1997, pp. 197–219.

Garland, Susan. "Aging Alone? Here's How to Plan for the Later Years."
The New York Times, 25 Mar. 2018, p. BU5.

Garner, Helen. "The Insults of Age." *The Monthly*, May 2015, www.the
monthly.com.au/issue/2015/may/1430402400/helen-garner/insults
-age.

Gawande, Atul. *Being Mortal*. Metropolitan Books, 2014.

Geewax, Marilyn. "Preparing for a Future that Includes Aging Parents."
NPR, 24 Apr. 2012, www.npr.org/2012/04/24/150587638/preparing-for-a
-future-that-includes-aging-parents.

Gen Silent. Directed by Stu Maddux, Interrobang Productions, 2010.

Gerber, Sara Zeff. "Solo Agers: A Challenge to Individuals and Society."
Aging and Society: Seventh Interdisciplinary Conference. 3 Nov. 2017.
Berkeley, CA.

Gilbert, Matthew. "The Worst Sitcom on TV? We Have a Winner."
The Boston Globe, 10 Oct. 2018, www.bostonglobe.com/arts/2018/10/10/the
-worst-sitcom-have-winner/dhVSCrTUv4Y5wMMXa8838H/story.html.

Gillick, Muriel. *Old and Sick in America: The Journey through the Health Care
System*. U of North Carolina P, 2017.

Glass, Annie. "Why Aging in Community?" Durrett, pp. 255–272.

Godwin, Gail. "Losing Ground." *Aging: An Apprenticeship*, edited by Nan
Narboe. Red Notebook Press, 2017, pp. 202–211.

Golant, Stephen. *Aging in the Right Place*. Health Professions Press, 2015.

Golden, Marita. *The Wide Circumference of Love*. Simon and Schuster, 2017.

Goldman, Marlene, and Sarah Powell. "Alzheimer's, Ambiguity, and Irony:
Alice Munro's 'The Bear Came over the Mountain' and Sarah Polley's
Away from Her." *Canadian Literature*, vol. 225, Summer 2015, pp. 82–99.
EBSCOhost.

Gonyea, Judith, and Kelly Melekis. "Women's Housing Challenges in
Later Life: The Importance of the Gender Lens." *Generations*, vol. 41,
no. 4, Winter 2017, pp. 45–53.

Gordon, Emily Fox. "At Sixty-Five." *The American Scholar*, 10 June 2013,
theamericanscholar.org/at-sixty-five/#.XCJVPVVKgdU.

Gorton, Kristyn. "'I'm Too Old to Pretend Anymore': Desire, Ageing and
Last Tango in Halifax." *Serializing Age: Aging and Old Age in TV Series*,

edited by Maricel Oro-Piqueras and Anita Wohlmann, Transcript, 2016, pp. 231–247.

Graham, Judith. "Power of a Sense of Purpose." *Chicago Tribune*, 7 Sept. 2017, sec. 5, p. 1.

Grandma. Directed by Paul Weitz, Sony Pictures Classic, 2015.

Graydon, Shari, editor. *I Feel Great about My Hands and Other Unexpected Joys of Aging*. Douglas & McIntyre, 2011.

Greer, Germaine. Afterword. *Ageing Women in Literature and Visual Culture*, edited by Cathy McGlynn et al. Palgrave, 2017, pp. 321–325.

Grigoriadis, Vanessa. "A Death of One's Own." *New York Magazine*, 8 Sept. 2003, nymag.com/nymetro/news/people/n_9589/index2.html.

Groen, Hendrik. *On the Bright Side: The New Secret Diary of Hendrik Groen*. 2017. Translated by Hester Velmans. Grand Central Publishing, 2019.

———. *The Secret Diary of Hendrik Groen, 83 ¼ Years Old*. 2014. Translated by Hester Velmans. Grand Central Publishing, 2017.

Grumbach, Doris. *Coming into the End Zone*. Norton, 1993.

Gubar, Susan. *Late-Life Love*. Norton, 2019.

Gullette, Margaret Morganroth. *Aged by Culture*. U of Chicago P, 2004.

———. "Ageism and Social Change." Cole et al., pp. 314–340.

———. *Agewise: Fighting the New Ageism in America*. U of Chicago P, 2011.

———. *Declining to Decline*. UP of Virginia, 1997.

———. *Ending Ageism, or How Not to Shoot Old People*. Rutgers UP, 2017.

Haines, Krista, et al. "Barriers to Hospice Care in Trauma Patients: The Disparities in End-of-Life Care." *American Journal of Hospice and Palliative Medicine*, vol. 35, no. 8, Aug. 2018, pp. 1081–1084. ncbi.nlm .nih.gov/pubmed/29361829.

Hall, Donald. "Death." *Essays after Eighty*. Houghton Mifflin Harcourt, 2014, pp. 89–97.

———. "Fucking." *A Carnival of Losses: Notes Nearing Ninety*. Houghton Mifflin Harcourt, 2018, p. 181.

Halliday, Lisa. *Asymmetry*. Henry Holt, 2017.

Hanauer, Cathi, editor. *The Bitch Is Back: Older, Wiser, and (Getting) Happier*. Harper Collins, 2016.

Hanc, John. "Longer and Better." *The New York Times*, 5 Mar. 2017, p. F4.

Hannon, Kerry. "Reaping the Benefits of an Aging Work Force." *The New York Times*, 4 March 2018, p. F7.

Harrington, C. Lee, et al., editors. *Aging, Media, and Culture*. Lexington
   Books, 2014.

Harris, Elizabeth. "Think Saving for Old Age Can't Be Fun?" *The New
   York Times*, 3 Nov. 2018, www.nytimes.com/2018/11/03/business/saving
   -retirement-games.html.

Harris, James C. "Lucian Freud's *Reflection (Self Portrait)*." *JAMA Psychiatry*,
   vol. 70, no. 5, May 2013, pp. 455–456.

Haruf, Kent. *Our Souls at Night*. Knopf, 2015.

Heid, Markham. "Alzheimer's: A Tutorial." *TIME: The Science of Alzheimer's*,
   edited by Jeffrey Kluger. Time Books, 2018, pp. 9–13.

Heilbrun, Carolyn. *The Last Gift of Time: Life beyond Sixty*. Dial Press, 1997.

Hepworth, Mike. *Stories of Ageing*. Open University Press, 2000.

The Hero. Directed by Brett Haley, The Orchard, 2017.

Herrera, José Rodriguez. "*Away from Her?* Sarah Polley's Screen Adapta-
   tion of Alice Munro's 'The Bear Came over the Mountain.'" *Brno
   Studies in English*, vol. 39, no. 2, 2013, pp. 107–121. *Academic Search
   Complete*, doi: 10.5817/BSE2013-2-7.

Heyman, Arlene. *Scary Old Sex*. Bloomsbury, 2016.

Hollander, Nicole. *Tales of Graceful Aging from the Planet Denial*. Thorndike
   Press, 2007.

Holmes, Tamara. "How to Plan for the Care of Your Aging Parents." *USA
   Today*, 26 Mar. 2018, p. 3B.

Holstein, Martha. *Women in Late Life: Critical Perspectives on Gender and
   Age*. Rowman and Littlefield, 2015.

"The Home." *Grace and Frankie*, season 4, episode 13, 19 Jan. 2018, Netflix.

Huddleston, Cameron. "Baby Boomers Are Giving Thousands to Their
   Millennial Children Each Year." *Pittsburgh Post-Gazette*, 2 Mar 2017,
   post-gazette.com/aging-edge/aging-edge-reports/2017/03/02/How
   -baby-boomers-are-losing-11-000-a-year-to-their-millennial-children
   /stories/201703020194.

Hulko, Wendy, et al. "Views of First Nation Elders on Memory Loss and
   Memory Care in Later Life." *Journal of Cross Cultural Gerontology*,
   1 Dec. 2010, pp. 317–342. *EBSCOhost*, doi: 10.1007/s10823-010-9130-x.

Hunt, Michael, and Gail Gunter-Hunt. "Naturally Occurring Retirement
   Communities." *Journal of Housing for the Elderly*, vol. 3–4, Fall/Winter
   1985, pp. 3–21.

———. "Re: NORCS." Received by Ellyn Lem, 18 June 2018.

Hurston, Zora Neale. *Barracoon: The Story of the Last "Black Cargo."* HarperCollins, 2018.

Ianzito, Christina. "My Surprising New Friend." *AARP Bulletin*, July/Aug. 2018, p. 30.

Illing, Sean. "Scientists Are Waging a War against Aging. But What Happens Next?" *Vox*, 6 May 2017, vox.com/conversations/2017/5/4/15433348/aubrey-de-grey-life-extension-aging-death-science-medicine.

The Intern. Directed by Nancy Meyers, Warner Bros., 2015.

Iris. Directed by Richard Eyre, BBC, 2001.

Jacoby, Susan. *Never Say Die: The Myth and Marketing of the New Old Age.* Vintage, 2012.

———. "We're Aging Fast, and Not Doing Anything about It." *The New York Times*, 26 Dec. 2019, p. A25.

Jamieson, Sara. "Reading the Spaces of Age in Alice Munro's 'The Bear Came over the Mountain.'" *Mosaic*, vol. 47, no. 3, Sept. 2014, pp. 1–17. *Project MUSE*, doi: 10.1353/mos.2014.0035.

Jen, Gish. "No More Maybe." *The New Yorker*, 19 Mar. 2018, pp. 77–83.

———. "The Third Dumpster." *Living in the Land of Limbo: Fiction and Poetry about Family Caregiving*, edited by Carol Levine. Vanderbilt UP, 2014, pp. 28–34.

Jenkins, Jo Ann. *Disrupt Aging*. Public Affairs, 2016.

Johnson, Claire. "My Filthy Little Heart. Love It? Or Lose It?" Hanauer, pp. 115–128.

Johnson, Mark. "Family Helps Senior Living Alone Stay Engaged." *The Milwaukee Journal Sentinel*, 20 Dec. 2015, p. 7A.

———. "Solo in Their Twilight Years." *The Milwaukee Journal*, 20 Dec. 2015, pp. 1A+.

Joint Center for Housing Studies. "Housing America's Older Adults." Harvard University, 2014, www.nado.org/wp-content/uploads/2014/09/Harvard-Housing-Americas-Older-Adults-2014.pdf.

Jonasson, Jonas. *The 100-Year-Old Man Who Climbed Out the Window and Disappeared*. Translated by Rod Bradbury. HarperCollins, 2012.

Jong, Erica. *Fear of Dying*. St. Martin's Press, 2015.

Jordan, Mary, and Kevin Sullivan. "The New Reality of Old Age in

America." *The Washington Post*, 30 Sept. 2017, washingtonpost.com
/graphics/2017/national/seniors-financial-insecurity/.

Kagan, Shelly. *Death*. Yale UP, 2012.

Karpf, Anne. *How to Age*. Picador, 2014.

Kenen, Regina. "After the Frogs and Princes Are Gone: Widows and the
Uncertainty in Current American Society." Aging and Society:
Seventh Interdisciplinary Conference. 3 Nov. 2017. Berkeley, CA.

Khong, Rachel. *Goodbye, Vitamin*. Henry Holt, 2017.

King, Jeannette. *Discourses of Ageing in Fiction and Feminism: The Invisible
Woman*. Palgrave, 2013.

King, Neal, and Toni Calasanti. "Men's Aging Amidst Intersecting Relations
of Inequality." *Sociology Compass*, vol. 7, no. 9, 2013, pp. 699–710.

Kinsley, Michael. *Old Age: A Beginner's Guide*. Tim Duggan Books, 2016.

Kluger, Jeffrey. "The Disease that Steals the Self." *TIME: The Science of
Alzheimer's*, edited by Jeffrey Kluger. Time Books, 2018, pp. 4–5.

———, editor. *TIME: The Science of Alzheimer's*, Time Books, 2018.

Knisley, Lucy. *Displacement: A Travelogue*. Fantagraphics, 2015.

Kolata, Gina. "More Americans Are Dying at Home Than in Hospitals."
The New York Times, 11 Dec. 2019, www.nytimes.com/2019/12/11/health
/death-hospitals-home.html.

Kozol, Jonathan. *The Theft of Memory: Losing My Father, One Day at a Time*.
Broadway Books, 2015.

Kritz, Fran. "The Alzheimer's Café." *Neurology Now*, Aug./Sept. 2016, pp. 8–9.

La Gorce, Tammy. "When Your Parents Remarry, Everyone Is Happy,
Right?" *The New York Times*, 22 Mar. 2018, www.nytimes.com/2018/03
/22/your-money/parents-remarry-inheritance-children.html.

Lamb, Sarah. "Beyond the View of the West: Ageing and Anthropology."
The Routledge Handbook of Cultural Gerontology, edited by Julia Twigg
and Wendy Martin. Routledge, 2015, pp. 37–42.

———, editor. *Successful Aging as a Contemporary Obsession: Global
Perspectives*. Rutgers UP, 2017.

Larson, Eric B., and Joan DeClaire. *Enlightened Aging: Building Resilience
for a Long, Active Life*. Rowman and Littlefield, 2017.

Lasalle, Mick. "'Enough Said' Review: Macabre Twist to Romance." *The
San Francisco Chronicle*, 26 Sept. 2013, www.sfgate.com/movies/article
/Enough-Said-review-Macabre-twist-to-romance-4846257.php.

———. "Michelle Pfeifer, Seen from a Distance, Gives Everything to 'Where Is Kyra?'" *The San Francisco Chronicle*, 12 Apr. 2018, www .sfchronicle.com/movies/article/Michelle-Pfeiffer-seen-from-a -distance-gives-12829415.php.

"The Last Acceptable Prejudice?" *AARP Magazine*, Oct./Nov. 2018, p. 4.

Le Guin, Ursula. "Space Crone." *Oxford Book of Aging*, edited by Thomas Cole and Mary Winkler. Oxford UP, 1994, pp. 71–74.

The Leisure Seeker. Directed by Paolo Virzi, Sony, 2017.

Leland, John. *Happiness Is a Choice You Make: Lessons from a Year among the Oldest Old*. Sarah Crichton Books, 2018.

Lewis, C. S. *A Grief Observed*. HarperCollins, 1961.

Lively, Penelope. *Dancing Fish and Ammonites*. Viking, 2013.

Loe, Meika. *Aging Our Way: Lessons for Living from 85 and Beyond*. Oxford UP, 2011.

———. *The Rise of Viagra*. New York UP, 2004.

Loh, Sandra Tsing. "Daddy Issues." *The Atlantic*, Mar. 2012, www.theatlantic .com/magazine/archive/2012/03/daddy-issues/308890/.

———. *The Madwoman in the Volvo*. Norton, 2014.

Lonergan, Kenneth. *The Waverly Gallery*. Grove Press, 2000.

Louis, Catherine Saint. "When Families Fall Out." *The New York Times*, 26 Dec. 2017, pp. D1+.

Lucky. Directed by John Carroll Lynch, Magnolia Pictures, 2017.

Lyall, Sarah. "One Last Thing for Mom." *The New York Times*, 2 Sept. 2018, Sunday Review, pp. 3+.

Macdonald, Barbara. *Look Me in the Eye*. Spinsters Ink Books, 2001.

MacFarquhar, Larissa. "The Memory House." *The New Yorker*, 8 Oct. 2018, pp. 42–55.

Macmillian, Amanda. "Why Being Single Is Less of an Alzheimer's Risk than It Used to Be." *TIME: The Science of Alzheimer's*, edited by Jeffrey Kluger. Time Books, 2018, p. 62.

March, Anna. "Gone Girl: What I (Don't) Owe My Mother." Hanauer, pp. 25–36.

"Marital Status of the US Population in 2017." *Statista*, 2018, www.statista .com/statistics/242030/marital-status-of-the-us-population-by-sex/.

Marshall, Barbara L. "Sexualizing the Third Age." *Aging, Media, and*

Culture, edited by C. Lee Harrington et al. Lexington Books, 2014, pp. 169–180.

Marshall, Leni. *Age Becomes Us: Bodies and Gender in Time.* State University of New York P, 2015.

———. "Thinking Differently about Aging: Changing Attitudes through the Humanities." *The Gerontologist*, vol. 65, no. 4, Aug. 2015, pp. 519–525. doi: 10.1093/geront/gnu069.

Marshall, Leni, and Aagie Swinnen. "'Let's Do It like Grown-Ups': A Filmic *Ménage* of Age, Gender, and Sexuality." Harrington et al., pp. 157–168.

Masotti, Paul, et al. "Healthy Naturally Occurring Retirement Communities: A Low-Cost Approach to Facilitating Healthy Aging." *American Journal of Public Health*, vol. 96, no. 7, July 2006, pp. 1164–1176, ncbi .nlm.nih.gov/pmc/articles/PMC1483864/.

Maxmen, Amy. "Questionable 'Young Blood' Transfusions Offered in the U.S. as Anti-Aging Remedy." *MIT Technology Review*, 13 Jan. 2007, www.technologyreview.com/s/603242/questionable-young-blood -transfusions-offered-in-us-as-anti-aging-remedy/.

McCann, Colum. *Thirteen Ways of Looking.* Random House, 2015.

McCullough, Dennis. *My Mother, Your Mother: Embracing 'Slow Medicine,' The Compassionate Approach to Caring for Your Aged Loved Ones.* Harper, 2008.

McGill, Robert. "No Nation but Adaptation: 'The Bear Came over the Mountain,' *Away from Her*, and What It Means to Be Faithful." *Canadian Literature*, vol. 197, Spring 2008, pp. 98–111. *EBSCOhost.*

McGlynn, Cathy, et al., editors. *Ageing Women in Literature and Visual Culture.* Palgrave, 2017.

McMurtry, Larry. *Terms of Endearment.* Simon and Schuster, 1975.

Meadows, Robert, and Kate Davidson. "Maintaining Manliness in Later Life." Calasanti and Slevin, pp. 295–312.

Meeuf, Russell. *Rebellious Bodies, Stardom, Citizenship and the New Body Politic.* U of Texas P, 2017.

Meier, Emily, et al. "Discussing a 'Good Death' with Patients." *Today's Geriatric Medicine*, Sept./Oct. 2016: 8–10, www.todaysgeriatricmedicine .com/archive/SO16p8.shtml.

"Men and Heart Disease." *Center for Disease Control*, 30 July 2019, www
.cdc.gov/heartdisease/men.htm.

The Meyerowitz Stories (New and Selected). Directed by Noah Baumbach,
IAC Films, 2017.

Miller, Jen. "The Parents around the Corner." *The New York Times*, 6 May
2018, p. 10.

Miller, William Ian. *Losing It*. Yale UP, 2011.

"Mom's the Word." *Family Guy*, season 12, episode 12, Fox, 9 Mar. 2014.

Moody, Rick. "Whosoever: The Language of Mothers and Sons." *Living
in the Land of Limbo: Fiction and Poetry about Family Caregiving*, edited
by Carol Levine. Vanderbilt UP, 2014, pp. 19–27.

Morales, Laurel. "Alzheimer's Underdiagnosed in Indian Country." *New
Hampshire Public Radio*, 28 Dec. 2015, www.nhpr.org/post/alzheimers
-disease-underdiagnosed-indian-country#stream/o.

"More Businesses Recruit and Hire Older Workers." *AARP Bulletin*,
Oct. 2017, p. 6.

Morris, Virigina. *How to Care for Aging Parents*. Workman, 2004.

Munro, Alice. "The Bear Came over the Mountain." *Family Furnishings:
Selected Stories 1995–2014*. Vintage, 2014, pp. 267–306.

Nevins, Sheila. *You Don't Look Your Age and Other Fairy Tales*. Flatiron
Books, 2017.

Nochlin, Linda. "Old Age/Old Age Style: Late Louise Bourgeois." *Louise
Bourgeois*, edited by Frances Morries. Rizzoli, 2008, pp. 188–196.

Nolan, William, and George Clayton Johnson. *Logan's Run*. Dial Press, 1967.

Norman, Abby. *Ask Me about My Uterus*. Nation Books, 2018.

Nuland, Sherwin B. *How We Die: Reflections on Life's Final Chapter*.
Vintage Books, 1995.

Nussbaum, Martha, and Saul Levmore. *Aging Thoughtfully: Conversations
about Retirement, Romance, Wrinkles and Regret*. Oxford UP, 2017.

Oaklander, Mandy. "Our Bodies, Our Selves." *TIME: The Science of
Alzheimer's*, edited by Jeffrey Kluger. Time Books, 2018, pp. 40–45.

Olive Kitteridge. Directed by Lisa Cholodenko, HBO, 2014.

Olson, Elizabeth. "Proof Is Elusive in Age Bias Cases." *The New York
Times*, 8 Aug. 2017, pp. B1+.

———."Swindlers Target Older Women on Dating Sites." *The New York*

Times, 25 July 2015, www.nytimes.com/2015/07/18/your-money/swindlers
-target-older-women-on-dating-websites.html.

O'Nan, Stewart. *Emily, Alone*. Viking, 2011.

Our Souls at Night. Directed by Ritesh Batra, Netflix, 2017.

Park, Alice. "Alzheimer's from a New Angle." *TIME: The Science of Alzheimer's*, edited by Jeffrey Kluger. Time Books, 2018, pp. 78–85.

Pausch, Randy, and Jeffrey Zaslow. *The Last Lecture*. Hyperion, 2008.

Pearson, Allison. *How Hard Can It Be?* HarperCollins, 2017.

Perry, Michael. *Montaigne in Barn Boots*. HarperCollins, 2017.

"Phil." *Better Things*, season 2, episode 5, 12 Oct. 2017, FX.

Phillips, Michael. "'The Intern' Plays like 'Driving Miss Texty.'" *The American Statesman*, 24 Sept. 2015, movies.blog.austin360.com/2015/09
/24/the-intern-plays-like-driving-miss-texty-our-grade-b/.

Pidd, Helen. "Sexual Activity Survey Debunks Myths Concerning Lives of Older People." *The Guardian*, 28 Jan. 2015, www.theguardian.com/uk
-news/2015/jan/28/older-sexual-activity-ageing-survey-manchester.

Pipher, Mary. "The Joy of Being a Woman in Her 70s." *The New York Times*, 13 Jan. 2019, Sunday Review, p. 10.

———. *Women Rowing North: Navigating Life's Currents and Flourishing as We Age*. Bloomsbury, 2019.

Pollan, Michael. *How to Change Your Mind*. Penguin, 2018.

Poniewozik, James. "The Best Shows of 2019." *The New York Times*, 2 Dec. 2019, www.nytimes.com/2019/12/02/arts/television/best-tv
-shows.html.

Poo, Ai-Jen. *Age of Dignity*. New Press, 2015.

Pour, Tara Bahram. "Promise You'll Never Put Me in a Nursing Home." *The Washington Post*, 8 Feb. 2016, www.washingtonpost.com/local/social
-issues/promise-youll-never-put-me-in-a-nursing-home/2016/02/08
/1ce8737c-cb62-11e5-a7b2-5a2f824b02c9_story.html.

Powers, Richard. *The Overstory*. Norton, 2018.

Rabin, Roni Caryn. "Mixed Results for Testosterone." *The New York Times*, 28 Mar. 2017, p. D4.

Ran. Directed by Akira Kurosawa, Nippon Herald Films, 1985.

Rau, Jordan. "Nursing Homes Routinely Mask Low Staff Levels." *The New York Times*, 8 July 2018, pp. 1+.

Rauch, Jonathan. *The Happiness Curve: Why Life Gets Better after 50*.
St. Martin's Press, 2018.

Reichert, Amy. *The Optimist's Guide to Letting Go*. Simon and Schuster, 2018.

Respini, Eva. *Cindy Sherman*. Museum of Modern Art, 2012.

"The Return of the Multi-Generational Family." *Pew Research Center*, 18
Mar. 2010, www.pewsocialtrends.org/2010/03/18/the-return-of-the
-multi-generational-family-household/.

Rhodes, Linda. *Should Mom Be Left Alone?* New American Library, 2005.

Riggs, Ransom. *Miss Peregrine's Home for Peculiar Children*. Quirk Books,
2011.

Rikleen, Lauren. "Older Women Are Being Forced Out of the Workforce." *Harvard Business Review*, 10 Mar. 2016, hbr.org/2016/03/older
-women-are-being-forced-out-of-the-workforce.

Rix, Sara. "Boomers Sail into Retirement—Or Do They?" *Public Policy and
Aging Report*, vol. 21, no. 1, Winter 2011, pp. 34–38, www
.seniorserviceamerica.org/resources/employment/.

Rukeyser, Muriel. *The Speed of Darkness*. Random House, 1968.

Saline, Carol. "Sex at Any Age." *Hadassah Magazine*, July/Aug. 2018,
pp. 32–34.

Salter, Jessica. "Artists Impose Own Likeness on Royal Portraits." *The
Telegraph*, 7 Sept. 2008, www.telegraph.co.uk/news/uknews/2700824
/Artists-impose-own-likeness-on-royal-portraits.html.

Santlofer, Jonathan. *A Widower's Notebook: A Memoir*. Penguin, 2018.

Sarton, May. *Endgame: A Journal of the Seventy-Ninth Year*. Norton, 1992.

Scharlach, Andrew. "Creating Aging Friendly Communities: From Theory
to Practice." Aging and Society: Seventh Interdisciplinary Conference.
3 Nov. 2017. Berkeley, CA.

Schreiber, Martin. *My Two Elaines*. Book Publishers Network, 2017.

Schuetze, Christopher. "Take a Look at These Unusual Strategies for
Fighting Dementia." *The New York Times*, 22 Aug. 2018, www.nytimes
.com/2018/08/22/world/europe/dementia-care-treatment-symptoms
-signs.html.

Segal, Lynn. *Out of Time: The Pleasures and Perils of Ageing*. Verso, 2014.

Sehgal, Parul. "Cindy Sherman Turns the Instagram Selfie Inside Out."
The New York Times Magazine, 5 Oct. 2018, pp. 62–69.

Serano, Julia. *Whipping Girl*. Seal Press, 2016.

Shakespeare, William. *The Tragedy of King Lear*. 1623. Folger Shakespeare Library. Simon and Schuster, 1993.

Shrednick, Andrea. Personal Interview. 8 Dec. 2017.

Sichelman, Lew. "Seniors Who Want to Stay in Longtime Homes Need to Plan Ahead." *Chicago Tribune*, 1 Dec. 2016, www.chicagotribune.com /classified/realestate/ct-housing-market-seniors-stay-longtime-homes -plan-ahead-20161201-story.html.

Simon, Scott. "Isolated and Struggling, Many Seniors Are Turning to Suicide." *NPR*, 27 July 2019, www.npr.org/2019/07/27/745017374/isolated -and-struggling-many-seniors-are-turning-to-suicide.

Simonson, Helen. *Major Pettigrew's Last Stand*. Allen and Unwin, 2014.

Slaughter, Anne-Marie. *Unfinished Business: Women Men Work Family*. Random House, 2015.

Smiley, Jane. *A Thousand Acres*. Knopf, 1991.

Smith, Ali. *Autumn*. Anchor Books, 2017.

Smith, Stacy, et al. "Seniors on the Small Screen." *Media, Diversity, and Social Change Initiative*, 2017, assets.uscannenberg.org/docs/Seniors_on _the_Small_Screen-Dr_Stacy_L_Smith_9-12-17.pdf.

Snapes, Laura. "Too Few Films about Older Women and Sex? Thank Heaven for *Book Club*." *The Guardian*, 31 May 2018, www.theguardian .com/film/2018/may/31/too-few-films-about-older-women-and-sex-thank -heavens-for-book-club.

Sommer, Jeff. "A Good Reason for Women to Retire Later." *The New York Times*, 8 July 2018, Business, p. 4.

Span, Paula. "Aging Parents' Willfulness May Be 'Mismatched Goals.'" *The New York Times*, 3 Sept. 2019, p. D5.

———. "A Better Kind of Nursing Home." *The New York Times*, 22 Dec. 2017, www.nytimes.com/2017/12/22/health/green-houses-nursing -homes.html.

———. "A Child's Death Brings 'Trauma that Doesn't Go Away.'" *The New York Times* 29 Sept. 2017, www.nytimes.com/2017/09/29/health /children-death-elderly-grief.html.

———. "How to Age in Place? Plan Ahead." *The New York Times*, 19 May 2017, p. D5.

———. "More Seniors Shun Marriage." *The New York Times*, 9 May 2017, p. D3.

————. "A Scan May Predict Alzheimer's. Should You Get One?" *The New York Times*, 6 Aug. 2019, p. D3.

————. "When Retirement Doesn't Quite Work Out." *The New York Times*, 4 Mar. 2018, p. D5.

Spiegelman, Art. *Maus*. Pantheon, 1996.

Starnone, Domenico. *Trick*. Translated by Jhumpa Lahiri. Europa Editions, 2016.

Steinke, Darcey. *Flash Count Diary: Menopause and the Vindication of Natural Life*. Sara Crichton Books, 2019.

Still Doing It: Intimate Lives of Women over 65. Directed by Deidre Fishel, Mind's Eye Productions, 2004.

Stoecker, Randy. "Elders in Society: Burden or Boon?" Aging and Society: Seventh Interdisciplinary Conference. 4 Nov. 2017. Berkeley, CA

Stoller, Silvia, editor. *Simone de Beauvoir's Philosophy of Age: Gender, Ethics and Time*. De Gruyter, 2014.

Stowe, James, and Teresa Cooney. "Examining Rowe and Kahn's Concept of Successful Aging: Importance of Taking a Life Course Perspective." *The Gerontologist*, vol. 55, no. 1, Feb. 2015, pp. 43–50. *Academic Search Complete*, doi: 10.1093/geront/gnu055.

Strout, Elizabeth. *Anything Is Possible*. Random House, 2017.

————. *Olive Kitteridge*. Random House, 2008.

"Study: Seniors' Relationship with Adult Children Influences Dementia Risk." *Massachusetts General Hospital Mind, Mood and Memory Newsletter*, July 2017, p. 2.

Swanson, Emily, and Ricardo Alonso-Zaldivar. "AP-NORC Poll: Adult Caregivers Overwhelmed and Undertrained." *Associated Press*, 5 Oct. 2017, www.apnorc.org/news-media/Pages/AP-NORC-Poll-Adult-caregivers -overwhelmed-and-undertrained.aspx.

Swartz, Aimee. "James Fries: Healthy Aging Pioneer." *American Journal of Public Health*, July 2008, ncbi.nlm.nih.gov/pmc/articles/PMC2424092/.

Swinnen, Aagje. "Reading Ageism in 'Geezer and Grump Lit': Responses to *The Secret Diary of Hendrik Groen, 83 ¼*." *Journal of Aging Studies*, vol. 50, Sept. 2019, pp. 1–10. *Academic Search Complete*, doi: 10.1016/j. jaging.2019.100794.

Taylor, Richard. *Alzheimer's from the Inside Out*. Health Professions Press, 2007.

Tavernise, Sabrina. "Centenarians Proliferate and Liver Longer." *The New York Times*, 21 Jan. 2016, www.nytimes.com/2016/01/21/health /centenarians-proliferate-and-live-longer.html.

Terrell, Kenneth. "What You Need to Know about America's Nursing Homes." *AARP Bulletin*, Nov. 2017, pp. 14–15.

Thomas, Kathy. "Dirty Work." Hanauer, pp. 75–87.

"Time's Arrow." *BoJack Horseman*, season 4, episode 11, 8 Sept. 2017, Netflix.

Tisdale, Sallie. *Advice for Future Corpses: A Practical Perspective on Death and Dying*. Simon and Schuster, 2018.

Toews, Miriam. *All My Puny Sorrows*. Knopf, 2014.

Trainwreck. Directed by Judd Apatow, Universal Pictures, 2015.

Trieschmann, Catherine. *One House Over*. Directed by Mark Clements, The Milwaukee Rep, 25 Mar. 2018, Milwaukee.

Trollope, Anthony. *The Fixed Period*. 1882. Oxford UP, 1993.

Turner, Kathleen M. "The Betty White Moment: The Rhetoric of Constructing Aging and Sexuality." *Aging Heroes: Growing Old in Popular Culture*, edited by Norma Jones and Bob Batchelor. Rowman and Littlefield, 2015, pp. 211–221.

Twigg, Julia. *Fashion and Age: Dress, the Body and Later Life*. Bloomsbury, 2013.

Twigg, Julia, and Wendy Martin. "The Challenge of Cultural Gerontology." *The Gerontologist*, vol. 55, no. 3, June 2015, pp. 353–359. *Academic Search Complete*, doi: 10.1093/geront/gnu061.

Urrea, Luis. *The House of Broken Angels*. Little, Brown, and Company, 2018.

Wallace, Steven, and Valentine Villa. "Women: A Demographic Lens." *Generations*, vol. 41, no. 4, 2017–2018, pp. 12–19.

Wang, Penelope. "Who Will Care for You?" *Consumer Reports*, Oct. 2017, pp. 28–39.

Waxman, Barbara. "Literary Texts and Literary Critics Team Up against Ageism." Cole et al., pp. 83–104.

Wentzell, Emily. "Erectile Dysfunction as Successful Aging in Mexico." Lamb, pp. 68–81.

Where Is Kyra? Directed by Andrew Dosunmu, Great Point Media, 2017.

Wickersham, Joan. "The Tunnel, or The News from Spain." *Best American Short Stories 2013*, edited by Elizabeth Strout and Heidi Pitlor. Houghton Mifflin Harcourt, 2013, pp. 285–307.

Williamson, Joan. Personal Interview. 22 Sept. 2017.

"Will Limiting Red Meat Help Stave off Alzheimer's?" *Tufts Health and Nutrition Letter*, Jan. 2017, p. 6.

Wolfgang, Kelly. "Hearing Loss and Dementia: Breakthrough Research Seeks Causal Link." *The Hearing Journal*, vol. 72, no. 9, Sept. 2019, pp. 22–26. *Free Access*, doi: 10.1097/01.HJ.0000582420.42570.de.

Wolitzer, Meg. *The Wife*. Scribner's, 2003.

Woodward, Kathleen. "Against Wisdom: The Social Politics of Anger and Aging." *Cultural Critique*, vol. 51, Spring 2002, pp. 186–218.

———. "Performing Age, Performing Gender." *NWSA Journal*, vol. 18, no. 1, 2016, pp. 162–89. *Academic Search Complete*, doi: 10.2979/NWS.2006.18.1.162.

Yadev, Kuldeep, et al. "Approximately One in Three US Adults Completes Any Type of Advance Directive for End-of-Life Care." *Health Affairs*, July 2017, healthaffairs.org/doi/abs/10.1377/hlthaff.2017.0175.

Zadoorian, Michael. *The Leisure Seeker*. William Morrow, 2009.

Zimmerman, Sheryl, et al. "New Evidence on the Green House Model of Nursing Care: Synthesis of Findings and Implications for Policy, Practice and Research." *Health Services Research*, vol. 51, no. 1, 2016, pp. 475–496. *Academic Search Complete*, doi: 10.1111/1475-6773.12430.

Index

About the Author

ELLYN LEM is a professor of English and gender studies at the University of Wisconsin–Milwaukee at Waukesha, where she teaches a variety of interdisciplinary courses on subjects ranging from children's literature to women in popular culture. Her first book, *The Work-Family Debate in Popular Culture*, was co-written with colleague Timothy Dunn and included a foreword by Anne-Marie Slaughter, one of the leading experts on work-life balance. Lem's scholarship also appears in anthologies on *The Hunger Games* and *Like Water for Chocolate* and in journals on subjects ranging from Jewish food literature, interdisciplinary approaches to teaching war, Arthur Miller, and Louise Bourgeois. She is also a regular presenter at national conferences on topics related to popular culture and literature. On campus, Lem directs the Honors Program and advises the student veterans.